BEGINNING RESEARCH IN POLITICAL SCIENCE

Carolyn Forestiere

UNIVERSITY OF MARYLAND, BALTIMORE COUNTY

D1716178

NEW YORK   OXFORD

OXFORD UNIVERSITY PRESS

Oxford University Press is a department of the University of Oxford.
It furthers the University's objective of excellence in research,
scholarship, and education by publishing worldwide.
Oxford is a registered trade mark of Oxford University Press
in the UK and certain other countries.

Published in the United States of America by Oxford University Press
198 Madison Avenue, New York, NY 10016, United States of America.

Library of Congress Cataloging-in-Publication Data

Names: Forestiere, Carolyn, author.
Title: Beginning research in political science / Carolyn Forestiere,
    University of Maryland Baltimore County .
Description: New York, NY : Oxford University Press, 2016.
Identifiers: LCCN 2016014870 | ISBN 9780190215965 (pbk. : acid-free paper)
Subjects: LCSH: Political science—Research. | Political science—Methodology.
Classification: LCC JA86 .F62 2016 | DDC 320.072—dc23 LC record available at
https://lccn.loc.gov/2016014870

9 8 7 6 5 4 3 2 1
Printed by R.R. Donnelley, United States of America

Dedicated to my husband, Asher Mikow

BRIEF CONTENTS

TABLE OF CONTENTS

PREFACE

LEARNING BY DOING

In 2005, shortly after arriving at UMBC as a new faculty member, I was asked by the chair of the department of political science to teach research methods to undergraduates. Once I agreed to teach the course, I set out to create a syllabus that would allow students to engage directly with the research process as early as possible in the semester. In this way, my course would emphasize the "learning-by-doing" approach. To this end, I selected important, standardized steps in the research process, and after presenting each step in the classroom, I provided explicit instructions on what my students needed to do to complete discrete tasks related to a single research project. These tasks began with the identification of a research topic and the writing of a brief literature review about the general topic. The next task was to ask an analytical research question within the topic, using a format that included several independent variables and a single dependent variable in the research question. From here, students could write theory and derive testable hypotheses about the relationships among their variables. Later in the semester, we covered research design, concept measurement, and different forms of quantitative and qualitative analysis. I wanted students to work with empirical material directly to test their hypotheses. To this end, I taught students how to perform and interpret the results from different types of statistical tests, assuming that they had no prior knowledge of statistics. I also included some qualitative analysis by requiring students to write interview schedules related to their independent and dependent variables, conduct a number of interviews with people representing their research population, and analyze the information they collected through content analysis. Toward the end of the semester, I included tutorials on how to present work in a final research report. The idea was that over the course of the semester, the individual assignments students turned in as we covered the steps would be stitched together to form a full-length research project.

CRITICAL ANALYSIS

Indirectly, I noted that the applied approach I adopted for my course also contributed to the realization of another important pedagogical goal, critical analysis. Early in my teaching career I had discovered that many students are not critical of the information they consume. This suggested to me that what was missing from my students' education was a menu of appropriate questions that could be asked whenever students engage with academic material. Such questions include how a particular sample may or may not reflect a research population, how social science concepts are operationalized in research, and how empirical findings—both quantitative and qualitative—are derived and interpreted. The questions themselves serve as a means to critically assess the research materials students read as part of their academic work or otherwise.

The truth is that many of the students we teach in undergraduate political science programs will not go on to become professional political scientists. To be sure, some do, and the formal education we provide—especially in a methods course—should prepare these students for the rigors of graduate school. But the overwhelming majority of the students in our classrooms will join the workforce in other ways. Hence, it is imperative that we think strategically about the political science curricula we provide in classrooms. A methods course should not only be about teaching students how to do research; it also should teach students how to consume research and other forms of information. The learning-by-doing approach can be helpful in this regard. Producing original research, even for just one semester, can help students become better consumers of information. Students learn that research is based on the strategic decisions scholars make in the design and execution of a research project and that these specific decisions can directly impact whatever conclusions are reached.

THIS BOOK

The outline and content of this book closely follow the pedagogical strategy I created for my first research methods course in 2006 and significantly revised in 2012 when I began to incorporate data from the World Values Survey, a public database with surveys about political, economic, and social values from around the world, as part of the students' projects. Each chapter contains information about each research theme and generally ends with examples taken from the political science literature, exercises to solidify student knowledge, and a "Paper progress" section with specific instructions on what students must do to complete a particular task associated with their research projects.

To structure the research project students do as they work with the book, the first step, at the end of Chapter 1, requires students to choose 1 of 16 possible topics that are associated with specific questions from the World Values Survey. The 16 topics were selected because of their relevance for study in political science and because the way in which the potential range of answers for each of the 16 survey questions is associated with each of the 16 topics listed in Chapter 1 produces a variable with ordinal measurement on a scale from 1 to 10. This becomes important later when students perform different types of data analysis on the World Values Survey data.

After students choose a research topic in Chapter 1, they are required to write a literature review. Chapter 2 concentrates on how to distinguish between different types of academic sources and how to search for studies related to a particular topic in the literature, the usefulness of creating annotated bibliographies as a means of staying organized, and how to write a streamlined literature review about a given topic. The chapter ends with examples from the political science literature, exercises, and the paper progress section so students can write their own literature reviews.

Once the literature review is complete, Chapter 3 covers how to ask analytical research questions in political science. Students are encouraged to think of their research questions in terms of independent and dependent variables. This chapter also includes a section called "Introduction to measurement," which describes different types of quantitative measurement. It is important to introduce the different measurement types at this juncture because at the end of this chapter, students must choose two independent variables that will be used to explain variation in their single dependent variable. Chapter 3 emphasizes that one of the independent variables must have nominal measurement and the other must have ordinal, interval, or ratio measurement. In addition, the variable with nominal measurement must either be a binary variable on its own (biological sex, for example) or be transformed from a variable with many categories into a variable with only two categories. These precise instructions are not arbitrary. By choosing a topic associated with a dependent variable with ordinal measurement on a scale from 1 to 10 and by choosing two independent variables with different types of measurement, students will be set up to perform certain types of data analysis (in a later chapter), such as the difference of means test (for the binary independent variable) and the computation of correlation coefficients (for the independent variable with ordinal, interval, or ratio measurement). Including independent variables with different types of measurement also matters for the way in which regression coefficients are interpreted in ordinary least squares regression (also covered in a later chapter).

Chapter 3 ("Asking questions in political science") also encourages students to think about different research populations for their analyses. Instructors should help students identify the specific research population that will be targeted in the students' research studies as early as possible in the semester; in fact, it is probably best if the instructor sets the research population for the entire group[1] because of how the research tasks associated with Chapter 10, "Qualitative analysis through case studies," are constructed. In addition to conducting statistical data analysis on the World Values Survey data, students are encouraged to interview people who represent their research population as a means to collect and analyze original qualitative data through content analysis. The precise research population and hence the decision of whom to interview should be determined as early as possible in the semester so that arrangements can be made for an "interview day." Instructors may choose from two possibilities. One possibility is to make the research population the millennial generation, which, assuming that the students in the course were born between the early 1980s and early 2000s, would allow students to interview each other in the classroom for the qualitative portion of the analysis. This choice is fairly straightforward and does not require institutional review. The second possibility is to think about different research populations, but this decision will require more work on the instructor's part because of the need to identify where students will go to interview people and to secure institutional review before interviewing takes place.

For example, for the past several years, in my classroom we have identified people ages 60 and older as the research population for the students' projects. As part of my course, I have organized field trips to a local retirement community so students could conduct in-depth interviews with a small number of people in this age range.[2] These interviews form a nonprobability convenience

---

1   Some instructors may not like the idea of limiting the World Values Survey dataset to include only observations for a particular research population. However, I have found that theory writing is easier when subgroups in the population are studied because certain factors related to the specific demographic characteristic can be highlighted as part of the explanation for why particular patterns between variables are expected. In addition, teaching the importance of generalization is also more straightforward when the data are limited to a particular demographic group.

2   The community we visit has a minimum age of 60 years for residents; this is why the research population for my course is this specific age group.

sample from the retirement community's population; the retirement community itself becomes the "case" that is examined for the qualitative portion of the students' research. Leaving the classroom to interview members of the local community has the additional benefit of adding a civic engagement activity to the course curriculum. In addition to helping students develop research skills and increase their capacity in critical analysis, leaving the classroom for a structured civic engagement activity can also promote the development of certain civic agency skills, such as empathy and understanding differences between people. A few weeks after the research projects are complete, my students return to the retirement community to debrief the residents regarding their work and to discuss with them the relevance of their research findings. In this way, students can disseminate their research to an external audience. Instructors must consult with their institution's institutional review board to determine the appropriate procedures for obtaining institutional approval for the students' projects if students leave the classroom to conduct interviews. Informed consent is required from all research participants although the information gleaned from the subjects is used for classroom purposes. More information about this important issue is provided in Chapter 3 and Appendix A.

Once an analytical research question has been identified, it becomes necessary to explain why students expect relationships between or among their variables. Chapter 4 thus introduces theory, why it is important, and how theory is created and used in research. This chapter also covers how to derive research hypotheses from theory. At the end of the chapter, students must write a theory to explain why they expect correlations to exist among their variables and to derive specific research hypotheses based on their theory that will be tested with empirical data once they learn more about quantitative and qualitative analysis.

Research design is covered in Chapter 5. Differences between quantitative and qualitative designs, experimental and observational designs, and comparative designs like the most similar systems design and the most different systems design are explained and an example of each type of design from the political science literature is included. Mixed methods designs that integrate elements from different designs into a single design are also explained. It is important to provide a description of several types of design so students do not develop the incorrect notion that all research is like the research they are doing as they work with this book. Rather, the specific design used for the student projects—a mixed methods design that integrates both quantitative and qualitative elements—is just one type of design among a number of possibilities. Once the student projects are complete, Chapter 12 will reintroduce this idea with a description of ways to modify the specific design students used for their project on political values and attitudes.

Chapter 6, "More on measurement," reminds students that many of the concepts we use in the social sciences defy precise measurement. The progression from concept to indicator and from indicator to variable is described, along with an explanation for how we can evaluate the indicators we choose for concepts with an assessment of reliability and validity. Several of the examples presented at the end of this chapter demonstrate how scholars have used survey questions from the World Values Survey as indicators for particular social science concepts, such as knowledge about democracy, environmental concern, tolerance, and public trust.

In Chapter 7, students begin to work with "real data" using a particular statistical program, IBM Statistics software (SPSS)*. SPSS was selected because of its relative ease of use, especially for newcomers to quantitative analysis. The chapters that deal with SPSS (Chapters 7–9 and 12) include screenshots with overlaid arrows and textboxes showing the order of commands that must be executed for each data manipulation. After learning how to download the World Values Survey data with SPSS from the World Values Survey's website, students can perform descriptive statistics on each of their three variables. In this chapter, students come to fully appreciate the differences in measurement among the variables since how a variable is measured is directly related to how it can be described quantitatively. For example, Chapter 7 explains that frequency distributions should be generated for variables with nominal measurement and for variables with ordinal measurement with fewer than five categories, whereas summary statistics are appropriate for variables with ordinal measurement with five or more categories and for variables with interval or ratio measurement.

Chapter 8 introduces two bivariate statistical tools—the difference of means test and the computation of correlation coefficients—so students can determine whether and how their variables are correlated in the World Values Survey sample. Since the World Values Survey uses a probability sampling method to obtain a representative sample for each country, making inferences from each country's sample to the overall population is reasonable. Chapter 8 explains this important process, with a description of how to interpret p values from the statistics derived from the difference of means test and correlation coefficient.

Since different forms of regression analysis are ubiquitous in quantitative political science research, Chapter 9 goes one step further in data analysis to

---

* SPSS Inc. was acquired by IBM in October, 2009.

introduce students to ordinary least squares linear regression. Like the previous two chapters, Chapter 9 includes detailed screenshots from SPSS to demonstrate how to set up regression equations, with explanations of how to interpret results. Again, the deliberate choice of one independent variable with nominal (binary) measurement and one independent variable with ordinal, interval, or ratio measurement allows students to interpret different types of coefficients, both in single-variable and in multivariate regression. Students are encouraged to evaluate the sign, size, and significance of regression coefficients to further assess whether their hypotheses are supported by the World Values Survey data. Instructors who prefer to leave regression out could omit Chapter 9 from a syllabus.

By the time students complete the three quantitative chapters, they should be ready to perform and interpret the different types of quantitative analyses on their own variables. Each chapter ends with an example of how the specific statistical tool covered in the chapter was used in selected research studies, exercises that utilize SPSS and the World Values Survey data, and a detailed paper progress section with instructions that explain how students can perform their own analyses using their three variables (two independent and one dependent). Since incorporating these activities into my course, many students have reported to me that learning SPSS as part of their undergraduate education has helped them in many ways. Of particular note, students can demonstrate to potential employers or graduate schools that they have some skills in quantitative analysis.

Chapter 10 introduces qualitative analysis. The chapter is organized around how to conduct a "case study" in four steps. The first step is determining what is to be studied, and this section describes different types of case studies (such as hypothesis-testing and illustrative case studies). The second step is gathering information for the case study. Tasks related to interviewing, observing, and studying documents are outlined. This section also explains how the identification of a nonprobability sample from an identified population—such as a convenience sample—is an important part of case study research. The third step is analyzing the information collected for the case study. This section describes content analysis and process tracing. The fourth and final step is writing up the case study. The instructions in the paper progress section of the chapter mirror these steps and explain how students should identify the case for their case study (i.e., where they will go to conduct interviews), write an interview schedule so detailed information about their independent and dependent variables can be collected for a convenience sample of people who represent their research population, conduct the interviews and analyze the data through content analysis, and finally write up their findings for the case study that will eventually be included in the final paper.

Once all research tasks are complete, students can write up their findings in a streamlined report. How to write final papers is the subject of Chapter 11. This chapter includes a description of each section of a final paper. I suggest that students write the "middle" of the paper first (the literature review, theory and hypotheses, methods and data, and findings from the empirical analyses) and the "frame" of the paper last (the introduction, conclusion, and abstract). Students may turn in various sections of their papers during the course of a semester so that feedback can be provided and incorporated into the final product. I have found that the feedback I provide and the opportunity to fix mistakes can reinforce student learning and promote greater levels of confidence among my students as they write and rewrite their assignments.

Students who use this book and follow all of its instructions will complete a full-length research project by the end of a single semester. The learning-by-doing approach gives students an opportunity to apply what is learned in each chapter to complete concrete tasks and eventually weave them together into a single narrative. The last chapter of the book, Chapter 12, explains how students can manipulate the design they used for the completion of their research on political values and attitudes for other types of projects in political science. The chapter also provides suggestions for how students can disseminate the findings of their work, either through undergraduate research conferences or in undergraduate research journals. At my own university, for example, I have worked with students to organize a yearly political science undergraduate research conference since 2007 so students who wish to further share their work can disseminate their findings as poster presentations to an audience of peers and faculty.

ACKNOWLEDGMENTS

Several colleagues, both at UMBC and at other institutions, have been instrumental in helping me identify and explain the most important research concepts used in this book. At UMBC, I thank the members of my department for their consistent, invaluable support and for sometimes talking with me at length about different parts of the research process and the best ways to present them to undergraduate students. They are all wonderful colleagues. In political science, they include Ian Anson, William Blake, Jeffrey Davis, Felipe Filomeno, Brian Grodsky, Devin Hagerty, Cindy Hody, Art Johnson, Tyson King-Meadows, Roy Meyers, Nick Miller, Tom Schaller, Brigid Starkey, and Lisa Vetter. I thank Emma Sellers, our program manager, for the excellent work she does and for making my work life easier. I also thank colleagues from other departments for their support and encouragement, including Lisa Dickson and Bob Carpenter from the economics department, Jason Schiffman from the psychology department, Simon Stacey and Delana Gregg from the Honors College, and Stephen McAlpine from interdisciplinary studies. At the administrative level at UMBC, I thank Janet McGlynn, Amanda Knapp, deans Diane Lee and Scott Casper, provost Philip Rous, and president Freeman Hrabowski, each of whom provided encouragement at various stages of the book-writing process. Outside of UMBC, I thank my good friends, Michelle Williams of the University of West Florida and Christine Ristaino of Emory University, for their optimism about the overall project and for helping me work through the review process. I also extend my gratitude to Sean Twombly of Pi Sigma Alpha, the National Political Science Honor Society, for helping me identify conferences in the United States where undergraduate students can present their research. Finally, I owe a special debt of gratitude to one particular colleague at UMBC, Laura Hussey, who also teaches research methods in my department. I single her out as being particularly generous with her time when I had to make decisions about how to present certain statistical concepts. I remain grateful for her assistance and the careful attention she paid to certain aspects of the text.

The students who read my chapters and completed my Research Methods in Political Science course have been instrumental in helping me think about and refine how I present certain concepts in this book. Many students made general comments about how they absorbed the information I presented in the chapters and I am appreciative of all their suggestions. Over the past few years, a number of students have served as research assistants, teaching assistants, or copy editors as I wrote and rewrote chapters. I am more than grateful for their enthusiastic assistance. First, I mention UMBC graduate student and Fulbright scholar Cheryl Camillo, whose expertise in qualitative methods helped me decide what to include in the qualitative chapter. I am grateful to Aidan Delisle, Ahmed Eissa, Alyssa Ramos, and Kelly Robier, who served as teaching assistants while I was writing this book. I also thank Christopher Winter, Rhyner Washburn, and Meghan Carpenter for their assistance at various stages of the book-writing process. Finally, thank you to Summer Akhtar, Zuhair Riaz, and Nathaniel Wong for helping me with the companion website materials, specifically the assessment questions.

I also thank my family and friends, who remained patiently supportive as I wrote this book. This includes my parents, Elaine and Joseph Forestiere, my brother, Brian Forestiere, and my in-laws, Victoria Mikow Porto and James V. Porto. I am also in debt to my "family friends," who allowed me to talk endlessly about the book itself and never failed to offer support. I acknowledge the friendship of Kalindi Kapadia, Cheryl Powell, Stephen Young, Bridgett Goldfarb, Martha Somerville, Bill Somerville, Luigina Castorani, Piero Arnetoli, Bernardo Vega, Alexander Bruno, Lynn Elliot, Darian Schiffman, Kirk Halgren, Leslie Parker, and Cassie Stallings.

My editor at Oxford University Press, Jennifer Carpenter, has been particularly helpful and I remain grateful to her for everything. She never swayed in her belief in the project and was wonderful to me at every step in the process, from securing a contract to completing the book. I would also like to acknowledge the assistance of Matthew Rohal, Michael Kopf, and Susan Brown during the copyediting and the book's production. Their careful attention to detail did not go unnoticed and I am immensely appreciative of their efforts. I also thank the reviewers of the manuscript, whose comments helped me identify both the greatest strengths and the greatest weaknesses in the text. I came to learn that the toughest comments were often the most useful in making the manuscript a stronger product.

I reserve the last paragraph for my immediate family. I am more than grateful for the love, support, and silliness of my two beautiful and brilliant children, Dax and Sky, who seemed to understand that their mother sometimes had to work at odd times to complete certain tasks related to something called "the book." And although it may seem strange to acknowledge a canine, I mention our sweet dog, Roux, who kept me company whenever I was working from home and who always demanded a portion of whatever snack I enjoyed. But the lion's share of my gratitude must be reserved for my husband and partner of more than 17 years, Asher Mikow. The expression "my better half" doesn't even begin to cut it. I will forever be grateful for his endless support, even when I was continually preoccupied with thoughts of research pedagogy, his willingness to take on more than his fair share of responsibility in our home during the two years when the book was written, and his never-ending belief in the merit and importance of the overall project. That this book could not have been done without his commitment to me and my work is an understatement to say the least, and it is for this reason that the book is dedicated to him.

CHAPTER 1

INTRODUCTION

The aim of the book you have in your hands is to help you develop tools that you can use to ask and answer analytical research questions in political science. Until now, you have probably been a consumer of research, someone who uses other people's research to develop your own base of knowledge. This book is designed so that you can do research and write research papers as early as possible in your academic career. In doing so, you will become a producer of research. Thus, the primary emphasis on what is learned in each chapter is the direct application of the material to specific research activities and writing assignments. When combined, these research activities and writing assignments will create a comprehensive project. Since you are probably using this book for a research-oriented course in political science, the final project for your course will likely be the papers you write as you work through the book. In addition, the book should be helpful to you as you continue your coursework since most upper-level or graduate courses in political science usually involve some aspect of research and academic writing. Even if you do not continue your study of political science once your formal collegiate experience is complete, what you learn from this book can be applied in different ways beyond the college classroom.

One of the most important goals of liberal arts education is the development of skills for **critical analysis**, which involves the objective evaluation of research conclusions to determine whether you accept or reject them. Critical analysis requires tools to question the methodology that other researchers utilized in research to reach conclusions. If the methodology in the determination of a specific conclusion is sound, you might accept it as being true. However, if the methodology is flawed in some way, you might reject the conclusion based on one or more problems you identify. One of the benefits of doing research early in your academic career is the ability to directly experience the research process for yourself, which allows you to witness the difficulties researchers face as they make decisions about how to answer research questions. By understanding each step of the process and by understanding that each step involves decisions researchers must make, you will be better equipped to critically evaluate the research process and conclusions of any future study you read. A research methods course is thus an important part of political science education. Not only will you become a producer of research with this book, but also, as part of the process, it is hoped that you will develop tools to help you with critical analysis and hence become a better consumer of research.

From the beginning it will be important for you to appreciate the connection between political science and politics. Although both have the same subject at their core—things that are political—you should note there is a crucial difference between political science and politics. Men and women who have the power to make decisions that affect a group of people are in politics; men and women in positions within the academic world who apply scientific principles to understand regularities in the political world are in political science. Political science differs markedly from politics. Simply put, political science is the study of the practice of politics. Although they are related, they are very different from one another. But someone who does not have a good understanding of politics will likely not become a good researcher in political science. Before a political scientist can ask a good question about the political world, it is important to become as familiar as possible with how politics works in different contexts.

THE STEPS OF THE RESEARCH PROCESS

Let's look at an example to see how an understanding of politics can help someone identify important research questions in political science. On April 17, 2015, the *New York Times* featured a story about the possible decline of U.S. influence during meetings of global economic organizations, such as the International Monetary Fund and the World Bank.[1] In the article, the perceived decline in American influence was attributed to a specific factor, the presence of intense conflict among American politicians in national-level institutions in the United States, both within and among the political parties. According to the author of the news story, the conflict may jeopardize the remarkable authority the United States has wielded since the end of World War II in

---

1   Jonathan Weisman, "At Global Economic Gathering, Concerns That U.S. Is Ceding Its Leadership Role," *New York Times*, April 17, 2015 (accessed May 20, 2015).

international trade negotiations. The news story suggested that political conflict, which produces competing and incompatible demands among parties, unions, and other organizations, has led to new actors, especially in Asia and particularly China, wielding more influence in the international economic sphere. These foreign actors may be in a serendipitous position to initiate and shape any new rules or regulations that would advantage their own workers and businesses, to the detriment of American workers and businesses. As evidence of this trend, the author references the creation of the Asian Infrastructure Investment Bank and the diminishing influence of already established international organizations like the International Monetary Fund and the World Bank, in which the United States has generally played an important role.

As political science researchers, we can use this news story about American influence during meetings of global economic organizations to identify a research topic we can explore for a research project. A **research topic** is a general subject from which different types of questions can be derived. Are there any potential research topics that can be identified from the news story? The story reported that American influence in global economic organizations may be on the decline because of intense domestic political conflict among American leaders. Based on this speculation, we might identify *the degree of American influence during meetings of global economic organizations* as a potential research topic.

To begin research on this topic, we can engage in the social scientific research *process*, which proceeds in a series of standardized steps. The chapters in this book are generally arranged around these steps so that you may be able to answer questions about different types of research topics. For many scholars, the first step in the research process is to study politics in different ways so that interesting and relevant research topics can be identified. Reading newspapers or news magazines, watching the news through reliable sources, following political blogs to understand different points of view, and learning about what happens in the political world are all helpful in this respect. A good topic should be interesting for you (after all, you are the one who will do the research) and relevant for others.

For many scholars, after an interesting and relevant topic has been identified, the next step in the research process is to review the scholarly literature to determine whether and how other scholars have studied research topics that are similar to yours. Reviewing the literature is important for the preparation of a formal literature review that will eventually appear in your final paper. This is the subject of Chapter 2. A literature review is a short written synthesis on previous research on a particular topic. It places a given study in the context of the overall literature and helps us understand more about the chosen research topic. Thus, using the example above, before we continue with the research process we should know whether and how other scholars have studied the degree of American influence in global economic organizations. This knowledge will supply us with information we can use to think about (1) what to include in the specific research question we will eventually pursue and (2) how we might think about a potential answer to that research question.

Once the literature review on your research topic is complete, the next step is to think about the specific question you will ask within your general research topic. The literature review will likely help you refine your thinking about the potential research questions you could ask. Most research questions that are posed in political science are analytical research questions. Analytical research questions require explanation, analysis, and interpretation. They are not simple questions that can be satisfied with simple answers. Rather, they generally ask how variation within variables related to the research topic can be understood. Variables are attributes or characteristics that can differ across observations. For example, one potential analytical research question based on the *New York Times* story could ask the following: How does one variable—the degree of conflict among American politicians in Washington, DC, generally influence a second variable—the degree of influence the politicians can exert at meetings of global economic organizations like the International Monetary Fund and the World Bank? Note that in this question, differences in the first variable (the degree of conflict among American politicians) are expected to have some impact on the differences in the second variable (the degree of influence the politicians can exert at meetings). The purpose of the research, then, is to derive an answer to this specific question. Since asking a good analytical research question is such an important step in the research process, how to ask a specific type of analytical research question in political science will be covered in detail in Chapter 3.

Once the literature review on a general research topic is complete and an analytical research question pertaining to the topic has been asked, we continue the research process by returning specifically to our analytical research question and asking *why* the degree of conflict among American leaders is expected to impact the degree of American influence at meetings of global economic organizations. We must think carefully about this to understand whether there is a *causal mechanism* at work between the degree of conflict among American leaders and the degree of American influence at meetings of global economic institutions. As mentioned in the previous paragraph, the degree of conflict and the degree of influence are variables. One ambition of the research is to determine whether an empirical relationship, or correlation, exists among the variables under study. The causal explanation that specifies why the first variable (the degree of conflict) should be correlated with the second variable (the degree of influence) is called a theory. Most research studies in political science include elaborate theories that explain why the variables under study are related to one another. This is not as simple as it may appear. In the social world, there are many variables that can lead to a particular outcome. Our job, in writing theory, is to isolate the causal effect that one variable has on another. We must explain why increased conflict among American leaders causes the degree of American influence to decline at meetings of global economic institutions. For a theory we might suggest that when there is a large amount of domestic conflict among American leaders in Washington, there is a spillover effect at international meetings, which makes it difficult for the leaders to identify and work toward common goals, even when their most basic interests at the international meetings are in alignment. When there is intense domestic political conflict, leaders representing different ideologies are predisposed to viewing themselves as adversaries in both domestic and international policy negotiations. Continual conflict at home breeds mistrust and discord, which prevents cooperative collaboration. As a result, leaders representing American interests at the meetings do not speak with one clear voice.

Once a theory has been written, it becomes possible to list the specific expectations for *how* the two variables in a study are related. These specific expectations are called research hypotheses. For example, based on the theory above, we might expect that as the degree of conflict among American leaders increases, American influence at meetings of global economic organizations decreases. Hypotheses are derived from the theory we have developed to explain why two or more variables should be correlated with each other. They must be specified in a way that allows us to test them with empirical data. If a research hypothesis derived from a theory is shown to be true, there is evidence that the theory from which the hypothesis was derived is supported as well. Theory and hypotheses, which are covered in Chapter 4, are important in analytical research.

The next step in the research process involves the specification of a research design, which is a plan for how a research question will be answered. There are many different types of research design. Most designs in political science, however, fall into one of three general categories that will be explored more fully in Chapter 5: quantitative or qualitative research designs, experimental or observational research designs, and comparative research designs.[2]

---

2   As explained in Chapter 5, these categories are not always mutually exclusive. For example, a research design can be quantitative and experimental at the same time.

For example, one way to answer a research question might be to plan a quantitative research design, which would involve developing quantitative measures for both sides of the research hypotheses and determining whether they are correlated with one another. To do this, we first need a quantitative measure for the degree of conflict among American leaders. Next, we need a measure for the amount of American influence at meetings of global economic institutions. What this means is that a number must be assigned for each concept (the degree of conflict and the amount of influence) for each international meeting we decide to include in our analysis. We could assess, for example, on a scale from 1 to 10 (or on any scale we deem appropriate), how much agreement there is among American leaders in Washington at the time of a single meeting of a global economic organization. Next, we could assess, on a scale from 1 to 10 (or, again, on any scale we deem appropriate), how much American influence was present at the same meeting. Before we can complete this task, we must understand what we mean specifically by "the degree of conflict among American leaders" and by "the amount of American influence at an international meeting." This is not an easy matter. It requires the identification of indicators to measure these important social concepts. How to identify indicators for social concepts like "conflict" and "influence" is the subject of Chapter 6.

As part of the research design, for quantitative research or otherwise, we must also decide how many meetings we want to study. Generally speaking, for quantitative research designs a larger number of observations (meetings of global economic organizations, in this case) is preferable to a smaller number of observations. We will likely need to construct a sample of observations that we collect from a larger population. Constructing a reasonable sample is one of the most important aspects of quantitative research. The sample must represent the population from which it is derived as closely as possible for any conclusions to be generalizable to observations that are not included in the research study. The purpose of the quantitative analysis, once all the data are collected for a number of different international meetings, is to determine how the variables that are derived from the indicators are numerically correlated with each other in the sample and whether the results are statistically significant. Quantitative analysis is covered in Chapters 7, 8, and 9.

Instead of a quantitative research design, another research strategy might be to develop a qualitative research design for the same analytical research question. Qualitative analysis is covered in Chapter 10. For a qualitative design we would study how the degree of political conflict among American leaders is related to American influence for a much smaller number of meetings of global economic organizations. Using fewer observations, this type of analysis allows us to go into much more detail for understanding how the degree of conflict among American leaders is related to the degree of American influence at one specific global economic meeting. Rather than developing quantitative indicators for each part of the hypothesis and doing quantitative analysis to determine how variables are correlated with each other, the ambition of a qualitative design is to explain through a concise and well-reasoned argument why one variable influenced another in a specific context. This strategy might entail doing interviews with a number of American politicians who attended a specific meeting of a global economic institution to ask detailed and in-depth questions about how the political environment in Washington either helped or hindered their ability to exert influence at the meeting. The analysis of such qualitative data provides rich information about how something works in practice.

It has become increasingly fashionable for researchers in political science to create mixed methods designs, in which elements of different types of designs are presented in the same research study. For example, with this strategy we could include both quantitative analysis (for many meetings of global economic organizations at the same time) and qualitative analysis (involving interviews with politicians who attended a small number of meetings). There are many ways to design research studies and scholars are increasingly mixing different types of designs together in single studies.

Finally, once our research is complete, we write a final report. This is where we present the work we have done as we progressed through the steps of research and provide an elaborate interpretation of our research findings. The end of a final report is often used to ask new questions and demonstrate how the research conclusions may be generalizable. Chapter 11 explains how to write a final report.

This book proceeds in a straightforward manner. Each subsequent chapter is generally presented as the next step in the research process. The steps are summarized in Figure 1.1.

DIFFERENT KINDS OF RESEARCH

As a field, political science is characterized by different kinds of research. Each kind serves a different purpose. First, there is **applied research**, which is used to solve a problem a researcher identifies. Usually this is a social problem, such as crime, poverty, or political apathy. The goal of the research is to develop recommendations that people in positions of power can utilize to implement programs or policies designed to mitigate the social problem in some way.

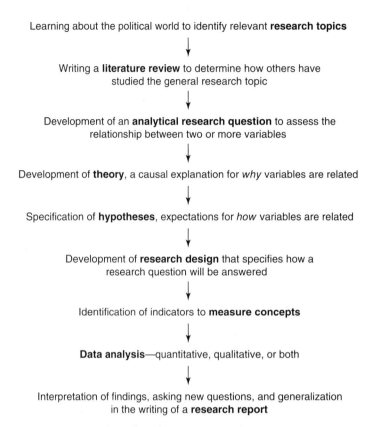

Learning about the political world to identify relevant **research topics**

Writing a **literature review** to determine how others have
studied the general research topic

Development of an **analytical research question** to assess the
relationship between two or more variables

Development of **theory**, a causal explanation for *why* variables are related

Specification of **hypotheses**, expectations for *how* variables are related

Development of **research design** that specifies how a
research question will be answered

Identification of indicators to **measure concepts**

Data analysis—quantitative, qualitative, or both

Interpretation of findings, asking new questions, and generalization
in the writing of a **research report**

FIGURE 1.1: The Political Science Research Process

Someone working with applied research for the project on American influence in international economic meetings would likely study the ways that fierce conflict among political leaders might be resolved, even temporarily, as a means to promote consensus for American interests.

A second type of research, **pure research**, is the type of research you will be doing as you work with this book. Scholars conduct pure research not necessarily to solve a direct problem, but to satisfy their curiosity about a question, to engage others in rigorous discussion about political topics, and to develop new information about how the political world works. Scholars who work with pure research in political science ask questions that are of interest to them and other scholars. Pure research follows the principles of social scientific thinking and is usually designed to discover regularities within the political world. Thus, a researcher studying American influence in international economic meetings would conduct the research to understand whether patterns exist in how certain variables, such as the degree of conflict among leaders and the degree of American influence, are correlated with one another.

Another issue to consider with different kinds of research involves the distinction between normative and empirical research. **Normative research** in political science is generally concerned with arguments about what ought to be or what should be in politics. Normative research is not geared to the development of new facts. Rather, it is concerned with making judgmental arguments about morality or values based on what a scholar believes a society should look like. A scholar who works with normative research takes certain assumptions for granted, such as the superiority of democracy as a regime type or the goal of social equality for a society. Rather than evaluating, for example, whether the distinction between democracy or authoritarianism leads to a particular outcome through empirical research, a normative researcher makes an a priori assumption that democracy is the better regime type. (Keep in mind that a second scholar could believe that authoritarianism is the superior regime type and base his or her arguments on that assumption.) Normative research is concerned with arguments about what should be or ought to be, given a set of assumptions the researcher makes concerning what he or she believes is best for a society. A scholar engaging in normative research, for example, would likely develop an argument to suggest that American policy makers should have a greater amount of influence in international trade negotiations.

The counterpart to normative research is **empirical research**, which is what you will be doing as you work with this book. Empirical research is not judgmental and does not take certain assumptions for granted. Differences in how the political world is constructed, for example, the difference between democracy and authoritarianism, are taken as conditions that explain differences in a particular outcome that is under study, such as economic growth. Empirical research uses the presence of evidence, rather than moral arguments, to support hypotheses. The purpose of empirical research is to develop a theory that explains why differences in an outcome exist, such as the degree of American influence in global economic institutions.

Finally, there is a distinction to be made between descriptive and causal research. The purpose of **descriptive research** is to describe an event or a process. Descriptive research is helpful and often performed when a particular event or process is not well understood. Its main goal, however, is not necessarily the development of theory that explains why particular variables are associated with one another, which is the purpose of **causal research**. Both descriptive and causal research are important because descriptive research is sometimes used to identify the specific elements that may eventually be included as part of an explanation in causal research.

Taking these distinctions together, the type of research you will do as you work with this book is pure, empirical, and causal. The purpose of the research is to ask analytical research questions about the political world and to answer them objectively with empirical data, using the principles of the social scientific framework as a general methodology with the hopes of identifying a causal mechanism that explains why the variables you identify for study should be correlated with one another.

PLAN FOR THE BOOK

This book differs from traditional research textbooks in political science. Like other textbooks, the book presents the steps of research in separate chapters and provides examples of how scholars have used research to answer questions. But the novelty of the book is that as you read the chapters, you will be given instructions on how to write a specific research paper. By the time you complete your reading of this book, it is expected that you will complete at least one full-length research paper. If that causes panic, do not worry. It may seem overwhelming, but the instructions at the end of each chapter are geared directly toward helping you complete each section of your eventual papers.

Thus, by the time you finish this book, not only will you have basic information about many of the standard steps in the social science research process, reinforced by the presentation of many examples as the information is presented, but also you will *apply* that knowledge as you work with your own papers. This is a "learning by doing" approach. The book is geared toward beginning students in political science who, by the time they are reading this book, will have likely completed some basic courses in the discipline. But the book makes the assumption that you have little knowledge of research in political science and presents the specific terminology most political science researchers utilize in a straightforward way, with the expectation that by the end of each chapter you will be able to apply what you have learned for a specific research exercise. For example, at the end of this introductory chapter you will identify 1 of 16 potential research topics about political values and attitudes that you will research as you work through this book. In Chapter 2 you will learn how to conduct a literature review on your specific research topic with the expectation that you will complete a literature review before you move on to Chapter 3, and so on.

From the outset, you must understand that the structure of the papers you will write using this book, from the identification of a research topic to the final generalizations you make about your conclusions, is very specific. The structure represents *only one potential structure* that you can use to answer research questions. It is relatively straightforward, but at the same time its simplicity renders it highly effective. The structure involves the specification of a particular type of analytical research question—one that involves a single dependent variable and two independent variables. (Do not worry if you have never heard of independent or dependent variables before now; you will be comfortable with these terms by the time you finish the book.) You will conduct your research with a mixed methods design, which means you will learn how to do specific types of both quantitative and qualitative analysis. For the project—which will be on some aspect of political values and attitudes—you will be shown how to use the data from the publicly available World Values Survey through a statistical program called Statistical Package for the Social Sciences (or SPSS for short) for the quantitative part of the analysis. Since you may be new to working with quantitative information, several chapters will be devoted to this particular research step. The first of the quantitative chapters covers how to derive descriptive statistics for the individual variables in your study. The next chapter covers how to conduct and interpret the results from two types of bivariate data analysis to test your hypotheses. The last of the quantitative chapters goes one step further and introduces regression analysis. The rationale for including this last quantitative chapter is motived by the fact that most quantitative studies in political science utilize some form of statistical regression. Hence, it is informative for beginning students in political science to have some idea about the goals of regression and how it works in practice. Once the quantitative analyses are complete, you are encouraged to conduct interviews, either with peers in your class or with members of your community, and to analyze the data you collect from the interviews for the qualitative portion of your analysis. At every step, you will be shown exactly what you need to do; each chapter ends with a section called "Paper progress" that contains specific instructions for each step in the research process. In addition, an entire chapter is devoted to the writing of a final research report so you can learn how to present the individual sections of your paper in a complete study.

Because the structure for the papers you are encouraged to write while reading this book is so specific, you may mistakenly believe that this approach to research is the only way to conduct research in political science. Yet nothing could be further from the truth. You should be aware as we begin that a vast array of possibilities exist when it comes to research design and research methods. As a result, some of the chapters will cover important information that may not be directly relevant for the papers you will write. Nonetheless, this information is necessary because as you write your papers, you should be aware of the other ways research can be completed. Note, too, that each chapter ends with a series of exercises to help solidify your knowledge about a particular research topic, which is followed by the paper progress section. The approach you should take as you read this book is as follows: (1) study the chapter, (2) do the exercises at the end of the chapter, and (3) follow the instructions to make progress on your paper.

As part of the description of the research themes, most chapters provide several examples of studies in political science that offer concrete applications of the ideas discussed in the text. Most of the examples involve recent studies (studies published within the past 2 to 5 years) from the most well-known journals in political science. These journals include *American Political Science Review, The Journal of Politics, American Journal of Political Science,* and *British Journal of Political Science,* among many others. In addition, the examples encompass a wide range of subfields in political science, such as American politics, comparative politics, and international relations. This is to provide a comprehensive survey of the work being done in a variety of subfields. Each study was chosen because of how it relates to a particular theme. In most cases, the study itself is described in some detail, followed by an explanation of how the study relates to the theme covered in the chapter.

Thus the reader of this book should be aware that the way the research is presented here represents only one way of conducting social scientific research. Although the methodological tools most political scientists employ have many things in common—literature reviews, theory development, and data analysis, for example—there is no single model of research that is appropriate for all research questions. Consequently, you should view the tools you learn in this book as basic building blocks that can be assembled in various ways to create different types of research projects. Although the instructions for the full-length paper in this book are specific, this particular format is not used by all researchers uniformly. The format a researcher chooses should be based on the research question and what is deemed most appropriate for the chosen design. In addition, a willingness to respond to problems that arise and to change a design when necessary is important.

One more point in this general introduction before we begin: because the book emphasizes application, many parts of the research process that are usually presented in traditional texts have been left out of this book. Furthermore, the treatment of some of the concepts in this book may not be as complete compared to that found in other books. These omissions are entirely deliberate. Including all of the potential information other texts provide while expecting a student to complete a full research project likely would be overwhelming for students. Hence, the approach in the writing of this book has been to present certain elements within each step of the research process. These elements should help you apply what you have learned as quickly and efficiently as possible. But keep in mind that what you have here represents only a part—albeit a big part—of the research process. Knowing how to utilize these elements in research effectively will greatly prepare you for the future writing of papers for your upper-level classes or for other research projects in political science or even for other disciplines in social science, such as sociology or economics.

GLOSSARY

APPLIED RESEARCH   Research that is used to solve a particular problem.

CAUSAL RESEARCH   Research whose main goal is the development of theory to explain why particular variables are associated with one another.

CRITICAL ANALYSIS   The objective evaluation of research conclusions to determine whether one accepts or rejects them.

DESCRIPTIVE RESEARCH   Research that is used to describe an event or a process.

EMPIRICAL RESEARCH   Research that uses the presence of evidence, rather than moral arguments, to support hypotheses.

NORMATIVE RESEARCH   Research that is generally concerned with arguments about what ought to be or what should be.

PURE RESEARCH   Research conducted to satisfy curiosity about a question, to engage others in rigorous discussion, and to develop new information.

RESEARCH TOPIC   A general subject from which different types of questions can be derived.

EXERCISES

1. Think about the difference between politics and political science. What within the general area of politics do you find interesting? How do you read, listen to, or watch political news? What can you do as you work through this book to increase your knowledge of politics so that you might identify potential research topics?
2. Explore the politics section of a major newspaper or a political blog to identify a news story or opinion piece that you find interesting. Read the selection carefully. Can you use the material in what you have read to identify a potentially interesting and relevant political science research topic?

PAPER PROGRESS

The research process usually begins by identifying a research topic that is interesting to you and relevant for study. To assist you in the writing of your paper on political values and attitudes, 16 research topics are listed below. Choose one of them; this will be the research topic that you will work with as you continue through the book.

Possible topics:

Life satisfaction

Perceptions of personal choice and control in one's life

Perceptions of public trust

Satisfaction with financial situation of household

Left/right ideology

Views on income differences among people in a society

Views on private versus state ownership

Views on government versus individual responsibility

Views on whether economic competition is good or harmful

Views on wealth accumulation

Views on whether taxation of the rich is an essential characteristic of democracy

Views on whether unemployment benefits are an essential characteristic of democracy

Views on whether reducing income inequality is an essential characteristic of democracy

Views on whether obedience of rulers is an essential characteristic of democracy

Views on whether gender equality is an essential characteristic of democracy

Views on how democracy is working

As you read through these topics, see whether one of them interests or excites you in some way. Have you read a newspaper story or heard something lately about one of them? Is the topic becoming more important over time? Is the topic something you think people are ignoring, but should not? Choose a topic you are willing to think a lot about. It must be something that will keep you engaged as you progress through the research process. Figure out why the topic is important to you and why it would be relevant for other scholars.

COMING UP

Once you choose a research topic, the next step will be to evaluate how other scholars have studied it. This is the subject of Chapter 2: Reviewing the literature. Reviewing the published literature about your topic helps you situate your own study within the literature and can greatly assist you in developing both your eventual research question and the causal theory you will write to explain why variables associated with your topic are expected to be correlated with one another.

REVIEWING THE LITERATURE

No topic of study is completely new. In addition to identifying an interesting and relevant research topic, one of the most important first steps in the research process is conducting a thorough search in the social science literature for information about how other scholars have studied the topic you have chosen. This step will help you write a concise and informative literature review that you will eventually include in your final report. A **literature review** is a short, written synthesis of previous research on a particular topic. A literature review traces the history of where ideas came from and how they developed over time. If the goal of research is dissemination to a larger audience, each research project should present itself as part of a larger whole, a piece of a puzzle, or a next step in our understanding of something. Only a thorough literature review can help a researcher identify which topics have already been studied, what the methods and conclusions of those studies were, and what the literature leaves unresolved.

Although researchers spend considerable time gathering and analyzing new information, substantial energy also goes into the study of what has already been done. This is central to the idea of research as an ongoing conversation with a community of people who have similar interests. The literature on the research topics that are interesting to you will help you craft a research question that other scholars should find interesting as well. This is why you should review the literature on your research topics before writing the specific analytical research question you will attempt to answer through your own research. In addition, the literature will help you think about the theory you will eventually write to explain why certain variables associated with your research topic should be correlated with one another. The literature review you write using the instructions provided at the end of this chapter will be crucial for helping you with Chapter 3, when you write your analytical research question, and Chapter 4, when you write the theory for why you expect the variables associated with your research topic to be correlated with one another.

USING THE BEST SOURCES FOR A LITERATURE REVIEW

The first step in writing a literature review is to identify the literature that is most relevant to your research topic. To do this effectively, you must first distinguish among different types of sources. This is important because not all types of information are the same. The different types of sources can be listed as a hierarchy of three tiers, as presented in Table 2.1.

Tier 1: Peer-Reviewed Research Articles and Academic Books

Generally, the best sources for academic research come from **peer-reviewed** research articles and/or academic books published by university or academic presses. Peer review is crucial for high quality. A published article or book that has been peer reviewed has been evaluated by outside experts in the field and has met the high standards of quality set by the publisher. Not all submitted research articles are published. Only a small number of articles and books make their way into print because of the intense competition most scholars face for a limited number of publication outlets. Since publishers often receive a large number of submissions, the peer-review process ensures that only the best work is ultimately printed.

The Peer-Review Process

When a scholar wants to publish a paper in a journal, he or she sends the paper—per the instructions provided by the journal—to an editor at that journal. The paper is usually accompanied by a business letter to introduce the paper and its main findings. If the editor believes that the paper could eventually be included in the journal based on what is called an "internal review" of the paper's topic, quality of methods, and conclusions, he or she will send the paper out for a "blind external review." This means that the editor will ask political scientists who have expertise in some area related to the paper's overall topic to read and comment on the paper without knowing who wrote it. Blind review allows reviewers to be as objective as possible in their praise or criticism of the research. Journals usually maintain long lists of such experts.

TABLE 2.1: DIFFERENT TYPES OF SOURCES

Tier 1	Tier 2	Tier 3
Peer-reviewed research articles	Academic reports	News magazines
Academic books	Working papers	Newspapers

Political scientists working in academia are expected to review papers for academic journals at some point in their careers. The instructor for your course likely has served in this capacity. Once the reviewer has read a paper, he or she writes detailed comments regarding the paper and returns this information to the editor along with a recommendation. For most journals, the possible recommendations are to accept, conditionally accept, revise and resubmit, or reject. An initial recommendation of accept is rare. An accept recommendation means that the reviewer has determined that the paper meets all the standards and requirements for a specific journal. More often than not, a reviewer will have at least some suggestions for how the paper can be made stronger. When this is the case, a reviewer may recommend to conditionally accept a paper, which means that a paper can be accepted for publication once the recommended changes are made. But even this is rare. Most journals have low acceptance rates, and recommendations such as revise and resubmit or reject are more common. A revise-and-resubmit paper usually has several areas of weakness that the author must fix before the paper can be considered for publication. Once changes have been made, the author sends the paper back to the editor so the paper can be considered again. At this point, the editor may make a final determination based on the changes, send the paper back to the original reviewers for a second evaluation, or choose new reviewers to make a final decision on the paper. If the changes are acceptable, the paper may be given the green light for publication. But if the changes do not convince the reviewers of the paper's merit, a second revise and resubmit or a rejection may be decided. When a paper is rejected, it will no longer be considered for publication at that particular journal. The researcher may then choose to make additional changes and send the article to another journal, where the peer-review process will start again. The peer-review process is lengthy and tedious but it does guarantee most of the time that only the best research papers get published. The acceptance rate for the most prestigious journals in political science is low, sometimes as low as 10% of all submissions.

Here is a list of some of the well-known journals in political science, arranged by subfield.[1]

GENERAL POLITICAL SCIENCE

American Political Science Review
American Journal of Political Science
The Journal of Politics

---

1   For a more complete list of highly rated journals, see Iain McLean et al., 2009, "Comparative Journal Ratings: A Survey Report," *Political Studies Review* 7 (1): 18–38.

British Journal of Political Science
Perspectives on Politics

INTERNATIONAL RELATIONS
International Organization
World Politics
International Studies Quarterly

COMPARATIVE POLITICS
Comparative Political Studies
Comparative Politics

THEORY
Political Theory

Finding Peer-Reviewed Research Articles

Your institution's library probably has some form of research website that provides access to well-known databases for the social sciences and, in some cases, for political science in particular. These databases utilize search engines that can be extremely useful when you want to find academic material based on **keywords** derived from your overall research topic. Keywords are words or phrases that best describe your project. If your research topic is political ideology, for example, you could enter "political ideology" as one of the keywords you use to search for literature. By parsing the research topic down to a few keywords, with just a few searches you can get an idea of how much work has been done on your topic. Work that has high relevance for your research should eventually be included in your paper's literature review. Some of the most ubiquitous search engines for peer-reviewed academic articles are Academic Search Premier, Worldwide Political Science Abstracts, Web of Science, and JSTOR.

Academic Search Premier searches more than 3,000 journals for articles and studies using keywords that you enter through the database's online interface. Once you access the database, there are several boxes in which to enter the keywords related to your research project. With Academic Search Premier, you can also request that the results include studies that have been peer reviewed and works that have the full text attached. In the beginning of the research process, it is a good idea to select both filters because of the limited time frame in an academic semester.[2]

---

2   For a more complete list of results, you could include studies that do not have the full text attached. In theory, you can locate the text of these additional studies, either in print in your institution's library or in an electronic format that is not included in Academic Search Premier. If your library does not own a copy of the work, most studies can be obtained through interlibrary loan, a service most major academic institutions now utilize.

In addition to Academic Search Premier, there are other databases that work in a similar way. Depending on what is available at your library, you may opt to use Worldwide Political Science Abstracts, Web of Science, or JSTOR to find peer-reviewed research articles. Keep in mind, however, that some databases do not provide access to the most recent articles or to articles in journals not carried by the specific database. This is why searching with several different databases is advised.

Publishing Academic Books

The process of publishing academic books is similar to the publication of journal articles. When a researcher wants to write a book on a particular topic, he or she writes a proposal and sends it to the editor of a press. The editor does an internal review to assess the overall quality of the proposal and to determine whether the subject of the proposed book fits with the press's overall publication mission. If the internal review is successful, the editor will then send the proposal out for external peer review. The peer-review process for a book is similar to that of journal articles and usually guarantees that only the most relevant, interesting, and academically rigorous books get published. For some publishers, the editor will also ask the scholar to send sample chapters or sometimes even an entire manuscript along with the proposal before deciding whether to offer a contract for a book.

Below is a list of the top 20 distinguished presses known to publish books in political science, as reported by James Garand and Micheal Giles.[3]

Cambridge University Press
Princeton University Press
Oxford University Press
University of Chicago Press
Harvard University Press
Cornell University Press
University of Michigan Press
Yale University Press
University Press of Kansas
CQ Press
University of California Press
Johns Hopkins University Press

---

3   For a more complete list of publishers, see James C. Garand and Micheal W. Giles, 2011, "Ranking Scholarly Publishers in Political Science: An Alternative Approach," *PS: Political Science and Politics* 44 (2): 375–83.

Brookings Institution Press
Georgetown University Press
MIT Press
Lynne Rienner Publishing
Stanford University Press
Routledge
Rowman & Littlefield
Columbia University Press

Finding Academic Books

For academic books, using the traditional library catalog and taking an actual trip to the library can be helpful. Your library should have an online interface through which you can use the same keywords you used in the peer-reviewed research article search to find the most relevant books that have been published on your topic. Once you identify the call number for a specific book and find the book on a library shelf, take some time to peruse the books *around* the book you found. Call numbers refer to topics, which means that similar books are grouped together at the library. Thus, although your catalog search for books may not have provided you with every possible book on your topic, it is possible to find related material simply by looking to the left and right of the books that the catalog search engine did return.

Reviewing books about your topic is essential because academic books usually provide a broader treatment of a general topic and are much more comprehensive in scope than research articles. As a result, academic books can provide important foundational knowledge about a research topic.

Tier 2: Academic Reports and Working Papers

Academic reports and working papers constitute a second tier of sources. These studies are written by scholars who work for universities, think tanks, research organizations, or government or private agencies. Academic reports and working papers typically involve preliminary research that has not yet been formally published. The major difference between these sources and the first-tier sources is that academic reports and working papers are not, by definition, peer reviewed. Nonetheless, the quality from second-tier to sources is usually high, and oftentimes the work eventually finds its way into an academic journal or book. Researchers often use academic reports and working papers in their literature reviews, especially for topics of recent relevance that have may not have yet received extensive coverage in peer-reviewed research articles or academic press books.

Finding Academic Reports and Working Papers

For academic reports and working papers, Columbia International Affairs Online and Public Affairs Information Service return results consisting of academic reports and working papers produced by academic and research institutions around the world. These databases are particularly helpful for identifying the most current research that is being done on a topic. Sometimes researchers will write a report or working paper before submitting the work to peer review. By searching for your topic through these interfaces, you will have access to the most current work available. The interface for Public Affairs Information Service looks a lot like the interface for Academic Search Premier, and after conducting your search you can filter the results according to peer-reviewed work. For Columbia International Affairs Online, you can search on one line only, but you can filter the results according to the type of work: working paper, policy brief, case study, etc.

Tier 3: News Magazines and Newspapers

The last tier in the hierarchy of sources contains information from news magazines and newspapers. This type of work tends to be shorter and often contains valuable descriptive information that can be used effectively to understand the details of a particular case. However, a researcher should be aware that information from news magazines and newspapers tends to be more journalistic than academic or scientific. In addition, news stories do not usually involve the construction of generalizable theory. Rather, they provide a narrative and analysis about something that has happened.

Finding News Stories

LexisNexis Academic provides access to news stories published in a wide variety of commercial sources, such as *The New York Times*, *The BBC*, *The Financial Times*, or *The Economist*. The LexisNexis Academic database has advanced search options where you can limit the time frame for the news stories you wish to study or choose to search for news stories in a particular language. For news searches, it is useful to choose a specific geographic location that you wish to study. Using more refined, descriptive, and detailed search criteria will likely result in the most useful sources.

Although the three tiers of sources in this hierarchy do not comprise the entirety of what is available for use,[4] most political scientists generally use

---

4   One omission in the tiers of sources is political blogs. Political blogs are useful in helping a researcher understand different points of view about a topic. In addition, blogs often contain links to academic material. For a list of political blogs, see https://personaldemocracy.com/blogs/top/ or http://www.realclearpolitics.com/best_of_the_blogs/.

them for their literature reviews. Beginning with these sources and using them extensively will ensure that your literature review contains the most relevant and complete information possible. It is up to the researcher to choose sources carefully to ensure that high-quality information is included in the literature review.[5]

DOING YOUR SEARCH

The first step in finding sources is to think of the different ways a topic could have been studied by others. Since you are using computer databases to identify materials, you must have a working idea of how the topics you wish to research can be identified in the literature. In other words, think about how other researchers have thought about their keywords.

Often, the best way to begin a literature search is to start with your paper's general topic to see how others have approached its study in peer-reviewed research articles and academic books. For example, imagine that you are doing a project on political participation in Australia. You should begin searching for literature by isolating your search to "political participation" to see how other scholars have approached the topic, not only in Australia but also in other areas. Keeping the search parameter generic should capture studies that have been done about political participation not only in Australia but also in other democracies or, even more specifically, in other parliamentary democracies. Although your precise research question may concern political participation in Australia, research on political participation in democracies or specifically in parliamentary systems is likely valuable for insights about political participation in general and may actually contain information about Australia. To begin, enter the term "political participation" in the search engine for databases and catalogs that search for both peer-reviewed research articles and academic books.

If the search engine returns a large number of items for this first search, you could repeat the search by adding or changing the keywords. You could include many keywords in a single search line using the Boolean connectors "and" or "or" to denote which terms you want included in the results lists. For example, if your primary interest is voting as a form of political participation in Australia, you could add the term "voting" to your search: "political participation" and "voting" (which would provide results that include both political participation and voting

---

5   Many students have begun to utilize sources found on the Web, such as Wikipedia. Although Wikipedia can be immensely helpful and provides specific pieces of information, it is incumbent on a researcher to verify any information taken from any source on the Web.

as keywords) or "political participation" or "voting" (which would provide re- sults that only include either political participation or voting). You could also include the term "Australia" with the connector "and" to capture any studies that focus on that country. This approach will reduce the results list to studies that concentrate specifically on political participation and/or (depending on the search) voting in Australia. If this approach continues to result in a large number of studies, you could add additional keywords to limit the results.

It is also possible that your initial search will not return many results. If this is the case, remember that there are multiple ways to phrase social science concepts and there may also be different ways the keywords are represented in the databases. Scholars who have worked on your topic might have used differ- ent words to represent the same concepts you are working with. Most search terms have several synonyms that other researchers may have used. If your search parameters are too narrow, you may not retrieve all possible studies on your topic. Political participation, for example, could also be thought of as po- litical engagement or political involvement. As another example, socioeco- nomic status could be referred to as income or livelihood. Political affiliation could be partisan identity or political identity. Be flexible, and try as many different terms as possible while looking for literature. Doing multiple searches with the different ways your topic could be phrased will guarantee that you find as much information as possible.

A Few Tricks

1. For most search engines, when entering a search term you can cut the last few letters of the term and add an asterisk (*) so that the search engine will look for all results that contain at least the first part of the term. For example, by entering "democra*," the search engine will return any results that contain the letters "democra," such as democracy, de- mocracies, democratizing, and democratization.

2. When you get your results, you can look at the different ways the key- words are provided for studies that are relevant for your research. This strategy can be particularly helpful if you are having trouble identifying synonyms for search terms.

3. Use caution in how you use connector words in the search. Using the connector word "and" in the same search line will return studies that contain *all* of the words in the line. On the one hand, if you search for political participation "and" political engagement "and" political in- volvement, the only studies that will be returned from the search will be those that contain all three terms somewhere in the paper. Using the

connector word "or" in the same search line, on the other hand, will return studies that contain only one of the terms. Thus, if you search for political participation "or" political engagement "or" political involvement, the search will return studies that include any one of the three terms, but not necessarily all three in the same study. The "and" connector is useful when you want to find studies that connect two or more ideas (say, political participation and Australia), but the "or" connector is better when you are using synonyms for the same general concept.

4. After you have developed a working list of relevant studies, use the search engine to order them by publication date. Review the most recent research that has been produced on your topic first. Reading the most recent study first and scrutinizing its literature review can help you find other studies for your own literature review. If a good study referenced another particular study, it is probably important for you to read it too. This method of finding sources can be helpful if your searches in the standard databases do not produce relevant material.

5. Likewise, if you have identified an older study that is particularly relevant for your research interests, you could do a literature search to see how many researchers have referenced that particular study in their own work. This method should also help you identify scholarship to include in your literature review. The Web of Science provides this service. You can enter the bibliographic information about a study in the Web of Science's search engine to identify other studies that have referenced one particular study.

WHAT TO DO ONCE YOU HAVE IDENTIFIED THE LITERATURE THAT IS MOST RELEVANT FOR YOUR TOPIC

Identifying the most relevant literature for your topic is the first step of the literature review process. Reading and understanding it is the second. At this step, it pays to develop some reading skills. You do not read scholarly research the same way you read a novel. With a novel, readers usually start on the first page and read consecutively until the end of the book. Reading scholarly work is different, however. It is best to start with the work's title. Can you identify the paper's topic from what you see in the title? If the title interests you, read the abstract of the work (most studies include an abstract that specifies the research question, the methods used to answer the question, and the main conclusions of the research). If the abstract contains information that you find relevant for your topic, read the introduction of the work. If the information in the abstract and introduction does not help you understand some part of your topic, set the study aside and choose a different one. Make sure that each scholarly work you review provides as much information as possible for understanding as much as possible about your topic. If a study is too far afield from your research topic, it should not be used in your literature review.

If the abstract and introduction compel you to keep reading, skim the next several pages to see what else is contained in the work. How are the subheadings organized? What is coming next? Once you are familiar with the study's organization, skip ahead to the results or conclusion section to learn the study's main findings. Then go back and read the study from start to finish. If you have an idea of what the study's findings are, rereading the study will be much easier and more informative.

One important function of the literature review process (i.e., searching for literature and reading how other scholars have conducted research on your topic) is to help you understand more about your topic and what sorts of questions remain unresolved within it. In addition, a good understanding of the literature on a particular topic can help you identify why there might be variation within variables associated your topic, for example, why some people participate in politics more or participate in politics less. Remember that the studies you are doing as you work your way through this book are pure, empirical, and causal (see Chapter 1). In the next chapter you will think about why there is variation in a particular variable associated with your research topic. For example, if your research topic is political participation, and voting in particular, you must understand why some people vote more and why some people vote less. Assessing studies in the literature about political participation in general and voting in particular can be invaluable in this regard because the literature will provide insight you may not have previously considered as you think about the specific research question you will eventually construct. The literature review serves a vital function: it helps you refine exactly what you wish to research and how you think about your topic, which is why it is one of the first steps in the research process. You need to know what other scholars have had to say about your topic.

As you read the studies you identify as important, you may find that the assumptions you have about your topic are challenged by different ways of thinking. This is all part of the process. Do not necessarily throw out your ideas, but let the literature guide how you think about them. For example, it is possible that others have considered exactly what you are thinking about your topic, but threw out those ideas when they discovered faulty reasoning and empirical inconsistencies in their analyses. Be flexible in how you change your own ideas when you think it is appropriate to do so. Nothing in the research world is permanently set in stone. All ideas are subject to change with the incorporation of new and better information. This is how we grow within the academy.

Staying Organized

Once you have read the literature you want to include in your literature review, it pays to be highly organized. In the academic world you must take detailed notes on everything you read. The amount of scholarship is immense. Perhaps you were surprised when you saw the number of results when you looked for literature about your research topic. It would be impossible for a single person to read and remember everything that is relevant for his or her topic. Hence, maintaining a database or file of your own notes is an important part of the research process. There are several programs you can use to organize your notes. Programs such as Zotero and Endnote are popular choices for organizing material. These programs are useful because they allow you to include bibliographic information for the articles, books, and other sources you read as a savable file that grows with each entry you add. You can also include your own notes in each bibliographic entry, thereby creating your own database. Some programs will also create a bibliography (works cited page) once you are finished with your paper.

Annotated Bibliographies

Writing a literature review begins with writing an annotated bibliography for each source that will eventually be included in the literature review. An **annotated bibliography** is a summary of each piece of scholarship that you read. The summary should be as complete as possible and include at least the following information:

- The study's research question;
- The relevance of the study's research topic (i.e., the reason the author argues the research question is important);
- A summary of the theory presented in the study;
- The methods and data the author used to answer the research question;
- The main results and conclusions of the study; and
- The potential generalizability of the study.

In addition, consider including particularly insightful quotes that you might eventually include in the text of your research paper. When you copy the quotes as part of your notes, include the page number(s) on which the original quote appeared in the source. By doing this, you will not have to return to the original source when creating citations in your paper. If you have taken good notes, your annotated bibliography will contain all the information you need when you write your literature review.

You should write an annotated bibliography for each individual piece of scholarship that you read. Once it is complete, enter the bibliographic information and text of your notes into the program you are using to keep track of your notes. In doing so, you create a searchable database of your own notes. This will be important as you continue your academic career. If in the future you write a paper on a topic similar to that of a paper you have already written, your annotated bibliographies will help you begin the organizing process for writing the new paper's literature review.

THE LITERATURE REVIEW

Annotated bibliographies as described above are a tool for you and you alone. The text of the notes you include in the annotated bibliographies will not appear directly in the final text of your research paper. Once you have compiled a number of annotated bibliographies, the real work on the literature review begins. Writing a good literature review in many ways is more of an art than a systematic task, and this is where good organization and creative writing skills meet in the development of an informative but streamlined synthesis of the literature you find relevant for your research topic.

Writing an effective literature review is not easy. Usually, it takes several tries before a researcher is satisfied that the literature review is as complete and concise as possible. It must be complete because it must cover as much literature as possible. Yet it must also be concise because the literature review is not the main focus of research papers. The literature review establishes the credibility of the researcher and presents how other scholars have approached similar topics. It must be presented in a way that does not take too much away from the main event, the original work in your paper.

The best way to begin an effective literature review is to thoroughly study your annotated bibliographies. If you have taken good notes, you will not have to return to the original work you read to write the literature review. Rather, the condensed notes you took for each source should suffice for your purposes as you begin to organize and write your literature review.

As you read your annotated bibliographies, look for patterns among your sources. Do different studies approach similar questions in different ways? Are the findings of these studies mostly consistent? Are there areas of significant disagreement? How have similar research questions been answered through time? What was the progression in our understanding of a particular idea? Pore over your annotated bibliographies to see what patterns emerge. Make a flow chart or a map or a diagram to keep the material organized. Once you believe you understand how to present all your sources in one document as a united whole, begin writing. The idea is to produce a streamlined report about what you have learned from the literature.

The first line in a literature review should contain some form of introductory statement that broadly summarizes as much of the literature as possible. A researcher typically begins with a statement about the research topic itself to highlight what the studies have in common. This statement is followed by a list of citations that speak to the topic. Some examples of introductory sentences follow. These examples reference a hypothetical study assessing the role electoral systems (plurality vs. proportional electoral systems) play in the number of parties in a party system.

If scholars mostly agree with regard to a particular outcome:

Scholars who concentrate on how electoral systems affect the number of parties in a party system generally agree that proportional electoral systems tend to lead to more parties, whereas electoral systems based on plurality tend to produce fewer parties in a party system (citations needed here).

If scholars have come to differing conclusions:

Scholars who concentrate on how electoral systems affect the number of parties in a party system have reached differing conclusions about how proportional and plurality electoral systems matter for the number of parties in a party system. Specifically, some studies show that electoral systems are the primary determinant of party fragmentation (citations needed here), whereas others suggest that social variables such as ideological cleavages matter more (citations needed here).

If scholars have used widely different approaches to their studies:

Scholars who concentrate on electoral systems have utilized different approaches to understand the effects electoral systems have on the number of parties in a party system. Some have studied the effect of electoral systems on party systems across several countries at the same time (citations needed here), whereas others have conducted in-depth case studies by investigating a single election in a single country (citations needed here) or subnational unit (citations needed here).

If our understanding of a particular idea has increased progressively throughout time:

Scholars who have endeavored to understand how electoral systems matter for the number of parties in a party system have made refinements in how the number of parties in a party system has been measured over time (citations needed here).

After each clause that describes how the literature can be summarized, include citations for the studies that match what you have said. In many political science journals, this usually involves a **parenthetical citation** that includes the author's last name, followed by the year of the work's publication. Some bibliographic styles include a comma between the author's last name and the year of publication. You must include citations of this type any time you write about work that is not your own. Even if you do not quote a specific part of a study, you should still use parenthetical references to direct the reader to the studies discussed in the literature review. More about citation styles will be covered later in this chapter.

Once you have created an effective introductory statement based on your assessment of how all the studies on your topic fit together, the next task is to write the literature review itself. The introductory statement in many ways is the key to understanding what comes next. This is not to say that your literature review will be one-dimensional, since there could be agreement, for example, in some areas and disagreement in others. The introductory statement, as well as the introductory statements to the different sections within the literature review, will be a guide to how the literature will be presented.

EXAMPLES FROM POLITICAL SCIENCE

Below are paragraphs from different papers in the political science literature that serve as examples of how to concisely organize literature. By studying these examples, you can begin to get a sense of how literature can be integrated into a single narrative. The best literature reviews provide substantial information without taking up too much space.

The bibliographic information for each article is listed first. The style used for these references is common for journals in political science and is good to learn for your eventual reference list. Following the bibliographic citation is a general summary of each article, written by the author of this book. The summary is provided so that you will have some context about each study before you read the paragraphs, which were taken verbatim from the original articles' literature reviews. The information in the literature review was not modified. The paragraphs presented here involve only part of what was presented in the original studies. Refer to the articles themselves to study how the authors presented their complete literature reviews. You should be able to find the articles using the databases presented earlier in this chapter, such as Academic Search Premier.

Morgan, Jana, and Melissa Buice. 2013. "Latin American Attitudes toward Women in Politics: The Influence of Elite Cues, Female Advancement, and Individual Characteristics." *The American Political Science Review* 107 (4): 644–62.

This paper argues that elite cues in Latin American countries influence men's attitudes toward women as political leaders. This is an important topic, especially in newer democracies, where women's participation in politics, and gender equity in general, may be underdeveloped. The paragraph below presents some of the literature on the authors' general topic, which appears on the second page of the article under the subheading "Contextualizing attitudes about women in politics."

The first sentence is about the study itself.

And here is the justification for the study—this part of the literature review reveals the "gap" that this study hopes to fill. Specifically, the study concentrates on how contextual factors influence support for women in politics in developing democracies.

This article develops a theory of attitudes regarding women in politics, integrating explanations at both the contextual and individual levels. A growing literature has demonstrated the significance of context for explaining gender gaps in political engagement and efficacy (Atkeson 2003; Desposato and Norrander 2009; Hansen 1997; Schwindt-Bayer and Mishler 2005), and previous research hints at the idea that the political, economic, and cultural environment has important effects on gender attitudes by establishing that cross-national

CONTINUED

Here is the encompassing summary sentence about the literature. Morgan and Buice note that many scholars are working in this area by putting a number of citations in the same line. They do not need to elaborate on each study. Instead, they have managed to create a summary statement that integrates them. If we were to look up each of the studies listed here, they would all have the same general topic.

differences in these attitudes cannot be explained by individual-level factors alone (Banaszak and Plutzer 1993a). But apart from a few notable exceptions (e.g., Banaszak and Plutzer 1993b; Inglehart and Norris 2003; Moore and Vanneman 2003), little research has explored how context shapes gender values, and virtually no studies have theorized about contextual effects on feminist attitudes in developing democracies. Here we take on the important task of theorizing and testing how context influences support for women in politics.

Bartels, Koen P. R., Guido Cozzi, and Noemi Mantovan. 2013. "'The Big Society,' Public Expenditure, and Volunteering." *Public Administration Review* 73 (2): 340–51.

This article challenges the claim that volunteering should increase as the size of the public sector decreases. Bartels, Cozzi, and Mantovan suggest precisely the opposite. As public spending decreases, volunteering will also decrease because of the lack of support structures and training for volunteers. The paragraph below summarizes the general literature on why people engage in volunteering activities.

Like the previous example, the first sentence in this paragraph provides a summary statement about the literature in general.

These two sentences manage to integrate a number of studies by listing the topic of the study, followed by its citation. If someone wanted to know more about the determinants of volunteering, reading the literature summarized in these two sentences would be a good place to start. Note that there is a citation after every summary theme—that is because each study dealt with volunteering in a different way.

The literature provides important insights about the determinants of voluntary work for the total population or specific segments. Studies focusing on the total population showed that people can decide to volunteer, or give money to charity, because of pure altruism or warm-glow altruism (Andreoni 1990), a desire to personally "make a difference" (Duncan 2004), impatience to receive a certain good (Bilodeau and Slivinski 1996), social pressure (Della Vigna, List, and Malmendier 2011), obliging social norms (Olken and Singhal 2009), or because giving can enhance their well-being (Meier and Stutzer 2008). The decision to volunteer can also be influenced by the socioeconomic or ethnic composition of the neighborhood community (Alesina and La Ferrara 2000; Atkinson and Kintrea 2001; Goodlad and Meegan 2005). All of these variables together create a complex picture of individuals with multiple motivations for volunteering (Clary, Snyder, and Stukas 1996).

Reynolds, Andrew. 2013. "Representation and Rights: The Impact of LGBT Legislators in Comparative Perspective." *The American Political Science Review* **107 (2): 259–74.**

This article investigates whether the presence of LGBT legislators in national parliaments influences variation in laws that grant homosexual citizens the same rights as heterosexuals. Since this is a relatively new topic in political science, Reynolds borrows insights from the literature that assesses the efficacy of other politically marginalized groups in society in the policy-making process, such as women or ethnic minorities. He begins his article with the following paragraph.

> Since little literature centers on LGBT legislators in the policy process, Reynolds includes studies about female and minority representation.

> Baldez 2003; Krook 2009; and Wolbrecht, Baldez, and Beckwith 2008 must all deal with increasing numbers of women in national legislatures.

> The beginning of the second paragraph claims that the literature on LGBT legislators is not very developed, providing legitimacy to this study on the effect of LGBT legislators on policy outcomes.

Over the last 20 years, the inclusion of women and ethnic minorities in national parliaments has increasingly been seen as an indicator of the strength of democracy in established democracies and as a *sine qua non* of democratization in the developing world. Much has been written about the growing numbers and influence of women members of parliament (MPs) in the legislatures of the world (for example, see Baldez 2003; Krook 2009; Wolbrecht, Baldez, and Beckwith 2008). In 2012, the Inter Parliamentary Union identified 7,443 female members of national lower houses (20% of the total). A similar literature is emerging on the existence and influence of ethnic minority MPs in national legislatures. One of the largest surveys to date of minority MP presence covers 50 nations and identifies more than a thousand MPs with an ethnic minority background (see Reynolds 2006). Such *descriptive* (sometimes called "passive" or "symbolic") representation does not necessarily imply that the group members vote together or that individual representatives see themselves as primarily "women MPs" or "minority MPs." But without some visible inclusion of the faces and voices of the historically marginalized, it is unlikely that the interests of such groups will be at the forefront of decision makers' minds.

The literature on openly lesbian, gay, bisexual, and transgender (LGBT) MPs in national parliaments is undeveloped. Although there have been important studies of their presence in individual national parliaments (see Rayside 1998 on Britain, the United States and Canada) as well as analyses of gay legislators in U.S. state legislatures (see Haider-Markel 2007, 2010; Haider-Markel, Joslyn, and Kniss 2000) there is very little cross-national research on the existence and influence of openly LGBT MPs in national parliaments.

TO CITE OR NOT TO CITE

In your literature review and indeed in all of your writing, you must cite any work in which you present an opinion or idea that is not your own. Sometimes new writers worry about when they need to include a citation. Not providing a citation for an opinion or idea you have borrowed from an outside source is a serious matter and can lead to charges of plagiarism. The best rule of thumb is to cite if you are unsure. That way you protect yourself. Your instructor should be able to work with you when you are unclear about when to cite something. But as a general rule, when in doubt, cite. In addition, you must always cite a source when you have included a direct quote. The citation should include the page number or numbers where the quote appears in the original article.

You must develop an understanding of the difference between an accepted fact or detail (which does not require a citation) and someone else's opinion or idea (which does require a citation).

Consider the difference among the following:

- A fact/historical detail: The United States utilizes a plurality electoral system for the election of Congress.

No citation needed. It is an established fact that the United States utilizes a plurality electoral system for the election of Congress.

- An opinion/idea: The use of the plurality electoral formula generally leads to a two-party system (Downs 1957).

Citation needed. You must cite this statement since it is a hypothesis that Downs developed in his book, *An Economic Theory of Democracy*.[6]

- A fact/historical detail: Voting is one manifestation of political participation.

No citation needed. This is a fact—voting is indeed one way that people participate in the political arena. It does not need to be cited.

- An opinion/idea: Lower voter turnout in the United States does not mean that Americans do not participate in politics because different ways of participating have been evolving over time (Norris 2002).

Citation needed. Since this is an idea explored in Norris's 2002 book, *Democratic Phoenix: Reinventing Political Activism*,[7] it must be cited.

- A fact/historical detail: Per capita income is higher in advanced industrial democracies than in developing countries.

---

6   Anthony Downs, 1957, *An Economic Theory of Democracy*, New York: Harper.
7   Pippa Norris, 2002, *Democratic Phoenix: Reinventing Political Activism*, Cambridge, UK: Cambridge University Press.

No citation needed. This is a fact—per capita income is higher in advanced industrial democracies than in developing democracies.

- An opinion/idea: High per capita income is generally linked with postmaterialist values, which include a concern for the protection of individual expression and enhancement of the quality of life (Inglehart 1997).

Citation needed. This is not a fact. Rather, it is a conclusion from Inglehart's 1997 book, *Modernization and Postmodernization: Cultural, Economic, and Political Change in 43 Societies*,[8] which studied many different societies at the same time.

- A fact/historical detail: The French, Russian, and Chinese revolutions began in 1789, 1917, and 1911, respectively.

No citation needed. These are facts—historical details like this do not require citation.

- An opinion/idea: Despite their differences, the French, Russian, and Chinese revolutions bear striking similarities that can be studied in a single research design (Skocpol 1979).

Citation needed. This observation is not a historical fact. Rather, it is the conclusion of an elaborate research project presented in Skocpol's 1979 book, *States and Social Revolutions: A Comparative Analysis of France, Russia and China*,[9] which identified remarkable similarities among different revolutions in different contexts.

CITATION AND REFERENCE STYLES

There is no one universal bibliographic or citation style that all journals and book presses use. Journals and book presses provide precise instructions on how they want authors to create bibliographies and citations. For journals, this information is usually found either online or somewhere in the journal itself (usually inside the front or back cover). For books, this information is either found online or sent to the author once a book proposal has been accepted. Many authors use the *Chicago Manual of Style* to format their citations and reference list.[10] The *Chicago Manual of Style* is common among journals and books in political science and is a straightforward style to learn. The American Political Science Association provides an

---

8   Ronald Inglehart, 1997, *Modernization and Postmodernization: Cultural, Economic, and Political Change in 43 Societies*, Princeton, NJ: Princeton University Press.

9   Theda Skocpol, 1979, *States and Social Revolutions: A Comparative Analysis of France, Russia and China*, Cambridge, UK: Cambridge University Press.

10 The Chicago Manual of Style Online has a guide that can be purchased through its website: http://www.chicagomanualofstyle.org/home.html/.

TABLE 2.2:   **EXAMPLES OF PARENTHETICAL CITATION STYLES**

One author	(Smith 2012)
Two authors	(Smith and Jones 2012)
Three authors	(Smith, Jones, and Adams 2012)
Four or more authors	(Smith et al. 2012)
Quote with page number	(Smith 2012, 1)

abbreviated version of the style on its website that students can use as a guide for citing and referencing different types of sources (e.g., journals, books, newspapers stories, government documents, and websites) (http://www.apsanet.org/files/APSAStyleManual2006.pdf/). Utilize this style as you write your papers.

Citations

Any time you reference someone else's work in your text, you must provide some form of citation. Many political scientists utilize parenthetical citations somewhere in the sentence where the citation is needed. Parenthetical citations include the authors' last names, the year of publication, and the page number, where appropriate, according to the rules presented in Table 2.2.

Revisit some of the sentences from the literature review excerpts presented earlier in this chapter to see how the authors presented the literature through parenthetical citations. Imitate this style as you write your own literature review.

References

A **reference list** is an alphabetical listing of all sources referenced or cited. It appears at the end of a study or research paper. A reference list is sometimes called a bibliography or works cited page. The formatting style for some of the most common types of sources is given in Table 2.3.

CONCLUSION

A good literature review serves everyone. For a researcher, reviewing the work of other scholars can help identify an interesting and relevant research question and provide insight about the eventual theory that will be offered as an explanation for why variables associated with the research topic are expected to be correlated with each other. For a reader, the literature review situates the study within a broader context and provides immediate access to the most important conclusions other authors have reached regarding the research topic.

TABLE 2.3: FORMATTING STYLES FOR DIFFERENT TYPES OF SOURCES

Books:

One author

Last name, first name. Year. *Book Title*. City of publication: Press.

Two authors

Last name first author, first name first author, and first name second author last name second author. Year. *Book Title*. City of publication: Press.

Three authors

Last name first author, first name first author, first name second author last name second author, and first name third author last name third author. Year. *Book Title*. City of publication: Press.

Four or more authors

Last name first author, first name first author, et al. Year. *Book Title*. City of publication: Press.

Edited book:

One editor

Last name, first name, ed. Year. *Book Title*. City of publication: Press.

Two editors

Last name first editor, first name first editor, and first name second editor last name second editor, eds. Year. *Book Title*. City of publication: Press.

Chapter in an edited book:

Last name, first name. Year. "Chapter Title." In *Book Title*, ed. first name last name of editor. City of publication: Press, first page number of chapter–last page number of chapter.

Articles:

Last name, first name. Year. "Article Title." *Journal Title*. Volume number (edition number): first page number of article–last page number of article.

Follow the same format for multiple authors of articles as for books.

Newspapers:

If the author name is known

Last name, first name. Year. "Title of Piece." *Newspaper Title*, Month day.

If the author's name is not known

"Title of Piece." Year. *Newspaper Title*, Month day.

GLOSSARY

ANNOTATED BIBLIOGRAPHY   A summary of each piece of scholarship that is read in the preparation of a literature review.

KEYWORDS   Words or phrases that best describe a research topic.

LITERATURE REVIEW   A short, written synthesis of previous research on a particular topic.

PARENTHETICAL CITATION   A specific citation style for work that includes the author's last name, followed by the year of the work's publication in parentheses; a page number should be included whenever the citation involves a direct quote.

PEER REVIEW The process through which work is evaluated by outside experts in a particular field.

REFERENCE LIST An alphabetical listing of all sources referenced or cited that appears at the end of a study or research paper.

EXERCISES

Use a research database to find articles from one of the mainstream journals in political science. Some good examples are *American Political Science Review* and *The Journal of Politics*. Scroll through several articles and study how the authors constructed their literature reviews. Articles may or may not have subheadings to identify the article's literature review, but you should be able to find the article's literature review from the article's content. Make notes of how introductory summary statements were written. Was there agreement in the literature? Have several authors studied similar topics and reached different conclusions? This exercise will be helpful as you begin to prepare your own literature review.

PAPER PROGRESS

In Chapter 1 you were asked to choose 1 of 16 potential research topics. The next step is to write a literature review about your topic.

Step 1: Find the studies that are most relevant for understanding what other scholars have concluded about your research topic.

Start by using one of the mainstream search engines likely available through your institution's library. Try to find journal articles and/or academic books that pertain to your research topic. Since you are going to use the World Values Survey for the quantitative portion of your analysis, you could also include the term "World Values Survey" along with your research topic in the search engine you are using to determine whether other scholars have used the data pertaining to your specific topic in the World Values Survey in their research.

Use the advice offered under "A few tricks" to help you with your search. For example, use the Boolean connectors carefully and try various manipulations of all the ways a researcher might have phrased your research topic to ensure you find as much literature as possible. Identify the keywords you find in relevant studies to help you understand different ways scholars have phrased your topic and use those as search parameters. Also, if you happen to find a recent article or book that concentrates on your research topic, read that study's literature review carefully to identify additional studies. Likewise, if you identify an older study that is particularly relevant for your topic, you could use Web of Science to identify studies that also referenced that work in their literature reviews.

Step 2: Read the studies.

Once you identify a number of relevant studies, start reading them. Many students often ask how many studies they should review for a paper. This is a difficult question to answer. The answer depends on what you would like to do with your paper once it is finished. On the one hand, if you are writing your paper for eventual publication, you must review as many studies as possible. A common criticism in the review process is the omission of important studies in the literature review. Therefore, being immersed as much as possible in the literature, understanding how ideas have developed over time, and knowing what scholars are concentrating on now are strongly advised. Identifying seminal studies is important, too. There are certain studies within the different subfields with which all researchers should be familiar. You may be able to identify these studies as you read the articles and books you find for your topic because most (if not all) researchers have also identified them in their literature reviews. Discussing and making reference to such seminal studies in your own study further establishes your credibility.

On the other hand, if you are writing this paper as an assignment for a course, your instructor may have a minimum number of studies that you must read for your literature review. This number will likely be somewhere between five and eight. If you limit the number of studies you use, you should ensure that the studies you do include are as relevant and informative as possible.

Step 3: Create annotated bibliographies for each study you have read.

One way to structure an annotated bibliography is to place the entire bibliographic citation at the top of a page and then follow it with important information about the study's content (research question, relevance, logic of argument, methods and data, results and conclusions, and generalizability). You should include any quotes with page numbers you think you might eventually use in your literature review or in other parts of your paper (such as the theory section you will eventually write). The goal is to create a bibliographic summary of each study you read for your own notes. Being systematic in this process will make the writing of the literature review much easier. Annotated bibliographies are not presented in the final version of a research paper, although your instructor may ask to see them at some point along the way.

Step 4: Find themes among the studies and write a literature review.

After writing annotated bibliographies, the hard work begins. Now you must incorporate all of the studies you have read into an integrated literature review, which, for your paper, will be presented in its own section called "Literature review." Make the literature review as complete and concise as possible. It should not be too short (one or two paragraphs is probably not enough) but it should not be too long because the literature review is not the main focus of the paper. For the paper on political values and attitudes you are writing with this book, a good literature review can be completed in roughly two to three double-spaced pages. You will know you have completed the literature review when you have exhausted the information from your annotated bibliographies and feel that you have been as concise and complete as possible.

COMING UP

Once the literature review of your general topic is complete, it is time to move on to the next step in the research process, which is asking an analytical research question. In the next chapter you will learn how to ask a specific type of analytical research question, one that involves two independent variables and one dependent variable.

CHAPTER 3

ASKING QUESTIONS IN POLITICAL SCIENCE

Now that you have identified a research topic (Chapter 1) and conducted a literature review (Chapter 2), the next step in the research process is to specify an appropriate question that you can answer through research. In this chapter you will learn how to construct analytical research questions. As mentioned in the introductory chapter, **analytical research questions** require explanation, analysis, and interpretation and will often produce answers that lead to additional questions.

ANALYTICAL RESEARCH QUESTIONS

Imagine that you are reading a newspaper and learn that Barack Obama won the most votes in North Carolina in the 2008 American presidential election, yet lost the state to Mitt Romney in 2012. In another news story you read that many countries around the world have begun to pass legislation that allows same-sex couples to marry legally. These are accepted facts. But as you digest this information, you may find yourself wanting to know more, since it is simply not enough to know that President Obama's vote share changed between 2008 and 2012 in North Carolina or that many countries allow same-sex marriage. If you find yourself asking additional questions, you are likely beginning your career as an analytical researcher. An analytical researcher asks different sorts of questions and will want to understand *why* Obama's vote shares changed between the two elections or *why* some countries allow same-sex marriage although others do not. In other words, the new questions identify *a puzzle* for each issue area, something that may not be fully understood right now and that requires a specific type of research. For many scholars in political science, the identification of an important and relevant puzzle to study through the specification of an analytical research question is one of the most important parts of the research process. Instead of simply asking how Barack Obama's vote share changed between two time periods or which countries allow same-sex marriage, an analytical researcher carefully assesses *why* something happened the way it happened or *why* something is the way it is.

Often in political science, the analytical questions researchers ask assess the relationship between two or more variables to determine whether patterns among them exist. **Variables** are attributes or characteristics that can vary across observations. Empirical relationships between variables are called **correlations**. Analytical research questions are usually designed so that correlations among variables can be identified. For example, taking from the examples above, a researcher might ask, How do the voting trends of the Latino community explain changes in the vote shares for President Obama in North Carolina between 2008 and 2012? or How does the political composition of a country influence the likelihood of that country allowing same-sex marriage? In these examples, the researcher is expecting the voting trends of the Latino community (for the first question) or the political compositions of countries (for the second question) to matter for the answer to each question. In other words, the researcher is hoping to discover a correlation between the two variables specified in each research question. These are good examples of analytical research questions because their answers are not immediately clear and they require an analysis and interpretation of empirical evidence so an answer to the question can be identified.

Many analytical research questions in political science are structured in a particular way. Does one variable influence another? Does variation in X influence variation in Y? For example, does the poverty rate of a city influence its crime rate? In this example we have two variables—the poverty rate and the crime rate—and by putting the two variables together in a single analytical research question, the ambition of the research is to determine whether there is a correlation between them. Analytical research questions are thus often designed to assess whether the relationships between the variables identified in the question form patterns in how the social world is constructed. Ultimately, the central purpose of this type of inquiry is to craft definitive statements about these ideas that we would expect to be true in other circumstances. For example, if we find that as the poverty rate increases, the crime rate also increases in one city in the United Kingdom, we might expect the same relationship to exist in other areas of the country. Other examples of such analytical research questions include the following: How does religion influence views on abortion? How does a country's regime type influence ethnic conflict? How does the style of media coverage for political events influence voter turnout rates? Each of these questions asks whether one variable is correlated with a second variable. Questions such as these are common in the social sciences and in political science in particular. They require the researcher to offer theoretical and/or empirical evidence to demonstrate that a correlation between two (or more) variables exists.

By asking the question in this way, we also imply that we are looking for some sense of causality between variables in our analyses. Because we rarely deal with the types of experimental laboratories often found in the natural sciences (where the notion of control is very important), definitively establishing causality, where we can say that a particular value in one variable caused a particular value in a second variable, is no easy task in social science. Many social science researchers attempt to establish causality through theory and by demonstrating through research that empirical correlations do indeed exist between variables. We will return to establishing causality more fully in the next chapter, but for now, understand that when devising an analytical research question, a researcher should have both an *expectation* (correlation) and an *explanation* (theory) for why one variable should be related to another based on causal reasoning. Remember, however, that just because two variables are shown to be correlated with each other, the relationship between them is not automatically causal. This observation is the basis for the important adage that most researchers know well: correlation is not causation. This is why good theory is important. Thus, a researcher investigating how the Latino vote influenced Obama's vote shares in North Carolina between 2008 and 2012 must think about whether (correlation) *and* why (causation) the Latino vote is associated with the difference in vote shares. Likewise, a researcher investigating same-sex marriage must think about whether (correlation) *and* why (causation) the political composition of a country is associated with its likelihood of allowing same-sex marriage. Take this into consideration whenever you construct a research question. Do not include variables in a research question arbitrarily. Always have an expectation for why two or more variables are expected to be associated with one another because eventually you will need to develop a causal theory for why one variable causes another. To summarize, analytical research questions (1) require explanation, analysis, and interpretation; (2) ask whether a correlation exists between two or more variables; and (3) require the elaboration of a causal theory to understand why correlations among variables should exist.

Independent and Dependent Variables

Analytical research questions are often written in such a way that the variables under investigation can be easily identified. More often than not, researchers speak in terms of dependent and independent variables. A **dependent variable** is what we wish to explain in our research. Dependent variables are sometimes called "outcome" or "effect" variables. An **independent variable** is what we use to explain variation in a dependent variable. Independent variables are sometimes called "change" or "impact" variables. Some researchers also use the letter Y to denote the dependent variable and X to denote the independent variable. In analytical research questions, independent variables are expected to occur before dependent variables. (This will be important later when we attempt to establish causality between the independent and dependent variables in a theory.) For example, in the question "How does regime type influence ethnic conflict?" we identify regime type as the independent variable and ethnic conflict as the dependent variable. By stating the question in this way, we signal that we think regime type has some influence on ethnic conflict and not the other way around (that ethnic conflict influences regime type). In the question "How do differences in religiosity influence views on abortion?" differences in religiosity is the independent variable, whereas views on abortion is the dependent variable. Again, the purpose of the research question is to assess whether variation in religiosity has some effect on the variation on views on abortion, not whether variation in views on abortion influences variation in religiosity. The idea is that a change in the value of the independent variable will precipitate a change in the dependent variable (see Figure 3.1).

Since independent and dependent variables are variables, they must *vary*. This may seem obvious, but the necessity of variation is often taken for granted. It is only through the assessment of variation that we can determine whether correlations between variables exist. Although this is true, a researcher often will include an independent variable in his or her analysis and only include one observational value on the independent variable. For example, if a researcher asks "How do differences in religiosity influence views on abortion?" and only includes people who are very religious in the research design, it will not be possible to answer the research question. In other words, it will not be possible to make a statement about how different levels of religiosity explain variation in views on abortion because there is no variation in the independent variable. All of the people studied in the research represent the same value for

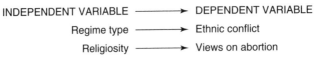

FIGURE 3.1:   Independent and Dependent Variables

the independent variable—they are all very religious. New researchers often make this mistake. They ask a question that they cannot answer with their research design. If the question were "How do differences in political affiliation influence views on abortion among very religious people?" it would be answerable using only one group of people. But if the question is "How do differences in religiosity influence views on abortion?" and only one group representing one value on the independent variable (very religious people) is studied, the research question cannot be answered because there is no variation in the independent variable. Put differently, when there is no variation in the independent variable, it is not possible to determine whether variation in the independent variable is correlated with variation in a dependent variable. Take another example. If a researcher asks how biological sex influences the probability of reelection and only studies men, it will not be possible to make a generalizable statement about biological sex as an independent variable since only one value on the independent variable (men) was assessed. To understand whether and how biological sex impacts the probability of being reelected, observations from both men and women are necessary in the research design.

Other Types of Variables

In addition to independent and dependent variables, other variables are sometimes included in research designs. The most common are antecedent and intervening variables. Although you will not identify these types of variables for the analyses you will perform as you continue through this book, you should still know what they are because other studies include them and you may choose to include a discussion of them as part of the discussion of your results once your data analysis is complete. Generally, the distinction between antecedent and intervening variables involves where they are placed within the expected relationship between the independent and dependent variables. **Antecedent variables** are those that are present prior to the variables included in the analysis. These variables may impact a dependent variable before the independent variable included in the analysis has an effect on the dependent variable. For example, a study that assesses how regime type influences ethnic conflict might specify each country's historical experience with ethnic conflict as an antecedent variable that might also influence the country's current level of ethnic conflict. Thus, each country's historical experience with ethnic conflict may have played some role in causing its current level of conflict. Although researchers may not formally include an antecedent variable in the analysis, it is still important to identify antecedent variables as alternative or contributing explanations for variation of the dependent variable.

By contrast, **intervening variables** interact with an independent variable in some way to produce an effect on the dependent variable. The placement of an intervening variable is generally between the independent and dependent variables. The intervening variable can help further explain the effect the independent variable has on the dependent variable. For example, a study that assesses how someone's religiosity influences views on abortion might identify placement on the left/right political scale as an intervening variable that helps connect how differences in religiosity influence abortion views. There may be a difference, for example, among religious people who identify either to the political left or to the political right and their views on abortion. Thus, although religiosity on its own is important, the identification of intervening variables allows you to consider how independent variables may interact with an intervening variable to influence the dependent variable in a systematic way.

PHRASING ANALYTICAL RESEARCH QUESTIONS

Many researchers working in political science ask questions in a straightforward way. Often, the main variables under study can be inferred from the title alone. Consider the titles of the following five studies that have been published in top journals in political science.

1. Jan H. Pierskalla and Florian M. Hollenbach. 2013. "Technology and Collective Action: The Effect of Cell Phone Coverage on Political Violence in Africa." *American Political Science Review* 107 (2): 207–24.
2. Peter K. Hatemi. 2013. "The Influence of Major Life Events on Economic Attitudes in a World of Gene–Environment Interplay." *American Journal of Political Science* 57 (4): 987–1007.
3. Jaroslav Tir and Shane P. Singh. 2013. "Is It the Economy or Foreign Policy, Stupid? The Impact of Foreign Crises on Leader Support." *Comparative Politics* 46 (1): 83–101.
4. David E. Campbell. 2013. "Social Networks and Political Participation." *Annual Review of Political Science* 16: 33–48.
5. Yann P. Kerevela and Lonna Rae Atkeson. 2013. "Explaining the Marginalization of Women in Legislative Institutions." *Journal of Politics* 75 (4): 980–92.

For each study, the dependent variable is readily identified. You should also be able to identify the independent variables in the titles of the first four studies (see Table 3.1). Furthermore, in the first three titles, expressions such as "the effect of," "the influence of," or "the impact of" give the reader a clear

TABLE 3.1:   IDENTIFYING INDEPENDENT AND DEPENDENT VARIABLES IN RESEARCH STUDIES

	Independent variable	Dependent variable
Pierskalla and Hollenbach	Cell phone coverage	Political violence
Hatemi	Major life events	Economic attitudes
Tir and Singh	Foreign crises	Leader support
Campbell	Social networks	Political participation
Kerevela and Atkeson	Not specified	Marginalization of women

indication of how the independent variable is expected to occur before the dependent variable. This wording provides an understanding that the authors want to establish a link between the independent and dependent variables (and presumably there is a theory behind each expectation to argue why different values in the independent variables cause different values in the dependent variables). Although the fourth study does not include a phrase to indicate the nature of the relationship between the independent and dependent variables, it can be inferred from the title that the researcher will argue that social networks influence political participation in some way. In the fifth study, the researchers clearly specify the dependent variable—the marginalization of women in legislative institutions—but leave independent variables out of the title.

Each of the variables identified in these paper titles can vary—there can be more or less cell phone coverage and more or less political violence, fewer or more major life events and positive or negative economic attitudes, fewer or more foreign crises and more or less leader support, more or less social networking and more or less political participation, and more or less marginalization of women in legislative institutions. Each of these variables varies, which means that the researchers can answer the research question they ask in their studies.

Let's take a closer look at two other examples of research questions from the political science literature. In 2007, three scholars published a paper in *Public Choice* to assess whether government involvement influences life satisfaction. They titled their paper "The Bigger the Better? Evidence of the Effect of Government Size on Life Satisfaction around the World."[1] Thinking of the title as a research question, can you determine the independent and dependent variables? Drawing from the five examples above, it is probably clear by now that government size is the independent variable and life satisfaction is the

---

1   Taken from Christian Bjørnskov, Axel Dreher, and Justina A. V. Fischer, 2007, "The Bigger the Better? Evidence of the Effect of Government Size on Life Satisfaction around the World," *Public Choice* 130 (3/4): 267–92.

dependent variable. In addition, the first part of the question, "The Bigger the Better?" should signal to us that there is likely some debate about this issue. Some scholars might have argued that bigger government causes more life satisfaction, whereas others might have argued that bigger government causes less life satisfaction. Which is it? On first glance, we do not know the answer to this research question, but we may have opinions based on our own experiences. One person may think bigger government leads to greater life satisfaction, whereas another person may think the opposite. Thus, before reading the paper, just from the title we can begin a theoretical debate about which value of the independent variable (bigger or smaller government) we think leads to greater or lesser life satisfaction. Like the examples above, the wording of the question allows us to think about variation in both the independent and the dependent variables. The independent variable (government size) can be big or small and the dependent variable (life satisfaction) can be high or low. By asking the question in this way and by ensuring the subsequent analysis captures observations on as many values of the variables as possible, the researchers can eventually provide an answer to the question based on the analysis and interpretation of empirical evidence. Hence, this is a good example of an analytical research question.

To answer their research question, the researchers first took data from a database called the World Values Survey (WVS). Specifically, they collected data on the dependent variable (life satisfaction) for 74 countries. Life satisfaction was measured by the WVS as a response to the question "How satisfied are you with your life these days?" Respondents could choose a number between 1 (not satisfied at all) and 10 (completely satisfied). The value the researchers used for overall life satisfaction is the percentage of respondents in each country that answered the satisfaction question with a score of 8, 9, or 10, the top three categories, indicating high levels of satisfaction. In their appendix, the researchers show that for the full sample, the lowest value on this particular scale is 9.55% (for India) and the highest value is 76.8% (for Denmark). This means that only 9.55% of the respondents in India answered the satisfaction question with an 8, 9, or 10, compared with 76.8% of the respondents in Denmark, and the remaining 72 countries fall somewhere in between. Clearly, there is variation here—according to the WVS, many more people are satisfied in Denmark than in India. For the independent variable, the researchers used a measure to assess direct government involvement in the economy at a number of different levels of involvement. These data were taken from the Penn World Tables. The lowest value for this variable is 6.01 (representing Japan) and the highest is 49.66 (representing Jordan). Thus, like the independent variable, there is variation in the dependent variable. What this means is that the researchers were able to perform statistical analysis to determine whether the two variables highlighted in their research question are empirically linked, that is, whether variation in the independent variable is correlated with variation in the dependent variable.

The lead author for another paper, Robert Inglehart, has been working on issues concerning ideas surrounding modernization and postmodernization for a long time. The title of one of his papers is "Changing Mass Priorities: The Link between Modernization and Democracy."[2] Again, the title alone provides important clues as to what the independent and dependent variables are: modernization is the independent variable and democracy is the dependent variable. In this paper, Inglehart and his co-author, Christian Welzel, argue that cultural variables, such as the values people in different societies hold, should be included in studies that assess levels of democracy. The problem is that culture is an elusive concept to measure; as a result, many researchers often leave it out when studying variations in democracy, choosing instead to include variables that are easier to quantify, such as aggregate economic indicators like per capita income. The contribution of Inglehart and Welzel's study is to demonstrate how certain cultural variables can be measured at the national level and then correlated with variation in democracy. The way to do this, the researchers suggest, is to use highly accessible survey data from sources like the WVS and to provide national averages for particular cultural variables such as religiosity or public trust for different countries. These averages, in turn, can be used to explain differences in democracy.

In the paper, the researchers assess many countries at the same time. Their ambition is to show how cultural variables can be measured at the national level as an indicator for differences in modernization and that the differences among the values that represent the level of modernization can be used to explain differences in democracy in different countries. Again, we see how the variables vary. Differences in modernization are expected to be associated with differences in democracy.

In both of the articles described above, you may have noted that a particular dataset, the WVS, was involved. The WVS "is a global network of social scientists studying changing values and their impact on social and political life, led by an international team of scholars, with the WVS

---

2   Taken from Robert Inglehart and Christian Welzel, 2010, "Changing Mass Priorities: The Link between Modernization and Democracy," *Perspectives on Politics* 8 (2): 551–67.

association and secretariat headquartered in Stockholm, Sweden."[3] The WVS website, which you will learn to access later in the chapter, includes a large comparative public opinion database with more than 250,000 interviews from the vast majority of the world's countries. The interviews have been conducted since the late 1970s and have been released to the public in a series of waves. The sixth and most recent wave was released in April 2014. It contains data for countries in which interviews were held between 2010 and 2014. You will use the survey questions available in the WVS as a means of identifying independent and dependent variables so that you can compose an analytical research question based on the research topic you chose in Chapter 1.

INTRODUCTION TO MEASUREMENT

Before we continue, you should understand something about measurement and **quantification**. Quantification involves turning words into numbers so that variables can be systematically analyzed. It is important to understand the main differences among variables now because the specific form a variable takes will directly influence what you can do with it in quantitative analysis. At the end of this chapter you will be required to identify the independent variables you will use to explain variation in a single dependent variable (one that is related to your research topic). To ensure that you can perform the different quantitative techniques you will learn in Chapters 7–9, you must have certain types of variables to analyze. Hence, it is best if you learn the different levels of measurement now so you can make the appropriate choices later in this chapter. Researchers work with several different levels of measurement: nominal, ordinal, interval, and ratio. Overwhelmingly, the WVS contains variables that have nominal and ordinal measurement.

Nominal measurement involves placing observations into discrete categories to create a variable. The categories do not have an inherent order to them and, as a result, they are not analyzed in terms of "less than" or "more than" statements. For example, to measure the concept of party choice in the United States, the WVS asks the following question: "Which party would you vote for if there were a national election tomorrow?" The possible categories for surveys conducted in the United States in 2011 are shown in Table 3.2.

---

3   See http://www.worldvaluessurvey.org/WVSContents.jsp for more information about the World Values Survey.

TABLE 3.2:   2011 POSSIBLE RESPONSES FOR V228, "WHICH PARTY WOULD YOU VOTE FOR IF THERE WERE A NATIONAL ELECTION TOMORROW?" FOR U.S. 2011

No answer
Don't know
Other
I would not vote
U.S.: Republican
U.S.: Democrat

The categories for a variable with nominal measurement should be both exhaustive and exclusive. The categories should be exhaustive so that every observation can fit into one of the possible categories. The categories should also be exclusive so that any one observation should fit into only one category. For example, someone who identifies as a Republican should not simultaneously be able to identify as a Democrat.

A special type of variable with nominal measurement is a **binary variable**. A binary variable contains only two categories. For example, one of the WVS questions asks respondents whether they were born in the United States or whether they are immigrants to the United States. Since there are only two possible responses, it is a binary variable (see Table 3.3).

Some indicators for concepts naturally result in binary variables because, given the survey question and range of possible answers, observations can fall into only one of two possible categories. Biological sex (male/female) is a good example of a binary variable.

Although some variables with nominal measurement are binary variables on their own, it is possible to condense the information from a variable with many categories to create a new binary variable with only two categories. Consider the measurement for ethnic group in the WVS for the United States in 2011. To measure ethnic group, the WVS asked participants to identify their ethnic group, which resulted in the categories listed in Table 3.4.

This variable with nominal measurement has five categories. There are two ways to condense this information so that it can be transformed into a binary variable.

TABLE 3.3:   POSSIBLE RESPONSES FOR V245, "RESPONDENT IMMIGRANT" FOR U.S. 2011

I am born in this country
I am an immigrant to this country

TABLE 3.4: POSSIBLE RESPONSES FOR V254, "ETHNIC GROUP"

U.S. white, non-Hispanic
U.S. black, non-Hispanic
U.S. other, non-Hispanic
U.S. Hispanic
U.S. 2+ races, non-Hispanic

1. First, you could use only two of the categories from the entire list if the desired goal is to compare two particular categories, for example U.S. white, non-Hispanic and U.S. black, non-Hispanic. Before you do this, however, you should ensure that each category in your new variable has enough representation to be meaningful in your study. You will be shown how to do this later in the chapter.

2. Second, you could group categories to create overarching categories. For example, you could leave the U.S. white, non-Hispanic category as it is and create a U.S. nonwhite category by combining the observations from the remaining categories (U.S. black, non-Hispanic, U.S. other, non-Hispanic, U.S. Hispanic, and U.S. 2+ races, non-Hispanic) into a new category. Once the U.S. nonwhite category has been created, the original variable will have been transformed from a variable with nominal measurement with five categories into a binary variable with only two categories.

As part of the activities associated with this book, you must transform any variables with nominal measurement you use into binary variables for the quantitative analysis you will do on the WVS data. You will learn how to do this in Chapter 7. Thus, if you are using any variable with nominal measurement that has more than two categories associated with it, variables such as party choice, religion, or ethnic group, you will be required to either (1) choose two categories within the variable to analyze or (2) combine the information from several categories to form new groups until only two categories remain.

Ordinal measurement involves placing observations into categories for which the ordering of the values representing the categories has meaning. In other words, a variable with ordinal measurement is one in which the ordering of values matters for understanding variation within the variable itself. The values generally represent a quantitative scale. Many of the questions in the WVS create variables with ordinal measurement. For example, some questions ask respondents to express their confidence in various institutions, such as churches, the armed forces, or the press. The WVS allows respondents to choose among four possible categories, wherein a value of 1 represents "a great deal" of confidence, 2 represents "quite a lot" of confidence, 3 represents "not very much" confidence, and 4 represents "none at all" (see Figure 3.2). The ordering of the values for these variables matters substantially because a respondent who selects a value of 1 with this particular measurement scheme has more confidence than a respondent who selects 2. In turn, a respondent who selects a 2 has more confidence than a respondent who selects 3, and so on. Many of the attitudinal variables in the WVS are structured this way.

When working with variables with ordinal measurement, it is important to understand how the values are ordered. For the confidence variable, note that lower numbers represent higher levels of support and higher numbers represent lower levels of support as shown in Figure 3.2. The ordering of the values will be important when you interpret the results of your data analysis. You should always know how your variables are ordered and what the lower and higher values in the variable mean.

Although variables with ordinal measurement are common in political science, one drawback to their use is the inability to infer the precise distance between the categories from differences in the values. We cannot, for example, say that someone who answers "a great deal" of confidence (the 1 category) has twice as much confidence as someone who answers "quite a lot" of confidence (the 2 category) or three times as much confidence as someone who answers "not very much" confidence (the 3 category). This is because the precise distance between the categories is not known.

The dependent variable you will work with throughout this book, as you will see, has ordinal measurement, except that instead of being from 1 to 4 as with the confidence variables described above, the dependent variable you will choose is on a scale from 1 to 10. Again, for any variable with ordinal measurement you should know what the lower numbers represent and what the higher numbers represent. For example, life satisfaction is measured from 1 to 10, with 1 representing completely dissatisfied and 10 representing completely satisfied.

As opposed to ordinal measurement, with **interval measurement** the distance between values on a variable can be assessed. In variables with interval measurement, the distance between one value and the next is uniformly the

1	2	3	4
A great deal	Quite a lot	Not very much	None at all

FIGURE 3.2: Response Structure for a Variable with Ordinal Measurement with Four Categories

same. For example, someone who was born in 1990 was born one year before someone who was born in 1991. Thus, not only can we say that someone born in 1990 is older than someone who was born in 1991, but also we can determine how much older the person is in years. Variables with interval measurement are useful in this way.

The last type of measurement is **ratio measurement**. Ratio measurement is similar to interval measurement in that the distance between the values can be meaningfully assessed, but unlike variables with interval measurement, variables with ratio measurement have a true zero associated with them. Ratio measurement is present any time we count something that starts from zero. Like the variables with ordinal and interval measurement, the differences between values matter. Someone who earns $40,000 a year earns more than someone who earns $20,000 a year. A legislator who submitted six amendments to a bill submitted more amendments than a legislator who submitted two. Thus, for these variables, lower numbers mean less of something; higher values mean more of something. However, the presence of a true zero in variables with ratio measurement allows us to make additional statements about the distance between the values associated with the variable. Someone who earns $40,000 a year earns twice as much as someone who earns $20,000. A legislator who submitted six amendments submitted three times more amendments than the legislator who submitted two. These types of statements are not possible with variables with ordinal or interval measurement.

In descriptive statistics and data analysis, which will be covered in later chapters, the distinction between variables with nominal measurement on the one hand and variables with ordinal, interval, or ratio measurement on the other hand means a great deal for how they can be used. For this reason, you must understand the differences among them before you choose the independent variables to include in your analytical research question. Later you will fully understand why this distinction is important.

COMING UP WITH AN ANALYTICAL RESEARCH QUESTION

In Chapter 1, you chose a research topic from a list of 16 possible research topics. These research topics were chosen deliberately because each has a specific survey question associated with it in the WVS. The variation in responses to the particular survey question will form your dependent variable. After you identify your dependent variable from the list, you must choose two independent variables, one with nominal measurement and one with ordinal measurement, from variables available in the WVS. Putting the independent and dependent variables together will form the basis for your analytical research question.

Step 1: Identify the Dependent Variable (DV) for Your Research Topic

The research topic you chose in Chapter 1 represents a general concept in social science: life satisfaction, left/right ideological placement, views on public trust, etc. To operationalize each concept, it is necessary to identify an indicator so that the concept can be measured and assessed empirically through a variable. The operationalization of concepts in social science will be covered more fully in Chapter 6. But for now, know that each research topic listed in Chapter 1 has been operationalized with a particular survey question in the WVS, and thus each topic listed in Chapter 1 already has a dependent variable associated with it. The dependent variables for each topic are listed below. Note that the range of possible responses produces a variable with ordinal measurement with values that range from 1 to 10. For example, for satisfaction with life, someone who responded with a 1 is completely dissatisfied with life, and someone who responded with a 10 is completely satisfied with life. Numbers between 1 and 10 represent intermediate categories. Someone who responded with a 2 is probably a little more satisfied than someone who responded with a 1, someone who responded with a 9 is a not as satisfied as someone who responded with a 10, and so on.

The first step in writing your analytical research question is to locate the research topic you chose in Chapter 1 from the list in Figure 3.3. Each topic is associated with a particular "V" designation. Make a note of the number following the V so that you will be able to locate your variable later when it is included with the many variables available in the WVS. Under the topic is the wording of the WVS question as it was asked to respondents, and under that is the range of possible responses. The range of responses for the survey question for your research topic is now your dependent variable.[4]

---

4   Keep in mind that for other projects you do in political science, for your courses or otherwise, you could choose any number of dependent variables for a particular topic. For example, imagine that your research topic were "support for right wing parties in Europe." A number of potential dependent variables could be identified for this topic. You could, for example, measure the percentage of votes each country's right-wing party received in the most recent election for the European parliament. Or, you could measure the percentage of votes each country's right-wing party received in the most recent national election. Or, you could measure the percentage of votes each country's right-wing party received in each country's most recent local elections. Each of these potential dependent variables falls under the general research topic "support for right-wing parties in Europe." Thus, the research topic is the general idea for which a number of potential dependent variables can be identified. But for the papers you will write, the heavy lifting, so to speak, has already been done for you because there is a specific dependent variable that has already been identified for each of the 16 research topics listed in Chapter 1.

V23: SATISFACTION WITH LIFE

(All things considered, how satisfied are you with your life as a whole these days? ... 1 means you are "completely dissatisfied" and 10 means you are "completely satisfied." Where would you put your satisfaction with your life as a whole?)

The respondent is completely   The respondent is completely
dissatisfied with life   satisfied with life

      1   2   3   4   5   6   7   8   9   10

V55: PERCEPTIONS OF PERSONAL CHOICE AND CONTROL IN ONE'S LIFE

(Some people feel they have completely free choice and control over their lives, while other people feel that what they do has no real effect on what happens to them. Please use this scale where 1 means "no choice at all" and 10 means "a great deal of choice" to indicate how much freedom of choice and control you feel you have over the way your life turns out.)

People do not have choice and   People have a great deal
control over the way life turns   ofchoice and control over the
out   way life turns out

      1   2   3   4   5   6   7   8   9   10

V56: PERCEPTIONS ON PUBLIC TRUST

(Do you think most people would try to take advantage of you if they got a chance, or would they try to be fair? ... 1 means that "people would try to take advantage of you," and 10 means that "people would try to be fair.")

People would try   People would try
to take advantage   to be fair
of you

      1   2   3   4   5   6   7   8   9   10

V59: SATISFACTION WITH FINANCIAL SITUATION OF HOUSEHOLD

(How satisfied are you with the financial situation of your household?)

Completely dissatisfied with fi-   Completely satisfied with financial situation of household   nancial situation of household

      1   2   3   4   5   6   7   8   9   10

<u>V95: LEFT/RIGHT IDEOLOGY</u>

(In political matters, people talk of "the left" and "the right."
How would you place your views on this scale, generally speaking?)

Left   Right

  1   2   3   4   5   6   7   8   9   10

<u>V96: VIEWS ON INCOME DIFFERENCES AMONG PEOPLE IN A SOCIETY</u>

(How would you place your views on this scale? 1 means you agree completely
with the statement on the left; 10 means you agree completely with the statement on the right; and if your views fall somewhere in between, you can
choose any number in between: "Incomes should be made more equal" vs.
"We need larger income differences as incentives for individual effort")

Incomes should be made more   We need larger income differ-
equal   ences as incentives for indi-
                                                vidual effort

  1   2   3   4   5   6   7   8   9   10

<u>V97: VIEWS ON PRIVATE VS. STATE OWNERSHIP</u>

(How would you place your views on this scale? 1 means you agree completely
with the statement on the left; 10 means you agree completely with the statement on the right; and if your views fall somewhere in between, you can choose
any number in between: "Private ownership of business and industry should
be increased" vs. "Government ownership of business and industry should be
increased")

Private ownership of business   Government ownership of
and industry should be   business and industry
increased   should be increased

  1   2   3   4   5   6   7   8   9   10

<u>V98: VIEWS ON GOVERNMENT VS. INDIVIDUAL RESPONSIBILITY</u>

(How would you place your views on this scale? 1 means you agree completely
with the statement on the left; 10 means you agree completely with the statement on the right; and if your views fall somewhere in between, you can choose

any number in between: "Government should take more responsibility to ensure that everyone is provided for" vs. "People should take more responsibility to provide for themselves")

Government should take more responsibility to ensure that everyone is provided for						People should take more responsibility to provide for themselves			
1	2	3	4	5	6	7	8	9	10

V99: VIEWS ON WHETHER ECONOMIC COMPETITION IS GOOD OR HARMFUL

(How would you place your views on this scale? 1 means you agree completely with the statement on the left; 10 means you agree completely with the statement on the right; and if your views fall somewhere in between, you can choose any number in between: "Competition is good. It stimulates people to work hard and develop new ideas" vs. "Competition is harmful. It brings out the worst in people")

Competition is good. It stimulates people to work hard and develop new ideas						Competition is harmful. It brings out the worstin in people			
1	2	3	4	5	6	7	8	9	10

V101: VIEWS ON WEALTH ACCUMULATION

(How would you place your views on this scale? 1 means you agree completely with the statement on the left; 10 means you agree completely with the statement on the right; and if your views fall somewhere in between, you can choose any number in between: "People can only get rich at the expense of others" vs. "Wealth can grow so there's enough for everyone")

People can only get rich at the expense of others						Wealth can grow so there's enough for everyone			
1	2	3	4	5	6	7	8	9	10

V131: VIEWS ON WHETHER TAXATION OF THE RICH IS AN ESSENTIAL CHARACTERISTIC OF DEMOCRACY

(Many things are desirable, but not all of them are essential characteristics of democracy. Please tell me for each of the following things how essential you think it is as a characteristic of democracy. Use this scale where 1 means "not at all an essential characteristic of democracy" and 10 means it definitely is "an essential characteristic of democracy": Governments tax the rich and subsidize the poor)

It is not an essential characteristic of democracy for governments to tax the rich and subsidize the poor

It is an essential characteristic of democracy for governments to tax the rich and subsidize the poor

1	2	3	4	5	6	7	8	9	10

V134: VIEWS ON WHETHER UNEMPLOYMENT BENEFITS ARE AN ESSENTIAL CHARACTERISTIC OF DEMOCRACY

(Many things are desirable, but not all of them are essential characteristics of democracy. Please tell me for each of the following things how essential you think it is as a characteristic of democracy. Use this scale where 1 means "not at all an essential characteristic of democracy" and 10 means it definitely is "an essential characteristic of democracy": People receive state aid for unemployment)

It is not an essential characteristic of democracy for people to receive state aid for unemployment

It is an essential characteristic of democracy for people to receive state aid for unemployment

1	2	3	4	5	6	7	8	9	10

V137: VIEWS ON WHETHER REDUCING INCOME INEQUALITY IS AN ESSENTIAL CHARACTERISTIC OF DEMOCRACY

(Many things are desirable, but not all of them are essential characteristics of democracy. Please tell me for each of the following things how essential you think it is as a characteristic of democracy. Use this scale where 1 means "not at all an essential characteristic of democracy" and 10 means it definitely is "an essential characteristic of democracy": The state makes people's incomes equal)

It is not an essential characteristic of democracy that the state makes people's incomes equal

It is an essential characteristic of democracy that the state makes people's incomes equal

1	2	3	4	5	6	7	8	9	10

V138: VIEWS ON WHETHER OBEDIENCE OF RULERS IS AN ESSENTIAL CHARACTERISTIC OF DEMOCRACY

(Many things are desirable, but not all of them are essential characteristics of democracy. Please tell me for each of the following things how essential you think it is as a characteristic of democracy. Use this scale where 1 means "not at all an essential characteristic of democracy" and 10 means it definitely is "an essential characteristic of democracy": People obey their rulers)

It is not an essential characteristic of democracy that people
obey their rulers

It is an essential characteristic
of democracy that people obey
their rulers

    1   2   3   4   5   6   7   8   9   10

V139: VIEWS ON WHETHER REDUCING GENDER EQUALITY IS AN ESSENTIAL CHARACTERISTIC OF DEMOCRACY

(Many things are desirable, but not all of them are essential characteristics of democracy. Please tell me for each of the following things how essential you think it is as a characteristic of democracy. Use this scale where 1 means "not at all an essential characteristic of democracy" and 10 means it definitely is "an essential characteristic of democracy": Women have the same rights as men)

It is not an essential characteristic of democracy that women
have the same rights as men

It is an essential characteristic
of democracy that women have
the same rights as men

    1   2   3   4   5   6   7   8   9   10

V141: VIEWS ON HOW DEMOCRACY IS WORKING

(How democratically is this country being governed today? Using a scale from 1 to 10, where 1 means that it is "not at all democratic" and 10 means that it is "completely democratic," what position would you choose?)

The country is not at all
democratic

The country is completely
democratic

    1   2   3   4   5   6   7   8   9   10

FIGURE 3.3: Survey Questions That Serve as Dependent Variables for the 16 Research Topics Listed in Chapter 1

Step 2: Choose Independent Variables (IV1 and IV2)

Now that you have your research topic and specific dependent variable, you must think about the rest of the research question. You now need independent variables that will be used to explain variation in your dependent variable. Think about the respondents themselves. Why would someone respond in one way and not another to the WVS question that represents your dependent variable? Are there attributes about the respondents that would systematically influence how they might answer the question representing your dependent variable? For example, would women respond differently than men? If so, then biological sex might be an important independent variable. Would more educated people respond differently than less educated people? If so, then education level might be an important independent variable. Would people who are more interested in politics respond differently than people who are less interested in politics? If so, then interest in politics might be an important independent variable.

One way to think about independent variables is to consider the studies you reviewed in preparation for your literature review. What insight did you glean from what you read? Were you able to identify particular variables you think you should include as independent variables? If so, you may wish to include them as part of your analysis.

Once you choose independent variables, you will be able to put your variables together in an analytical research question. Later you will be able to conduct data analysis to determine which independent variables are empirically correlated with your dependent variable. Think of *two* possible independent variables that might influence variation in the dependent variable. Choose carefully—as explained earlier in the chapter, you do not want to choose independent variables arbitrarily. *You will eventually have to explain why each independent variable is expected to correlate in some way with the dependent variable in a causal theory.*

For example, if the dependent variable is views on income differences (V96), what distinguishes people who believe that incomes should be made equal from people who believe that we need income differences as incentives? One possible independent variable to explain why people respond differently to this question is whether the respondents listed hard work as an important quality to teach children. (One of the questions in the WVS asks respondents to list 5 of 11 potential qualities that are important to teach children. In addition to hard work, these qualities include core values such as independence, feeling of responsibility, imagination, tolerance, thrift, determination, religious faith, unselfishness, obedience, and self-expression.) People who list hard work as one of the 5 top qualities to teach children may put a premium on competition and believe that economic winners, defined as those who earn the most in a society, should be those who work the hardest. Hard work is what determines what people earn in the work place. If hard work is not encouraged as a core value, people might not work at all or believe that they are responsible for themselves. Consequently, someone who responds that hard work is an important quality to teach children might be more likely to also respond that income differences are necessary as incentives.

But remember that variables vary. If the independent variable and dependent variable are associated with one another, then the respondents who do *not* list hard work as an important quality for parents to teach children should also think that incomes should be more equal. We also need an explanation for why this expectation is true. People who think parents should teach children other qualities first might believe that hard work should not be the end goal of one's life. For these respondents, other qualities such as unselfishness, imagination, and tolerance may be more important and, hence, people who do not indicate that hard work is one of the top five important qualities to teach children might think that income differences among people should not be large because all people should have access to a certain level of income and standard of living. Thus, as you choose your independent variables, *be sure to think about how different values of the independent variable might be associated with different values of the dependent variable.*

Look at the lists of independent variables in Table 3.5. Although these lists are long, they do not contain all the questions that were asked during the administration of the WVS in the 2011 interviews. Generally, the variables included on these lists are the ones that broadly have something to do with politics. Note that the possible independent variables are presented in two columns, Column A and Column B. Choose one independent variable from Column A and one independent variable from Column B. Column A includes survey questions that produce variables with nominal measurement. Examples include party choice, ethnic group, or religion. Some of these variables are binary variables on their own, whereas others are not. Later in the chapter you will learn how to access the WVS's online interface so you can see the categories associated with the variables with nominal measurement listed in Column A. This is important because if a variable in Column A is associated with more than two categories, you must

TABLE 3.5: POSSIBLE INDEPENDENT VARIABLES

Column A Nominal measurement	Column B Ordinal, interval, or ratio measurement
V12: Important child qualities: independence	V7: Important in life: politics
V13: Important child qualities: hard work	V9: Important in life: work
V14: Important child qualities: feeling of responsibility	V10: Important in life: religion
V15: Important child qualities: imagination	V23: Satisfaction with your life
V16: Important in life: tolerance and respect for other people	V51: On the whole, men make better political leaders than women do
V17: Important child qualities: thrift, saving money and things	V55: How much freedom of choice and control over own life?
V18: Important child qualities: determination, perseverance	V56: Do you think most people would try to take advantage of you if they got a chance, or would they try to be fair?
V19: Important child qualities: religious faith	V58: How many children do you have?
V20: Important child qualities: unselfishness	V59: Satisfaction with financial situation of household
V21: Important child qualities: obedience	V70: It is important for this person to think up new ideas and be creative, to do things one's own way
V22: Important child qualities: self-expression	V71: It is important to this person to be rich, to have a lot of money and expensive things
V24: Most people can be trusted	V72: Living in secure surroundings is important to this person, to avoid anything that might be dangerous
V25: Active/inactive member: church or religious organization	V74: It is important to this person to do something for the good of society
V28: Active/inactive member: labor union	V78: Looking after the environment is important to this person; to care for nature and save life resources
V29: Active/inactive member: political party	V79: Tradition is important to this person; to follow the customs handed down by one's religion or family
V30: Active/inactive member: environmental organization	V84: Interest in politics
V57: Marital status	V90: Political action recently done: signing a petition
V60: Aims of country: first choice[5]	V91: Political action recently done: joining in boycotts
V62: Aims of respondent: first choice[6]	V92: Political action recently done: attending peaceful demonstrations
V64: Most important: first choice[7]	V93: Political action recently done: joining strikes
V66: Willingness to fight for your country	V95: Self-positioning on political scale
V67: Future changes: less importance placed on work in our lives	V96: Income inequality
V69: Future changes: greater respect for authority	V97: Private versus state ownership of business

(continued)

5   Aims of country: first choice (choices are a high level of economic growth, making sure country has strong defense forces, seeing that people have more say about how things are done at their jobs and in their communities, and trying to make our cities and countryside more beautiful).

6   Aims of respondent: first choice (choices are maintaining order in the nation, giving people more say in important governmental decisions, fighting rising prices, and protection of freedom of speech).

7   Most important: first choice (choices are a stable economy, progress toward a less impersonal and more humane society, progress toward a society in which ideas count more than money, and the fight against crime).

TABLE 3.5:   POSSIBLE INDEPENDENT VARIABLES (*Continued*)

V80: Most serious problem in the world[8]	V98: Government responsibility
V81: Protecting environment versus economic growth	V99: Competition good or harmful
V144: Religious denomination	V100: Hard work brings success
V145: How often do you attend religious services?	V101: Wealth accumulation
V147: Religious person	V110: Confidence: the press
V228: Which party would you vote for if there were a national election tomorrow?	V112: Confidence: labor unions
V229: Employment status	V113: Confidence: the police
V230: Sector of employment	V114: Confidence: the courts
V235: Are you the chief wage earner in your house?	V115: Confidence: the government (in your nation's capital)
V237: Family savings during past year	V116: Confidence: political parties
V238: Social class (subjective)	V117: Confidence: parliament
V240: Sex	V118: Confidence: the civil service
V245: Respondent immigrant	V119: Confidence: universities
V237: Language at home	V120: Confidence: major companies
V248: Highest education level attained	V121: Confidence: banks
V248_CS: Education (country specific)	V122: Confidence: environmental organizations
V249: What age did you complete your education?	V123: Confidence: women's organizations
V254: Ethnic group	V124: Confidence: charitable or humanitarian organizations
	V125_005[9]: Confidence: the North American Free Trade Agreement
	V126: Confidence: the United Nations
	V127: Political system: having a strong leader who does not have to bother with parliament and elections
	V128: Political system: having experts, not government, make decisions according to what they think is best for the country
	V131: Democracy: governments tax the rich and subsidize the poor
	V134: Democracy: people receive state aid for unemployment
	V137: Democracy: the state makes people's income equal
	V138: Democracy: people obey their rulers
	V141: Democracy: how democratically is this country being governed today?
	V142: How much respect is there for individual human rights nowadays in this country?
	V152: How important is God in your life?
	V166: Older people get more than their fair share from the government
	V181: Worries: losing my job or not finding a job

---

8   Most serious problem in the world (choices are people living in poverty and need, discrimination against girls and women, poor sanitation and infectious diseases, inadequate education, and environmental pollution).

9   The V125 variables include international organizations relevant for each country surveyed. For the 2011 U.S. WVS data, the relevant organization is the North American Free Trade Agreement.

V182: Worries: not being able to give one's children a good education

V183: Worries: a war involving my country

V184: Worries: a terrorist attack

V186: Worries: government wire-tapping or reading my mail or email

V187: Under some conditions, war is necessary to obtain justice

V190: In the last 12 months how often have you or your family: gone without medicine or treatment that you needed?

V191: In the last 12 months how often have you or your family: gone without a cash income?

V212: I see myself as a world citizen

V217: Information source: daily newspaper

V226: Vote in elections: local level

V227: Vote in elections: national level

V231: Nature of tasks: manual versus intellectual

V239: Scale of incomes

V241: Year of birth

V242: Age

transform it into a binary variable. By contrast, Column B includes survey questions that produce variables with ordinal, interval, or ratio measurement. You can leave the variables in Column B as they are; they do not require any transformation. Choosing one variable from each column will allow you to perform the different types of quantitative analysis you will learn in Chapters 7, 8, and 9.

To access the entire list of variables contained in the WVS and to see how the two variables you selected (one from Column A and one from Column B) are measured precisely, go to http://www.worldvaluessurvey.org/wvs.jsp. From here, on the left side, first select Data and Documentation, then Online Analysis from the choices that appear, and then the rectangular tab for the 2010–2014 wave of the survey. You will see a list of countries. Check the country you would like to work with, which should be the country in which you reside. For example, if you are using this book as part of a course you are taking in the United States, choose the United States; if you are using this book as part of a course you are taking in a different country, choose that country. (Making sure you use the data for the country you are in will be important for the qualitative part of the study since you will need to interview either your class peers or members of your community about your topic.) Once you select a country, click Next at the top right of the page. You should see a list of all the variables that were asked about in the survey. Although the majority of the variables are present in Table 3.5, you may be interested in a variable that was not included.

On the WVS website, you can see how the variables are measured for each question in the survey for a particular country and year by clicking the variable number, which is located to the left of the variable name.[10] Doing this before you fully decide on an independent variable is important for several reasons. Once you select an independent variable, you should check for three things: (1) that the variable is actually present in the particular wave and country you are using; (2) that there is variation in the variable (remember that variables must vary); and (3) what the categories are for any variable with nominal measurement because the variable may need to be transformed into a binary variable. You can achieve these tasks easily by working with the WVS's online interface.

First, you should guarantee that the survey question you are interested in is actually populated for the wave of the survey for the country you are working with. The overwhelming majority of survey questions were asked for every country, but sometimes a particular variable for a particular country is not contained in the survey. Put differently, the question may have been asked in the survey for one country, but not for another. For example, V125_00 is the confidence a respondent has in the European Union. Clicking on this variable for the United States reveals that this particular question was not asked during the administration of the surveys to respondents in the United States. You may note, too, that a number of variables are associated with V125 and that most of them were not included in the surveys of American respondents. This is because many versions of V125 are associated with organizations and agencies that do not have relevance for people in the United States, such as the Asia–Pacific Economic Cooperation Conference (V125_01) or the Arab Maghreb Union (V125_03). These organizations do not impact respondents in the United States the way they would a respondent in either the Asia–Pacific region or the Middle East. V125_00, the question assessing confidence in the European Union, was most likely included in the surveys for the countries that belong to the European Union. Thus, if you are interested in one of the questions associated with V125, make sure the variable is populated with data. You can do this by clicking on the specific variable number and seeing whether the survey question has data associated with it. V125_05 is the confidence a respondent has with the North American Free Trade Agreement. Clicking on the variable name reveals that this question was asked during the administration

---

10 Do not use the "back" command in your browser as you look at different variables. Clicking on the back command will take you back to the original screen in the WVS (where you will need to select Online Analysis, the sixth wave, and the country you are working with again). When you want to see another variable, simply click on the survey questions tab at the top of the screen. This will take you back to the list of variables.

of the surveys in the United States. Because the survey questions list includes questions that were not posed to all respondents of the WVS around the globe, you should do a quick check to ensure that all of the questions you wish to use as variables were asked on the survey you are working with before deciding to include them as independent variables. If a question was not asked during the administration of a particular survey, you will see "not asked in survey" when you click on the variable's number.

Ensure that the two independent variables you choose are represented in the WVS. If you choose a variable that is not represented by a question in the WVS, you will, in essence, ask a question that cannot be answered with available data. Think of it this way—you may be interested in something that was not asked during the survey, but you cannot go back and pose additional questions to the thousands of people who already completed it. You must work with the data you have at your disposal. This is why it pays to scrutinize the variables carefully to determine which are the most interesting to you or which can serve as proxies, or replacements, for the ideas you wish to capture as independent variables.

Second, it is important to determine whether a potential independent variable has variation associated with it. Remember that one of the essentials in asking a research question is to ensure that the variables you use in an analytical research question vary. If the answers to a particular question do not involve much variation, it is probably best to choose another question that can serve as an independent variable. For example, V4 in the WVS is "important in life: family." Clicking on V4 for the 2011 United States reveals that 90.9% of American respondents felt that family was very important. Another 7.3% of respondents felt that family was rather important. This lack of variation violates the important principle that variables must vary. If 98.2% (90.9% + 7.3%) of a sample responds that family is either very or rather important, it will not be informative to use "important in life: family" in data analysis as an independent variable because almost all of the respondents expressed a similar response. Contrast this with V7, "important in life: politics," for which there is much more variation among the American respondents. The breakdown for V7 is 11.2% very important, 41.8% rather important, 34.9% not very important, and 11.0% not at all important. This spread of values is more useful for data analysis because the responses are more dispersed. You should examine the underlying variation in the variables you choose before settling on them completely to ensure that there is at least some variation in each of your two independent variables. You can access this information through the online interface by clicking on the variable name. The WVS online interface produces useful tables about how the values within the variable are distributed. Try doing this for V4 (importance in life: family) and V7 (importance in life: politics) so you can see how the WVS provides information about each variable's variability. You should do this for each independent variable you would like to include in your study.

Third, accessing your variables through the WVS website is also important for your variable with nominal measurement if the variable is associated with more than two categories; eventually you must transform it so that it only has two categories. It is a good idea to think about how that will happen now, although you will learn how to change the variable in Chapter 7. As mentioned earlier, to make this transformation you must either (1) choose two categories to compare from the original list of categories or (2) condense information from multiple categories into new categories to create a binary variable based on the original categories. Clicking on the variable number to the left of the variable name for the country and year you are investigating provides the information you need to make this decision.

Step 3: Think about Your Research Design

The people who answered the questions in the WVS are adult citizens. This means that the **unit of analysis** for the WVS data is "individuals." The unit of analysis specifies what is being studied and the level at which data are collected for each of the variables in an analysis. Since in the WVS the unit of analysis is individuals, we know that every measurement is taken at the level of an individual respondent.

At this point, you are encouraged to think about a particular demographic characteristic you can use to limit the WVS data for the country and year you would like to study. Once you choose this particular demographic characteristic (such as age or biological sex) and limit the WVS's dataset to include only observations that are representative of that demographic characteristic, the **research population** for your study will change. (Keep in mind, however, that the unit of analysis for the WVS dataset—individuals—stays the same.) A research population is a group of observations that have a particular set of attributes or characteristics in common. For example, since you are likely using this book in a research-oriented college-level course, your instructor may have already chosen a particular research population for you to study.

One approach could be to study people in the millennial generation, specifically people who are between 18 and 35 years of age. If you do this, then your research population is individuals who are between 18 and 35 years of age. For the quantitative part of your study, you will be able to limit the data in the WVS to include only this group of people. Then, for your qualitative analysis (your case study), you could interview a number of classmates who are also taking your research course. Your academic institution would thus become the case for your case study (this will be explained in more detail in Chapter 10). In this way, the data for the quantitative analysis (data from the WVS that are limited to people ages 18 to 35 years of age) and the qualitative analysis (interview data that you generate by conducting a number of interviews with your peers in your classroom) will be collected for the same research population (assuming that most of the people in your classroom are between the ages of 18 and 35).

However, you could choose another age group or a different demographic characteristic to create a different research population. If you make such a decision, you must (1) limit the data in the WVS so that only people who represent the age group or demographic factor you choose remain in the dataset; and (2) conduct interviews with individuals who represent the new group of people for your qualitative analysis. Limiting the data in WVS is not difficult. However, before you choose a research population based on a single demographic characteristic, you are strongly advised to think in advance about where you will go to conduct your interviews. For example, you may wish to concentrate only on older people and make older people your research population. If you do this, you will use only WVS data from survey respondents who are ages, say, 65 and above. Then, for the qualitative analysis, you could visit a retirement community and interview only people who are ages 65 and above. The retirement community would then become the case you explore through qualitative analysis.

Alternatively, you may wish to study only women. In this case, you would organize the data by biological sex in the WVS and not use any data from male respondents. Then, for qualitative analysis, you could make arrangements to do interviews with women who belong to a specific women's organization. The women's organization would become the case that you are studying for the qualitative case study of your research.

Your research population can be any demographic characteristic. However, be sure that the demographic characteristic you choose does not exclude too many respondents from the WVS. Before deciding on a research population, use the online interface on the WVS website to ensure that there are enough respondents within your proposed research population for meaningful study. For example, say you want to specify Jewish people as your research population. Religious denomination in the WVS is V144. Clicking on the number to the left of the variable's name using the online analysis tool shows the distribution for the variable for the 2011 WVS dataset for the United States (Table 3.6).

TABLE 3.6: RELIGION OF THE U.S. POPULATION, 2011 WVS SURVEY

Religion	Number of people in dataset	Percentage of people in dataset
None	736	33.0
Buddhist	14	0.6
Hindu	9	0.4
Jew	41	1.9
Muslim	7	0.3
Orthodox	6	0.3
Other; not specified	351	15.7
Protestant	541	24.2
Roman Catholic	480	21.5
No answer	46	2.1

Note that there are only 41 Jewish respondents in the 2011 wave of the WVS for the United States. Likewise, there are only 14 Buddhist respondents, 9 Hindu respondents, 7 Muslim respondents, and 6 Orthodox respondents represented in this wave. It would not be wise to choose any of these religions as the research population, not because they are not important, but because there is not enough variation in the WVS to perform quantitative analysis properly. In addition, it is possible that not every respondent within your research population answered the questions associated with your dependent and independent variables, which would reduce the number of observations even further when you conduct your data analysis. To ensure that data analysis can be performed appropriately, you should have at least 100 respondents within your research population. Ideally, however, this number will be even higher. With this in mind, there is enough representation among people who identified as Protestant (541 respondents) or Roman Catholic (480 respondents). Hence, you could choose people of these religions as your research population, but not the others. Furthermore, if you do choose people of one of these religions as the research population, you must identify where you could find people of those faiths, perhaps a Protestant church (if Protestant people comprise your research population) or a Catholic church (if Catholic people comprise your research population). The important point is to ensure (1) that there are enough respondents representing your research population in the WVS dataset for the wave and country you want to use and (2) that you can identify a place to which you can travel to conduct interviews with individuals who represent the research population. The place will become the case for your case study.

One word of caution, however: if you choose a research population that is *other* than the millennial generation in the course you are taking while using this book, with the intention of doing interviews outside of your classroom, your project will need institutional review board (IRB) clearance. See Appendix A for a description of institutional review. Such clearance is necessary whenever researchers interact with human participants. IRB clearance is obtained from your academic institution. Your instructor should be able to work with you on securing IRB approval for your projects at your institution. There may be an expedited process your instructor can utilize in the classroom that can extend institutional review to an entire class of students at the same time. Regardless, it is a good idea to think about this now so that you can obtain approval for your project as early as possible. You should be able to begin the process of securing IRB approval as soon as you identify your research question and where you will go to interview people who represent your research population if you leave your classroom to conduct the interviews.[11]

One last word of caution concerning your research population: it is important that you not include the characteristic that you used to define the research population as one of your independent variables. For example, if you specify the millennial generation or older citizens as your research population, you should not include age as an independent variable. You have already selected a particular age group to study and thus there will be little variation in age among the observations in your new dataset. Likewise, if you specify women as your research population, you would not include biological sex as an independent variable.

Step 4: Write Your Analytical Research Question

Once you have identified your single dependent variable and chosen your two independent variables (one from Column A and one from Column B), you can now write your analytical research question. Start with an introductory clause (such as "The effect of," "The influence of," or "The impact of") and then add both independent variables, your dependent variable, and your research population (Figure 3.4). In doing so you will write an analytical research question.

You may have noted that this "question" does not have a question mark associated with it. This is not a problem. The title still implies that an analytical

FIGURE 3.4   Writing an Analytical Research Question

research question is being asked. Wording the title in this way indicates that the relationship between the key variables in the question will be assessed. How you want to phrase the question is a matter of style.

One challenge you may find as you write your research question is exactly how to word it, given that some of the variables you may work with from the WVS are verbose. For the dependent variable, the list of 16 possible paper topics provided you a relatively concise way to present the general concept of the dependent variable you chose for the wording of your research question. For example, V97 is "Views on private versus state ownership." If this is your dependent variable, you can use the wording "Views on private versus state ownership" for the dependent variable in the research question. Most of the independent variables are also fairly straightforward and will not require you to come up with a generalized way of presenting them in the research question. This is the case for variables such as confidence in political parties, interest in politics, satisfaction with life, or biological sex. Thus, for example, you could ask, "How do biological sex and confidence in political parties influence views on private versus state ownership among people in the millennial generation?" This question is relatively streamlined. For other variables, however, you may need to think about how they will appear in the research question since their presentation in the WVS is somewhat long. For example, the wording for V228, "Which party would you vote for if there were a national election tomorrow," is too long-winded to include verbatim as an independent variable in a research question. For inclusion in the research question, it might be better to call this "party choice" or "party affiliation" so that the wording of the research question is more manageable.

CONCLUSION

Asking good questions is one of the most important steps in the research process. Analytical research questions are common in political science. They require explanation, analysis, and interpretation. Such questions often assess how variation in one or more independent variables is correlated with variation in a dependent variable. The dependent variable is what the research hopes to explain. The independent variables are what the researcher uses to explain variation in the dependent variable. In addition, the unit of analysis specifies what is being studied and the level at which data are collected for the independent and dependent variables. In the WVS, the unit of analysis is individuals. All data in the WVS were taken at the level of an individual respondent. However, for the research you will complete using the WVS data, you are encouraged to think of a particular demographic factor to create a specific research population for your analysis.

This chapter also introduced different levels of measurement. Overwhelmingly, the WVS contains variables with nominal and ordinal measurement. Nominal measurement involves placing observations into discrete categories to produce a variable. By contrast, ordinal measurement involves placing observations into categories for which the ordering of the values contains meaning. The distinction is crucial for different types of data analysis.

GLOSSARY

ANALYTICAL RESEARCH QUESTION A special type of research question that requires explanation, analysis, and interpretation and that often produce answers that lead to additional questions.

ANTECEDENT VARIABLE A variable that is present prior to the variables included in the analysis.

BINARY VARIABLE A variable containing only two categories.

CORRELATION An empirical relationship between variables.

DEPENDENT VARIABLE What is being explained through research.

INDEPENDENT VARIABLE A variable used to explain variation in a dependent variable.

INTERVAL MEASUREMENT A type of measurement in which the distance between values on a variable is the same.

INTERVENING VARIABLE A variable that interacts with an independent variable in some way to produce an effect on the dependent variable.

NOMINAL MEASUREMENT A type of measurement in which observations are placed into discrete categories that do not have an inherent order and are not analyzed in terms of "less than" or "more than" statements.

ORDINAL MEASUREMENT A type of measurement in which observations are placed into categories for which the ordering of the values representing the categories has meaning.

QUANTIFICATION Turning words into numbers so that variables can be systematically analyzed.

RATIO MEASUREMENT A type of measurement in which the distance between values can be meaningfully assessed, but unlike variables with interval measurement, variables with ratio measurement have a true zero associated with them.

RESEARCH POPULATION A group of observations that have a particular set of attributes or characteristics in common.

UNIT OF ANALYSIS Specifies what is being studied and the level at which data are collected for each of the variables in an analysis.

VARIABLES Attributes or characteristics that can vary across observations.

EXERCISES

1. Access the websites of some political science journals and look at the titles of the articles listed in the table of contents for the most recent editions. Locate journals like *American Political Science Review, American Journal of Political Science, British Journal of Political Science, International Organization, Comparative Political Studies, Annual Review of Political Science,* or *The Journal of Politics.* You might also want to look through journals from a particular subfield, such as comparative politics or international politics. Do the titles of the articles allow you to identify the independent and dependent variables in the analysis? Can you infer what the variables are by the way the title is worded? If not, read the abstracts of the articles. More often than not, researchers will clearly state their research question somewhere in the abstract. Can you identify the dependent variable from the abstracts? That is, can you determine what the researcher hopes to explain? Also, can you identify each study's unit of analysis and/or research population from the paper titles or abstracts?

2. Go to the WVS website and look at the list of questions for the country and wave you are using for your research project. Without reviewing Table 3.5, see whether you can identify the level of measurement for different variables that are produced by the questions in the WVS. For example, V29 is "active/inactive membership: political party." The precise question for the variable (also listed on the website) is, "Now I am going to read off a list of voluntary organizations. For each organization, could you tell me whether you are an active member, an inactive member, or not a member of that type of organization?" The possible responses to

this survey question are thus active member, inactive member, or not a member. Since these responses form discrete categories that cannot be interpreted through a "more than" or "less than" scale, the variable has nominal measurement. Another example, V84, is "interest in politics." The precise question in the WVS is, "How interested would you say you are in politics?" The possible responses are very interested, somewhat interested, not very interested, and not interested at all. Since these responses are on a scale whereby someone who is very interested is more interested than someone who is somewhat interested, and someone who is somewhat interested is more interested than someone who is not very interested, the variable for "interest in politics" has ordinal measurement. Try this exercise for a number of survey questions until you are comfortable identifying the difference among the different levels of measurement.

PAPER PROGRESS

In Chapter 1 you were asked to choose a research topic for your eventual paper on political values and attitudes. Now that you have your topic and have conducted a literature review, you can write the analytical research question you will pursue with your research. Here we revisit the steps you should complete before moving on to the next chapter.

Step 1: Identify the survey question in the WVS that is associated with your research topic and that will serve as your dependent variable. Note that your dependent variable is a variable with ordinal measurement and has a range of values from 1 to 10. Also make note of how the values are ordered, in other words, what the 1 in the range means and what the 10 in the range means. Go to the WVS website to ensure that the variable is present in the survey for the country and year you are investigating and that the variable has some variation associated with it.

Step 2: Identify survey questions that will serve as your independent variables. Variation in these independent variables will be used to explain variation in your dependent variable. Make sure you have a reason for why you included each independent variable because eventually you will need to write a causal theory for why variation in the independent variable causes variation in the dependent variable. Choose *two* independent variables, one from Category A (survey questions that lead to variables with nominal measurement) and one from Category B (survey questions that lead to variables with ordinal measurement[12]). If the survey question you chose from Column A has more than two categories associated with it, decide now how you will transform it into a binary variable. Use the WVS Online Analysis tool to help you make this decision. You must either (1) choose two categories within the variable to analyze or (2) combine the information from several categories to form new groups until only two categories remain.

Step 3: Think about your research design and identify a particular demographic characteristic that you would like to use to create the research population you will analyze. For this project, you will either remain in your classroom and interview your fellow classmates (and thereby choose age as the demographic characteristic) or leave your classroom to interview people who represent what you chose as your research population. Work with your instructor to obtain IRB clearance if you choose a demographic characteristic that will create a research population that will take you out of the classroom when you collect qualitative-level data. As mentioned previously, your instructor likely will be able to provide IRB training in your classroom with your class and apply for expedited institutional review for the class as a group since the project is a class exercise.

Step 4: Write your analytical research question using the example provided earlier in the chapter. Use an expression such as "The effect of," "The influence of," or "The impact of" to begin the question. Include your two independent variables, then the dependent variable, and, finally, your research population. Streamline the wording of the question as much as possible if the presentation of the variable in the WVS is too long-winded.

COMING UP

You should have your research question in hand as you begin the next chapter, which covers writing theory and deriving hypotheses. In this step you provide an answer to your research question by specifying an explanation (theory) and expectation (hypotheses) for the relationship between your independent and dependent variables.

---

12 Overwhelmingly, the survey questions in the WVS lead to variables with ordinal measurement. There are some variables with different levels of measurement, such as year born (interval) or age (ratio), that you could choose as independent variables as well.

CHAPTER 4

THEORY AND HYPOTHESES

Do you vote? It appears that many young people do not. Consider Table 4.1, in which age is shown to have an inverse relationship with voting. In the 2012 American presidential election, overall voter turnout was 62%. However, among 18- to 29-year-olds, turnout was much lower, at 45%. In the 2010 British parliamentary election, voter turnout was 65%. Yet, among 18- to 24-year-olds, it was 44%. Clearly, there is variation in the proportion of voters to nonvoters in different age groups.

Furthermore, according to the WVS, a large proportion of young people in the United States and Great Britain responded that they are not at all interested in politics. In the United States, almost 18.7% of young people responded that politics is "not important at all." In Great Britain, 26.1% of young people responded this way (Table 4.2).

The data demonstrate that young people do not vote as often as older people and that many younger people also do not believe that politics is

TABLE 4.1: VOTER TURNOUT RATES FOR DIFFERENT AGE GROUPS IN THE UNITED STATES AND UNITED KINGDOM

Age	Voter turnout (%) United States, 2012 presidential election	Age	Voter turnout (%) United Kingdom, 2010 parliamentary election
18–29	45	18–24	44
30–44	60	25–34	55
45–64	68	35–44	66
65+	72	45–54	69
		55–64	73
		65+	76
All ages	62		65

Source: Center for Information and Research on Civic Learning and Engagement (http://civicyouth.org/) and UK Political Info (http://ukpolitical.info/)

TABLE 4.2:   PERCENTAGE OF VOTERS IN THE UNITED STATES AND UNITED KINGDOM IN DIFFERENT AGE GROUPS RESPONDING THAT POLITICS IS "NOT IMPORTANT AT ALL"

Age	Percentage responding that politics is "not important at all"	
	United States	United Kingdom
15–29	18.7	26.1
30–49	6.8	16.4
50+	4.9	20.9

Source: World Values Survey, U.S. 2011 and U.K. 2005.

important. These trends are a major cause for concern among democratic theorists who believe that active participation among all age groups is necessary for vibrant democratic practice. Yet many young people are neither participating in nor interested in politics. What explains such apathy among young people in the United States and United Kingdom?

THEORY

Tables 4.1 and 4.2 show that young people are not voting as much as old people and that young people are more likely to not view politics as important. But the data cannot tell us the reason *why* this is the case. Many researchers have investigated youth apathy as a general topic and have come up with different answers to suggest reasons for the different degrees of apathy among young people. These answers are often written as **theories**. A theory is a generalized explanation for an observable outcome. Often, the particular outcome in question is a single value or range of values for a dependent variable using variation in an independent variable as part of an explanation for why something is the way it is. In other words, a theory posits that a value of at least one independent variable is the reason why there was a specific outcome in a dependent variable. Continuing the example from above, if the dependent variable is voter turnout or interest in politics among young people, the theory should identify the most important independent variables that can explain why some young people are voting or interested in politics and why some young people are not. It should explain why there is variation in the dependent variable. For example, think about what would separate young people into different groups based on one of the dependent variables noted above: interest in politics. Try to identify independent variables that would help us understand why there are different levels of political interest among young people and think about why those independent variables matter. Are there any independent variables you can identify? Below are some possibilities, along with an explanation for why each one matters for explaining differences in interest in politics among young people. As you read these theories, note how the explanation covers different values for each independent variable and associates those values with a specific outcome of the dependent variable.

- Political socialization: Many young people are not interested in politics *because* they were not introduced to political ideas by their families, schools, or communities when they were children. They may not come from politically active parents and thus are not subject to norms or customs concerning political participation. The lack of civic education in their schools or the lack of political resources in their communities may reinforce these outcomes. They do not see politics as important. Conversely, other young people are interested in politics *because* they come from politically active families. They were taught about the importance of voting by their schools or communities. They had exposure to civic education classes and their communities may have had resources to help young people learn the importance of political participation. These young people were politically socialized from an early age. They developed the habit of engaging in political participation early in their adulthood because they were brought up in a culture where political participation is considered important, essential, and a right.
- Information asymmetries: Many young people are not interested in politics *because* they do not possess the appropriate information to participate meaningfully in politics. They may not read or watch the news or be aware of the salient issues facing their government. They may not know about political parties or the political process or how their interests are represented at different levels in the political system. Conversely, other young people are interested in politics *because* they are much more knowledgeable about politics. They actively seek information about current events. They are aware of the most pressing issues facing their societies and have developed reasoned opinions about them. They know which parties best represent their interests.
- Intimidation: Many young people are not interested in politics *because* they are intimidated by the formal political process. They may not know the rules concerning registration, voting, and other forms of political participation. They may not believe that they can contribute meaningfully to the democratic political process. Conversely, other young people are interested in politics *because* they are not intimidated by the formal

political process and look forward to participating in their democracy through voting and other means of participation. They understand the rules associated with voting: how to register, where to vote, and what to bring (identification, for example). They are confident that their participation is meaningful.

Each of these theories explains variation in political interest among young people. They are written in a way that provides a specific reason, or a value of an independent variable, for why differences exist in how interested young people are in politics. The theory explains why variation in the independent variable (the absence or presence of political socialization, greater or fewer information asymmetries, or more or less intimidation) should lead to a particular outcome of the dependent variable, either less or more interest in politics.

These theories were written in a straightforward way. Note how the word *because* is used to establish causality between a value of the independent variable and a specific outcome of the dependent variable. Not all theories are written exactly in this way, but if we want to understand variation in the level of political interest among young people, we must consider events and influences that occurred *before* the degree of political interest in a single individual became apparent. For example, the political socialization theory suggests that families, schools, and communities are important for teaching political values and for encouraging young people to participate politically in their communities. When families, schools, and communities are active in the political sphere and teach children the importance of political participation, the theory suggests that those children are more likely to have more interest in politics because the children have been politically socialized to care about politics. When these influences are absent, the probability of a young adult being interested in politics becomes less likely. There is a temporal element to the theory. Any political socialization must occur before a young person becomes more or less interested in politics. This is true for the other theories as well.

Causal Explanations

The development of **causal explanations**, explanations that establish cause-and-effect relationships among variables, is a good way to think about theory building. Despite the usefulness of establishing cause and effect, it is often hard to do. Generally, researchers in the social sciences do not have testing laboratories where each variable influencing an outcome can be strictly controlled so that the effect of one particular variable on another can be assessed. Rather, as we will see in the next chapter, social science researchers often design observational studies that attempt to establish correlations and patterns among variables after events have already occurred. The studies are considered observational because events are observed after they have happened. However, although two variables can be shown to be empirically linked (correlation) for a group of observations, it is not possible through quantitative analysis alone in observational designs to show that one variable caused another (causation). Thus, the famous adage mentioned in the first chapter: correlation does not imply causation.[1] This is why theory is important.

It is relatively easy to find empirical correlations among variables. Areas that are characterized by poverty, for example, are usually associated with higher rates of crime. But to establish any causality between poverty and crime in a theory, we must satisfy certain requirements and then state why poverty leads to crime before we can say that there is a causal mechanism at work in a theory.

Generally, most researchers agree that there are three requirements to establish causality:

1. The observed cause and the observed effect must be empirically correlated.

   Finding an association or relationship among variables is necessary before causality can be established. If two or more phenomena are not related, then one cannot be said to cause the other. If crime and poverty do not co-vary, in other words, if the two are not empirically correlated, one cannot cause the other.

2. The observed cause must precede the observed effect.

   Sometimes it is difficult to pinpoint exactly when a phenomenon started. For example, if we want to argue that increased poverty causes a higher rate of crime, we must establish that poverty was present before there was crime and explain in a theory why higher or lower levels of poverty cause higher or lower levels of crime. This is important because another researcher could make the opposite argument, that higher levels of crime cause higher levels of poverty and that lower levels of crime cause lower levels of poverty. In this case, this second researcher could have an equally convincing argument that crime came before poverty, which would mean that poverty could not cause crime. Thus, establishing the temporal order of events is crucial before causality can be established.

---

1   The next chapter will contrast observational research designs with experimental ones, in which establishing causality is more straightforward.

3. The variation among two variables cannot be explained away by the presence of a third variable, which actually caused the variation in both of the original variables.

Even when a researcher can show that two variables are empirically correlated and that one preceded the other, it is still possible that the first variable did not cause the second. In this case, the observed relationship between crime and poverty could be **spurious**, that is, the two variables under investigation are indeed empirically correlated, but in truth the relationship between them is not causal. In many cases in which two variables are empirically correlated, there is an unidentified third variable that explains the variation in both the first and the second variables. In other words, for the relationship between poverty and crime, it is possible that a third variable exists that would explain both problems, although poverty and crime are empirically correlated (requirement 1) and although a state of poverty can be shown to occur before crime increases (requirement 2). This third variable might be a decline in access to high-quality education or an increase in the unemployment rate. Each of these variables could have caused both poverty and crime independently. As a result, until these are ruled out as possible variables that explain the variation in both the independent and the dependent variables, a causal relationship between poverty and crime cannot be established. In other words, when a third variable that explains variation in both the independent and the dependent variables is found to exist, a causal relationship between the independent and dependent variable cannot be established.

The third requirement to establishing causality is crucial in the social world, where many variables often intersect to cause an outcome. More often than not, the social world cannot be explained by the presence of a single independent variable. Rather, many variables are involved when a phenomenon is observed. Thus, to establish causality, it is important to eliminate alternative variables that might cause observed variation in both the independent and the dependent variables. It is important to carefully think through all of the possible causes for a particular phenomenon. Again, just because two phenomena are correlated does not mean one caused the other. The relationship between them could be spurious.

Probabilistic and Generalizable Theories

Although the premise of social science research is that we can identify patterns in human behavior, the truth is that many social theories are in continual flux. This is the reason that there are few laws in social science. First, it is difficult to predict social phenomena with 100% accuracy. There are too many ways in which humans differ from one another to suggest that one theory can explain everything humans do. This is why political science theories are considered probabilistic and not deterministic. **Probabilistic theories** of causation suggest that the likelihood of an event occurring is either higher or lower for a particular reason, that is, the presence of a certain value of one or more independent variables. In political science we work with probabilistic theories because we accept that we cannot correctly predict all social behavior.

Contrast this with **deterministic theories** that posit that an outcome is, by definition, the only possible result associated with a particular cause. It would be difficult in the social sciences to develop deterministic theories. As a result, our theories suggest that outcomes are more or less probable given a number of independent causes. For example, the political socialization theory does not suggest that differences in political socialization will always cause differences in voting patterns among young people. Rather, the political socialization theory posits that a young person is more likely to vote if he or she was politically socialized as a child. Thus, the political socialization theory is probabilistic.

In addition, the best theories are the ones that are generalizable. This means that a good theory should be applicable to as many contexts as possible and not only to the set of observations that were included in the original study. If a theory has success in explaining events across time and space, it is a strong theory. For example, imagine that empirical analysis finds that differences in political socialization indeed influence differences in voting patterns among young people in one particular place. If the theory behind the analysis is strong, other scholars should be able to use the theory to explain voting patterns among young people for other moments in time and in other places. The theory may be able to explain voting patterns among other age groups as well.

Theory Building

The information we use to build a theory usually comes from a combination of three sources of information: inductive observations, deductive reasoning, and insights from the literature. Information from each of these sources combines to form an explanation for an observed phenomenon or, for our purposes, variation in a dependent variable. Let's return to the example about the level of interest in politics from the beginning of the chapter to investigate how theories are made.

1. *Inductive observations* involve information you have at your immediate disposal. For example, you may be interested in politics and you may be interested in politics for a specific reason. In addition, you may have

friends who are also interested in politics, and you believe that their reasons for being interested in politics are similar to your own. The small group of cases to which you have access might lead you to conclude that all young people are interested in politics for the same reason that you are interested in politics. However, it is most likely that your theory will not be applicable to all young people. Although there is some probability that other young people are like you and the people you happen to know, it remains possible that (1) other young people are interested in politics for different reasons or (2) some young people are not interested in politics at all. Inductive observations provide information to start us thinking of explanations for observed phenomena, but they can lead us to faulty conclusions once we try to generalize to a larger set of observations. The truth is that most people, when thinking about the answer to research questions, begin with the information they have at hand. This is a good start, but the process of theory building only begins with inductive observations. You must consider other explanations before devising a plausible and generalizable theory. Otherwise, your explanation of events would be too narrowly based and you might commit an **individualistic fallacy**, which is inferring a characteristic about a group based on observations from only one individual or case. You would commit an individualistic fallacy if you assumed that everyone had the same motivations for participating in politics as you do. There are many reasons that explain why young people are more or less interested in politics; your experience with being interested in politics is just one possible reason, which may not be generalizable to everyone.

2. *Deductive reasoning* begins with a general premise that is used to generate expectations about how variables are related to one another. With deductive reasoning, you use logic and reason to explore many different generalized explanations, independent of direct empirical information, to identify a particular idea that can explain many observations at the same time. For example, you can use deductive reasoning to think in the abstract about why young people differ in how interested they are in politics. Maybe political interest among young people is driven by variables such as where they live, what organizations are active in their communities, or how committed they are to other areas of their lives. Deductive reasoning allows you to devise a number of plausible explanations that might have some power in explaining why there is variation in the dependent variable. If considered appropriate, each of these explanations could become part of the theory that will eventually be constructed.

But be careful in how you apply the general propositions you develop to individual observations when engaging in deductive reasoning. You will not want to commit an **ecological fallacy**, which is inferring characteristics about any one individual based on a general trend found within a group. In other words, you cannot assume that every possible observation will conform to the general premise you have devised.

3. Finally, a researcher may borrow good ideas and explanations about the relationships between variables from the established literature. This is part of the reason why studying the literature is so important and why you were encouraged to complete your literature review *before* writing both your analytical research question and the theory for your own work. Researchers who have thought extensively about the topics you are studying have much to teach you about how to think about them. Political theories are not simple. Good theories often take years to write. They most likely involve many moving parts and require careful elaboration for why correlations between independent and dependent variables are expected.

The literature contains a record of how scholars have thought about political outcomes over time and most likely contains valuable insight about why there is variation in the political world. It is thus essential that you use the ideas you gleaned from the literature review you wrote in Chapter 2 to help you shape the theory you will write about the variables you are including in your analysis. Using the literature in this way is common. For example, the literature most likely contains many studies that have already examined the level of political interest among young people. Part of the theory section in a paper on differing levels of political interest among young people should include what the literature has concluded about why such differences exist. In this way, the literature review serves two purposes: (1) to trace the evolution of ideas pertaining to a research topic over time and (2) to generate ideas about why there is variation in a dependent variable. Doing an extensive literature review on topics related to your general topic will thus help you determine which parts of established theory you can use as part of your own theory. You can use the theory established in the studies you find to help you develop new theory or provide refinements or extensions to the theories that already exist. For example, imagine that you are attempting to use differences in political socialization to explain differences in voting among young people. If several studies in the literature have offered theories to explain why differences in political socialization matter as an important independent variable for explaining variation in political participation, you could use that important theoretical insight in your own study. Be sure to provide the appropriate citations, however, when you incorporate existing theory into your own analysis. Your literature review should be full of references to specific works, but your theory may also contain numerous citations if you have borrowed insights from the literature in the development of the theory you present in a study.

Competing Theories

The complexity of the social world means that there is rarely one explanation for the entirety of the outcomes we wish to study. Even when a single theoretical argument meets all the criteria for causality and seems convincing in explaining an outcome, new research may challenge the implications or conclusions the theory attempts to establish. As a result, in the literature there likely exist several competing theories that attempt to explain variation in a single dependent variable. Some researchers devote considerable time and energy to determining which theory holds the most **explanatory power**, or the power of a theory to explain as much of an outcome as possible by evaluating them at the same time. For example, the purpose of one of the studies mentioned in Chapter 3 ("The Bigger the Better? Evidence of the Effect of Government Size on Life Satisfaction around the World") is to determine which of two theories—classical economic theory or public choice theory—better explains differences in life satisfaction, the dependent variable, in 74 countries. The size of the state sector is the primary independent variable (i.e., how much money is spent in each country on the government itself). Classical economic theory suggests that public goods and institutions are provided by states to correct for market inefficiencies and that there is equilibrium between such public goods and market inefficiencies so that the state efficiently spends its money on the goods and services the private market cannot provide. When this is the case, classical economic theory suggests, people are neither inclined nor disinclined to be more or less satisfied and, as a result, the size of the government should have no impact on citizens' life satisfaction. But public choice theory maintains that the incentives for politicians to overspend government money on themselves are stronger than any one individual's capacity to control spending. This means that over time, overspending leads to inflated budgets and increased regulation. When this is the case, public choice theory suggests, people will likely have lower life satisfaction because their tax money is spent, or wasted, on the state itself. The research study thus posits these two competing theories, one that suggests that the size of the state is optimal and appropriate (classical economic theory) and one that suggests that the size of the state is much too large (public choice theory). The subsequent data analysis presented in the paper provides strong support for public choice theory: "when it comes to overall government consumption, the evidence quite clearly supports the public choice view that excessive government spending is detrimental to individuals' quality of life" (Bjørnskov et al. 2007, 287)[2].

Bjørnskov et al. deliberately set out to determine which of two theories better explains the relationship between an independent variable, the size of state sector, and a dependent variable, life satisfaction. Many studies are structured in this way, given the number of theories that have been investigated in the literature. Researchers often use their empirical analyses to determine which theory has the most explanatory power. If, during your literature review, you find such debates or controversies surrounding your dependent variable, you could use the theory section of your paper to "take a side" and argue which theory, based on causal reasoning, you believe will likely be supported through empirical analysis.

HYPOTHESES

A theory provides a general explanation for *why* patterns exist among variables. To determine whether a theory has explanatory power, it is necessary to identify one or more **research hypotheses** that can be empirically tested. A research hypothesis is an expectation of how two or more variables are related. Hypotheses are derived from theories. To support a theory, hypotheses derived from them should be empirically true.

The Null Hypothesis

An important concept with regard to research hypotheses is that of the **null hypothesis**. Although there are different ways to specify a null hypothesis, for our purposes we can specify the null hypothesis as a statement that no relationship exists between an independent and a dependent variable. For example, if we wish to determine how age influences the probability of voting, the null hypothesis is the expectation that age is not related to voting or, in other words, that someone's age has no relationship with his or her probability of voting. Specifying the null hypothesis is important because the purpose of many quantitative analyses is to determine whether the null hypothesis concerning

---

2   Christian Bjørnskov, Axel Dreher, and Justina A. V. Fischer, 2007, "The Bigger the Better? Evidence of the Effect of Government Size on Life Satisfaction around the World," *Public Choice* 130 (3/4): 267–92.

the relationship between two variables can be rejected. We will return to this point in Chapters 8 and 9. For now, be aware that it is necessary to specify a null hypothesis for each research hypothesis you write. Take, for example, the theory concerning the relationship between political socialization and interest in politics from the beginning of the chapter. In this case, the null hypothesis is as follows:

> **Null hypothesis** (often denoted as **H0**): Political socialization is not associated with interest in politics.

Writing Research Hypotheses

The research hypothesis is what we wish to test against the null hypothesis. Research hypotheses are usually specified in a particular way, which includes a value of an independent variable and the expectation for how that value leads to a particular value of the dependent variable, followed by a mention of the comparison group.[3] If/then statements and words such as "increases" or "decreases" and "more likely" or "less likely" are often used in hypotheses to denote the direction of the expected relationship between the independent and dependent variables.

Take, for example, the theories concerning interest in politics from the beginning of the chapter. We can use these theories to derive hypotheses to specify precise expectations about the relationship between the independent and dependent variables.

Theory: Political Socialization

Research hypothesis 1 (often denoted as **H1**): People who were not politically socialized as children will exhibit a lower interest in politics as adults than people who were politically socialized as children.

Note that the first part of the research hypothesis provides a specific value of the independent variable (the absence of political socialization) and then provides a specific expectation of the dependent variable (lower interest in politics). The wording at the end of the hypothesis also suggests that a comparison is being made between two groups of people, people who were not politically socialized as children and people who were politically socialized as children. This is important. The idea is that different values of the dependent variable are

---

3   In some disciplines, the research hypothesis may not specify a precise direction for the relationship between the independent and dependent variables. In this case, the null hypothesis that there is no relationship between two variables is tested against the research hypothesis, which simply specifies that there is a relationship between two variables without specifying the precise nature of that relationship. Most research studies in political science, however, do entail a specific expectation that is derived from a theory.

expected for different values of the independent variable, based on what was established in the theory.

Hypotheses that mean the same thing can be written in different ways. For example, consider the following hypothesis: the wording differs from that of the research hypothesis already given, yet still expresses the same expectation.

H1: If someone was not politically socialized as a child, then he or she will have less interest in politics than someone who was politically socialized as a child.

This new hypothesis essentially means the same thing as the previous one: that one particular value of the independent variable (lower political socialization) is associated with a particular value (or range of values) of the dependent variable (greater interest in politics) and that a comparison is being made between two groups of people (people who were politically socialized as children and people who were not politically socialized as children). How you write your hypothesis is up to you, but ensure that the specific expectation you have for the relationship between your variables for different values of your independent variable is clear. In the examples provided later in this chapter, you will see that hypotheses can be written in different ways.

An important element of hypotheses is that they must be **testable**, which means they must be stated in a way that allows us to evaluate them empirically and determine whether a specific hypothesis, based on data, is either true or false. Hypotheses must be tested with information gleaned from observation or experience, not from reason or logic. For example, once we measure precisely what we mean by political socialization and what we mean by interest in politics, we can gather data on both variables and then determine whether correlations between the variables exist.

To continue this discussion, let's consider the two other theories mentioned at the beginning of the chapter to explain differences in interest in politics among young people, which utilize information asymmetries and intimidation as independent variables. The hypotheses provide the expectations derived from the theories.

Theory: Informational Asymmetries

Null hypothesis: The amount of information someone has about the political process is not related to the level of interest he or she expresses for politics.

Research hypothesis 2 (also denoted as H2): People who have less information about the political process are less likely to be interested in politics than people who have more information about the political process.

Theory: Intimidation

Null hypothesis: Different levels of intimidation are not related to different levels of interest in politics.

Research hypothesis 3 (also denoted as H3): People who are intimidated by the political process are less likely to be interested in politics than people who are not intimidated by the political process.

EXAMPLES FROM POLITICAL SCIENCE

The following examples of recent studies demonstrate the relationship between theory and hypotheses. In some examples one theory is presented, followed by a number of hypotheses. In others, there is a theory elaborated for each hypothesis. The presentation of this information here is based on how it was presented in the articles. The theory is summarized before the hypotheses are presented, but the hypotheses are taken verbatim from the original articles. Refer to the articles themselves for a more complete explanation of the theories.

As you read the following examples, think about causality and whether you agree with the researchers' theories about the relationship between the independent and dependent variables studied through the analysis. At the very least, each pairing of variables should be empirically correlated, the independent variable should occur before the dependent variable, and there should not be a third variable that actually explains variation in both the independent and the dependent variables. If you believe that each of these criteria has been met and that the theory presents a plausible explanation for why there is a relationship between the independent and dependent variables, causality may be established. Also, note that hypotheses can be written in different ways.

Nordås, Ragnhild, and Christian Davenport. 2013. "Fight the Youth: Youth Bulges and State Repression." *American Journal of Political Science* 57 (4): 926–40.

Independent variable: the absence or presence of youth bulges (defined as large youth cohorts, people ages 15–24)
Dependent variable: the level of state repression

This study suggests that a state's decision to resort to repressive tactics has something to do with the size of the youth population. This is because young people "particularly males, dominate insurgent armies, protests, images of terrorists and rioters, and are the most frequently associated with violent crime" (Nordås and Davenport 2013, 929). As a result, elites in repressive governments pay particular attention to the youth population, its size, and its behavior and will resort to repressive tactics to ensure that young people do not engage in activities that would destabilize the regime.

Authorities employ such tactics to thwart any emerging threats and to signal to other young people that further dissent will not be tolerated. Several hypotheses are derived from the theory, which are tested with information from more than 150 countries between 1976 and 2000. The dependent variable is the level of state repression, which is measured on a 5-point scale that assesses the degree to which there are state violations of human rights such as imprisonment, detention, torture, and murder among a population. The data are taken from a dataset called the Political Terror Scale. In the first hypothesis, the independent variable is the presence or absence of a youth bulge, defined in the research as a large youth cohort (people ages 15–24). In the second hypothesis, the independent variable is the size of the youth cohort.

H1: Countries that experience youth bulges are likely to have higher levels of state repression than countries that do not experience youth bulges.

H2: The relationship between youth bulges and repression is nonlinear, and states will increase repression levels when the percentage of 15- to 24-year-olds reaches a "critical level" of 20% of the total population.

The authors also suggest that there are additional independent variables that likely matter for varying levels of state repression. The first is the level of political dissent in the country. The hypothesis suggests that repression will be higher in areas where a nation's youth are already involved with dissent. This is because authorities do not want any form of dissent to escalate and threaten the regime. The second involves political institutions, specifically democracy. Democratic officials do not have the same types of incentives or options as officials in authoritarian regimes. Democracies often have restrictions on what the state can do and overtly repressive acts have potentially important consequences for reelection potential. Thus, the authors posit the last two hypotheses:

H3: States will increase repression levels more in contexts of dissent than in contexts of no overt dissent, and this effect will be stronger the larger the youth bulge in the country.

H4: The relationship between youth bulges and state repression is stronger in nondemocratic states than in democracies.

In the subsequent data analysis, the authors found that repression increases with the size of the youth population, providing support for Hypothesis 1. They also found that repression occurs more quickly in nondemocracies, which supports Hypothesis 4. But they did not find support for the other hypotheses. The level of existing dissent does not seem to increase repression. Furthermore, contrary to their expectation, there does not appear to be a "critical level" of youth size (Hypothesis 2) that must be reached before states become more repressive. These findings suggest that the researchers' overall theory is only partially supported. The authors take some time in the discussion and conclusion sections of the paper to speculate about why this might be. Researchers often do this when the results contradict their expectations by engaging in ex post theorizing to try to understand why a particular result was obtained. We will return to this idea in Chapter 11.

Newman, Benjamin J. 2014. "My Poor Friend: Financial Distress in One's Social Network, the Perceived Power of the Rich, and Support for Redistribution." *The Journal of Politics* 76 (1): 126–38.

Independent variable: socioeconomic differences among friends
Dependent variable: differences in political attitudes toward the perceived power of the rich and support for redistribution

How do friends and social networks influence our attitudes about welfare and redistribution? This paper suggests that having friends who are economically distressed can foster negative attitudes about the rich and create a desire for increased income redistribution. The theory for this idea is borrowed from other studies in social science that suggest that friendships across different groups of people can increase tolerance and decrease the perception of negative stereotypes. Newman focuses specifically on friendships across socioeconomic groups to determine the effect that having friends in worse-off socioeconomic groups can have on political attitudes. Furthermore, Newman suggests that having a friend who has a friend in an out-group also has an effect: friends in an in-group who know that another in-group friend has an out-group friend who is suffering may also generate more positive attitudes toward the out-group as a whole. Thus, it is not only having an economically disadvantaged friend that matters, but also having a friend who has an economically disadvantaged friend. This is important because of how people develop a sense of empathy and identification that extends beyond the self.

Newman specifies three hypotheses derived from this theory and uses data from the 2005 Citizenship, Involvement, Democracy Survey conducted by the Center

CONTINUED

for Democracy and Civil Society at Georgetown University to test them. The data include 1,001 interviews of adults in the United States. The first hypothesis involves how people perceive class-based unfairness and suggests that people who have friends who are suffering economically will be more likely to perceive unfairness in the overall political economic system, whereas the second and third hypotheses introduce how friends interact within social networks. Specifically, the amount of political discussion within the networks is expected to have strong effects on attitudes about the rich and income redistribution.

H1: Individuals who have friends that are experiencing economic hardship should be more likely than those who do not to perceive class-based unfairness in the political economic system, such that the rich are viewed as having undue power and influence.

H2: The degree of political discussion within one's social network should moderate the effect of having economically struggling friends on one's own attitudes, such that having an economically struggling friend will exert the strongest effect on attitudes (i.e., the perceived power of the rich) among individuals who actively discuss politics with their friends.

H3: Within social networks with high levels of political discussion, having economically distressed friends should indirectly enhance support for government income redistribution by increasing the perceived power of the rich.

The results from the data analysis strongly support all three hypotheses. Having friends who struggle economically in one's social network increases negative attitudes toward the rich. There was also a strong association between having economically disadvantaged friends with whom to discuss politics and the belief that the rich wield too much political influence. In other words, rich and poor people can be friends with each other, but unless they discuss politics together, there is no effect on how the richer friend views the power of the rich. Finally, the results also suggest that having economically disadvantaged friends with whom there is ample political discussion increases support for income redistribution from the rich to the poor.

Ezrow, Lawrence, Jonathan Homola, and Margit Tavits. 2014. "When Extremism Pays: Policy Positions, Voter Certainty, and Party Support in Postcommunist Europe." *The Journal of Politics* 76 (2): 535–47.

Independent variable: political party ideological positioning
Dependent variable: voter support for parties

This paper examines how party positioning influences party support in new democracies, specifically in postcommunist democracies. In established democracies, parties that steer their ideological positions close to the political center, where the position of the median voter is located, tend to win more votes than parties that represent more extremist ideologies. But Ezrow and his colleagues suggest that this tendency is not applicable to newer democracies, where a party's centrist position may actually cause it to lose votes. The main reason for this expectation involves the level of certainty that noncentrist parties provide in their political messages to voters. Parties in the center tend to promote ambiguous messages designed to capture as many voters as possible. But these types of parties in newer democracies are not as attractive because voters need certainty and want to know exactly what their vote represents. As Ezrow, Jonathan, and Tavits suggest, "citizens reward parties that present extreme party positions, because these parties are more successful at communicating clear policy stances than moderate parties" (Ezrow, Jonathan, and Tavits 2014, 536).

This theory led the authors to two main hypotheses, which were tested using data from 31 countries between 1996 and 2007.

H1 (The Established Parties Hypothesis): In established democracies, the closer the party is to the mean voter position on the left–right scale, the *higher* its vote share.

H2 (The Postcommunist Parties Hypothesis): In postcommunist democracies, the closer the party is to the mean voter position on the left–right scale, the *lower* its vote share.

The findings from the data analysis (using data from the Comparative Study of Electoral Systems) suggest that voters in both established and newer democracies tend to shun parties with uncertain political positions and that in newer democracies, the messages of extremist parties are clear, which means the extremist parties win more support. This suggests that if centrist parties in newer democracies want to win more votes, centrist parties must be more specific in the articulation of their preferred policy programs, rather than behaving in an ambiguous manner designed only to capture as many votes as possible.

Beath, Andrew, Fotini Christia, and Ruben Enikolopov. 2013. "Empowering Women through Development Aid: Evidence from a Field Experiment in Afghanistan." *American Political Science Review* 107 (3): 540–57.

Independent variable: the presence or absence of development aid programs that mandate female participation

Dependent variable: differences in attitudes toward women

In this study, Beath, Christia, and Enikolopov suggest that development assistance programs can empower women in societies notoriously characterized by the overt repression of females. Development programs can relieve such repression by mandating that women participate actively in any decision making involving how to use the development aid. The programs can also mandate that women take a primary role in deciding which projects a community will pursue. Such participation ensures that women are not excluded from decisions that affect an entire community. Furthermore, participation in development programs can potentially alter the traditional imbalance between males and females by influencing how males perceive their female counterparts.

To determine whether there is support for this theory, the researchers specify a number of hypotheses, which they tested by administering a survey in 500 villages in Afghanistan. Half of the villages had development programs (national solidarity programs) that mandated female participation and half did not. As you read each pairing of theory and hypothesis, note that the independent variable for each of the hypotheses is the development program—either the program mandates female participation or it does not. What differs for these hypotheses is the dependent variable; for this study there are five unique dependent variables, each presented in a separate hypothesis. This is a good example of a study with one independent variable and multiple dependent variables.

Theory: Female participation in development programs can demonstrate and affirm women's capacity and effectiveness in decision making. By participating, women challenge stereotypes that they cannot meaningfully contribute to local governance. This leads to the following hypothesis:

H1: A development program mandating female participation will increase the acceptance of women's involvement and role in local government.

Theory: Female participation in development programs gives women increased opportunities to leave their homes more often and with fewer restrictions and to interact with other females in ways that benefit their community. The programs also allow women the opportunity to influence economic decisions concerning the community, which could spill over to other areas of economic activity. This leads to the following two hypotheses:

H2a: A development program mandating female participation will increase socialization among women.

H2b: A development program mandating female participation will increase women's engagement in economic activity.

Theory: Participating in community-level decisions might have additional spillover effects because women's empowerment in the community could influence women's roles in the home. Hence, the researchers specify another hypothesis:

H3: A development program mandating female participation will increase women's engagement in household decision making.

CONTINUED

Theory: Finally, participation in the development programs could lead to many additional improvements for women in society because mandated participation over time should relax some of the restrictions traditionally placed on women, such as girls attending school or women working outside the home. This leads to a final hypothesis:

H4: A development program mandating female participation will improve perceptions of women's status in society.

In the subsequent data analysis, the researchers found support for several of the hypotheses. As a result of the development programs that mandate women's participation, both men and women became more accepting of women's participation in local government and income-generating activities. The development programs, however, did not have an effect on the position of women in the household or attitudes toward women in general. The researchers thus conclude that the programs' effects were limited to areas that were linked to the program itself (like local governance), but did not spill over to other areas such as the role of women in the household or in general society.

CONCLUSION

Writing theory is often difficult, yet it is essential in political science. One of the main goals in social science research is the development of generalizable theories that can be applied to explain outcomes in different contexts. A theory is a generalized explanation for an outcome. Theories are usually derived from inductive observations, deductive reasoning, and the established literature on the research topic. To determine whether a theory can be supported, one or more research hypotheses must be specified. Hypotheses must be stated in such a way that they may be tested with observable information. They posit the direction of a relationship between at least two variables. Generally, a hypothesis will include a value of an independent variable and the expected value of the dependent variable based on the theory, with reference to a comparison group. Evidence that suggests a research hypothesis is true can lead to the rejection of a null hypothesis and lend support for a given theory.

GLOSSARY

CAUSAL EXPLANATIONS   Explanations that establish cause-and-effect relationships among variables.

DETERMINISTIC THEORIES   Theories that posit that an outcome is the only possible result associated with a particular cause.

ECOLOGICAL FALLACY   Inferring characteristics about any one individual based on a general trend found within a group.

EXPLANATORY POWER   The power of a theory to explain as much of an outcome as possible by evaluating multiple theories at the same time.

INDIVIDUALISTIC FALLACY   Inferring a characteristic about a group based on observations from only one individual or case that belongs to the group.

NULL HYPOTHESIS   A hypothesis that states that there is no relationship between an independent and a dependent variable.

PROBABILISTIC THEORIES   Theories of causation that suggest that the likelihood of an event occurring is either higher or lower for a particular reason (i.e., the presence of a certain value of one or more independent variables).

RESEARCH HYPOTHESES   An expectation of how two or more variables are related.

SPURIOUS   When two variables under investigation are empirically correlated, but the relationship between them is not a causal one.

TESTABLE   A property in which a statement can be evaluated empirically with data to determine whether a specific hypothesis is either true or false.

THEORY   A generalized explanation for an observable outcome.

EXERCISES

1. Using the example in the beginning of the chapter, think about other independent variables that influence interest in politics. What besides political socialization, information asymmetries, and intimidation might influence a young person's interest in politics? Write a theory for why you expect that new variable to influence interest in politics. Then write a null hypothesis and a research hypothesis that you derive from your theory.

2. From Table 4.3, identify one independent and one dependent variable. You should have an expectation that the variation in the independent variable influences variation in the dependent variable. Write a theory for why the two variables should be associated with one another. Make the theory as encompassing as possible for different values in the independent variable. Next, write a null hypothesis stating that no relationship exists between the

TABLE 4.3:   THEORY WRITING EXERCISE PAIRING INDEPENDENT AND DEPENDENT VARIABLES

Independent variables	Dependent variables
Political news consumption	Political participation
Civics education	Voter turnout
Political party membership	Political knowledge
College-level education	Amount donated to political parties

two variables. Then, write a research hypothesis that you derive from your theory. You can repeat this exercise several times utilizing different combinations of the variables.

3. Using your library's online research portal, locate the following articles and study them to see how the theory and research hypotheses are presented. For each article, summarize the overall theory presented and identify the research hypothesis (or hypotheses). Define the null hypothesis for each research hypothesis you identify.

Kam, Cindy D. 2012. "Risk Attitudes and Political Participation." *American Journal of Political Science* 56 (4): 817–36.

Colgan, Jeff D. 2010. "Oil and Revolutionary Governments: Fuel for International Conflict." *International Organization* 64 (4): 661–94.

Kittilson, Miki Caul, and Leslie Schwindt-Bayer. 2010. "Engaging Citizens: The Role of Power-Sharing Institutions." *The Journal of Politics* 72 (4): 990–1002.

Rueda, David. 2008. "Left Government, Policy, and Corporatism: Explaining the Influence of Partisanship on Inequality." *World Politics* 60 (3): 349–89.

Portney Kent E., and Jeffrey Berry. 2014. "Civil Society and Sustainable Cities." *Comparative Political Studies* 47 (3): 395–419.

PAPER PROGRESS

By now you should have completed a literature review on your research topic. In addition, you should have specified an analytical research question that includes two independent variables and one dependent variable. Now it is time to write the theory for why you expect there to be a causal relationship between each of your independent variables and your dependent variable for the research population you have identified. You must also specify a null hypothesis and a research hypothesis for each independent variable.

Step 1: Write your theory

As you write your theory to explain why you expect there to be a correlation between your independent and dependent variables, try to keep the three criteria for establishing causality in mind; if one of the three criteria can be challenged, your theory cannot be supported. Consider the possibility of spurious relationships between your variables.

Your theory should be as encompassing as possible. For each independent variable, include a reason that different values of the independent variables should be associated with different values of the dependent variable. For your variables with nominal measurement (which by this point should be a binary variable if the original variable with nominal measurement had more than two categories associated with it), you must explain why one particular category is expected to be associated with one range of values of the dependent variable and why the second category is expected to be associated with a different range of values of the dependent variable. In other words, make sure your theory explains why you have a specific expectation on the dependent variable for each of the two categories. Next, for your variable with ordinal measurement, explain why lower values of the variable are expected to be associated with a particular range of values of the dependent variable and why higher values on the variables are expected to be associated with a different range of values of the dependent variable. Make your explanations as complete as possible for each of your two independent variables. This will create a theory for why you expect variation in your dependent variable among the respondents who represent your research population.

Step 2: Write your hypotheses

Once you have completed your theory, you must specify the hypotheses you will test when you perform your data analysis. For each independent variable, first write a null hypothesis. Then write your research hypothesis. When you write the research hypothesis, write out the specific expectation you have about the relationship between one value of your independent variable, along with the comparison group at the end.

For example, if your independent variable with nominal measurement is biological sex and your dependent variable is views on state ownership, and you believe, based on the theory you have written, that women will have more favorable views toward state ownership than men, you could write the following hypotheses:

> Null hypothesis 1: Biological sex is not associated with views on state ownership.
> Research hypothesis 1: Women are more likely to have more favorable views toward state ownership than men.

For your independent variable with ordinal, interval, or ratio measurement, you should specify the direction of your expectation, along with the comparison group. For example, if your independent variable is scales of income and you believe that people with lower scales of income will have more favorable views toward state ownership than people with higher scales of income, you could write the following hypotheses:

Null hypothesis 2: Scales of income is not associated with views on state ownership.

Research hypothesis 2: People with lower scales of income are more likely to have more favorable views toward state ownership than people with higher scales of income.

COMING UP

The work we have done to this point is about what we are studying. The next chapter covers research design, which is a plan that describes how a research question will be answered. Two researchers can ask similar questions, review similar literature, and even write similar theory and hypotheses, but execute their studies in different ways. This is why research design is important.

CHAPTER 5

RESEARCH DESIGN

Now that you have conducted a literature review, asked an analytical research question, and generated a theory and testable hypotheses, the next step is to determine *how* your study will proceed. This is why **research design** is important. A research design is a plan that describes how a research question will be answered. Two researchers can envision similar projects by asking similar research questions, reviewing similar literature, and generating similar theories and hypotheses, but the two researchers can execute their projects in different ways. Each study's research design specifies the information that will be used to answer the research question. Often, this information is contained in a section of a final paper called "Data and methods."

DIFFERENT TYPES OF RESEARCH DESIGN

Researchers in political science use different classification schemes for their research designs. The different designs within each scheme have particular attributes that signal how a research question will be answered, what types of information will be used, and how research conclusions may be generalized to observations within the research population that were not formally studied in the analysis. Researchers will usually use some space in a paper to explain the research design that was used to answer a research question. It is important to understand the differences in research designs for two reasons: (1) so you will be able to classify your own studies appropriately; and (2) so you will understand the research strategies employed by the authors of the studies you read in the future. In addition, note that the choice of a particular research design for a study is not arbitrary. Rather, it is often based on the nature of the research question and the amount and quality of information a researcher has at his or her disposal.

As demonstrated in Table 5.1, the classification schemes for many research designs include quantitative versus qualitative research designs, experimental versus observational research designs, and comparative research designs (most similar systems versus most different systems). See Table 5.1 for basic definitions of each of these designs. The designs within the categories are not mutually exclusive. A single research design could fulfill different types of design across the categories. For example, a researcher could construct a quantitative observational study based on a comparative most similar systems design.

Understanding these general definitions will be helpful as we continue with the rest of this chapter. Before defining the different types of design more precisely, however, you should understand two particularly important research concepts for any research design: (1) a study's unit of analysis and research population and (2) the types of samples that can be constructed when designing a study. Both elements of research influence the potential generalizability of research conclusions.

TABLE 5.1:   CLASSIFICATION FOR RESEARCH DESIGNS

Type of design	Basic definition
Quantitative versus qualitative	**Quantitative research design**: uses numerical measures for a large number of observations in a sample to produce a conclusion about correlations between variables. **Qualitative research design**: uses the analysis of nonnumeric information for a small number of observations to produce a conclusion about how and why something happened in a particular way.
Experimental versus observational	**Experimental research design**: allows the researcher to control the assignment of values on an independent variable (sometimes called a treatment) to test its effect on a dependent variable. The ability to control the assignment of values on the independent variable allows a researcher to identify precise causal mechanisms between independent and dependent variables. **Observational research design**: designs in which the researcher does not have control over the assignment of values within an independent variable. In these studies, the ambition of the analysis is to identify patterns among independent and dependent variables without the ability to manipulate the assignment of values on the independent variable.
Comparative	**Most similar systems design**: the observations included in the study are inherently similar to each other on a number of important dimensions so that variation in an independent variable can be used to explain variation in a dependent variable. The similarities among the cases are said to be held constant since they do not vary (and hence cannot be used as independent variables). **Most different systems design**: the observations included in the study differ from one another, but manifest the same value on the dependent variable under consideration. The ambition of the analysis is to identify a single value for an independent variable that explains why the value on the dependent variable is the same for the different observations.

THE UNIT OF ANALYSIS AND THE RESEARCH POPULATION

For any type of design, it is helpful from the start to identify a research study's unit of analysis and research population. Remember from Chapter 3 that the unit of analysis refers to the general grouping of what is being studied. It could be individuals or countries or policies. For example, take a study that attempts to evaluate the relationship between civics education and political participation in the 50 U.S. states. The unit of analysis for this study is states, which means that data are collected at the level of each individual state. In other words, each individual state will receive a score on the independent and dependent variables in the study. For civics education, this information could include the percentage of high schools in each state that require some form of civics education. For political participation the information could include voter turnout in each state. The unit of analysis specifies the level at which information is collected.

When we identify a particular characteristic to limit the observations within a unit of analysis, the unit of analysis stays the same, but the research population changes. The research population is the set of all possible observations within a particular unit of analysis with particular characteristics in common. For example, imagine that the research study mentioned previously concentrates on how differences in civics education influence differences in political participation in southern states in the United States. In this case, the unit of analysis is still "states" because all measurements are taken at the level of each state, but the research population is now southern states because only southern states are included in the analysis. This means that any conclusions derived by the analysis should be first applied to southern states. It may be possible to generalize findings from a study that uses a specific research population to other observations within a unit of analysis (other states, for example), but this must be done carefully.

SAMPLING AND GENERALIZATION

More often than not, it is not possible to investigate every potential observation within a research population. This is because some research populations are very large. As a result, for most studies it is necessary to select a **sample** to study and to use that sample to understand trends within a population. A sample is a microcosm of a larger population, a smaller group within a larger group. Knowing how a sample is generated is important for **generalization**, the application of conclusions to observations within a research population that were not formally studied. The way a sample is selected matters for how conclusions derived from the sample can be applied to the population.[1]

The purpose of using a sample of data from a research population is to make inferences from the sample that can be applied to the population. Hence, it is important that samples represent the research population as closely as possible. **Sample bias** occurs when a sample does not adequately reflect a population. This happens when particular observations are systematically excluded or when particular observations are overrepresented in the sample. Sample bias should be avoided whenever possible because it can lead to faulty inferences about the overall population from which a sample was derived. For example, imagine that you just read a newspaper article claiming that more than 80% of young people in your country utilize social media extensively. Based on this, you decide to set up a research study to understand how much students at your education institution are involved with social media and whether the experience of students at your institution matches what was reported in the newspaper story. You decide to set up a table outside a recreation hall at 7:00 pm on a Wednesday evening and ask people to fill out a brief survey as they walk by. After 100 people fill out your survey, you tally the results and observe that only 40% of the respondents utilize social media extensively. Why is there such a large discrepancy between the newspaper story and your own study? The problem likely is linked to sample bias and how your sample was derived. Perhaps students who enjoy activities at a recreation hall on a weekday evening, and hence enjoy face-to-face contact with other students, are systematically less inclined to participate heavily in social media. As a result, using the sample obtained by surveying people entering a recreation hall at 7:00 pm on a weekday to understand trends in social media use is not appropriate for generalizing to

---

1   Note that even when it appears that an entire population has been captured in a set of observations, it is still likely that the population is really a sample of a larger population of potential observations. For example, imagine a study that attempts to understand the relationship among a number of variables for the 50 U.S. states for a particular year. Although superficially it appears that the entire population has been captured by the study because all 50 U.S. states are involved in the design, we can still make statements about the research population that we would expect to be true in other contexts. This is because data were not collected for every conceivable time frame (one year before or one year after the year the data were collected for the 50 U.S. states, for example). As a result, even when data exist for every possible observation for a particular moment in time, the data can be treated as a sample in empirical analysis. Keep this in mind as you read studies in which a sample of every possible observation is included in an analysis. Again, although the dataset contains information about every state in a country, or every local government in a state, or every policy produced by a government (as examples), the information collected is still treated as a sample because it is possible to make inferences about the sample that we would expect to be true in other circumstances for the research population at a different time.

the overall population of young people. The possibility of sample bias is why the process of constructing a sample is an important part of the research process.

In general, researchers often make reference to two main categories of samples, probability samples and nonprobability samples. Probability samples are based on **randomization**, which means that each potential observation, in theory, has an equal and independent chance of being included in the research study. The explicit purpose of probability samples is to generalize to the larger population from which the sample was derived. Nonprobability samples are not based on randomization. Although generalization to the population from which a nonprobability sample was derived is possible, it must be done carefully because nonprobability samples are more likely to contain sample bias.

Probability Samples

A **probability sample** is based on randomization. The purpose of probability samples is to reduce sample bias as much as possible so that information from the sample can be used to make inferences about the population from which the sample was derived. Here, we should distinguish between population parameters and sample statistics to understand how probability samples work. **Population parameters** are particular characteristics about the research population. Population parameters are often unknown because of the inherent difficulties in gathering information from very large groups of observations, like large populations of people. Thus, the purpose of a probability sample is to use specific information from the sample to make inferences about the population. A specific piece of information derived from a probability sample is called a **sample statistic**. If a probability sample is selected carefully, it should be possible to use the sample statistics derived from probability samples to infer population parameters.

Take the example presented previously in which a news story reported that 80% of young people in a certain country use instruments of social media extensively. If it is true that 80% of young people in the country (the research population) use social media extensively, then approximately 80% of any probability sample we derive from the population should also use social media extensively. In other words, if the sample is derived from an established probability method, the sample statistics should mirror the population parameters closely. However, it is unlikely that the percentages describing the degree of social media use between any probability sample and the population from which the sample was derived will be *exactly* equal to one another. Rather, there is a range of averages associated with different possible samples (say between 78% and 82%) that we believe contains the true population value. This is an important point.[2] Probability samples rely on probability theory, which means that there is always a degree of error that is expected between a sample statistic we derive from a probability sample and the true population parameter. This is called the **sampling error**. Every time we derive a new probability sample, there is an expected degree of error between a sample statistic for the probability sample and the population's parameter (although it is possible that the sample statistic will be equal to the population parameter; it is just not likely).

To help us assess the relationship between a sample statistic and the population parameter, we use what are called the margin of error and confidence interval for a particular confidence level. The **margin of error** is a measure of the precision of our estimate (using a sample) of the true population parameter. The margin of error and the sample mean are then used to generate a **confidence interval** that may contain the true population parameter. For example, if the margin of error is 2% and the average for a particular variable in the sample is 80%, the confidence interval becomes 78%–82% because we add one margin of error and subtract one margin of error from the sample mean. But how much can we trust this result? For this, we need the confidence level. The **confidence level** is the probability that the way we have generated these statistics produces a result that contains the true population parameter. For most work in social science, the confidence level is set at 95%. Note that this does not mean we are 95% confident that the true population parameter is within a particular confidence interval. Once the sample is collected, the population parameter either is within the range or is not. What the confidence level tells us is that this method of deriving sample statistics will produce a range that contains the true population parameter 95% of the time. It is the percentage of samples that is expected to contain the population parameter.

It is also important to note that the margin of error, confidence interval, and confidence level are closely linked to sample size. Assuming the selection method for the sample follows the appropriate rules of probability sampling, the bigger a sample, the closer a sample statistic will be to the population

---

2   We can take a number of samples for any population and compare the statistics we obtain from the samples with each other. If we plot the sample statistics on a graph (for example, the average value for a particular variable in each sample), over time the graph will start to look like a bell curve, or normal distribution. The bell curve will become more evident if we increase the number of data points on the graph (i.e., as we take more samples from the population) and if we increase the number of observations in each sample. This property, through which a normal distribution is created by the sample statistics, is called the **central limit theorem**. Knowledge about normal distributions is important for many applications of statistical inference, especially when a particular population parameter is not known.

parameter. In technical terms, a larger sample allows us to reduce the margin of error for a given confidence level, which makes inferences between the sample and the population more trustworthy.

For most survey research, randomly selecting 1,000 individuals from a population will often produce a margin of error of 3% at 95% confidence. For example, imagine that you want to know how many people in a country approve of a particular leader. You generate a probability sample of 1,000 people, call each of those 1,000 people on the phone, and determine that 54% of the people you called approve of the leader. But how representative is this particular sample statistic of the overall population? First, note that we cannot say that 54% of the people in the population approve of the leader. Rather, we can say that 54% of the people in the probability sample approve of the leader. Probability theory then tells us that for probability samples of 1,000 people, adding and subtracting one margin of error to and from the sample statistic (54% approval) will produce a confidence interval (51%–57%) that most likely contains the true population parameter (what the true percentage of approval is in the population). Furthermore, the 95% confidence level tells us that 95 of 100 times, we expect the results from the survey to be reflective of the true population parameters.

Since the margin of error and the confidence interval are linked to sample size, we could increase the precision of the confidence interval by increasing the number of people in the sample. For example, imagine that we had the resources to call 2,000 people instead of 1,000 people. Increasing the probability sample's size to 2,000 reduces the margin of error from 3% to about 2% for 95% confidence. Thus, if could now call 2,000 people and ask whether they approve of the leader, we would be able make the confidence interval more narrow. Now, imagine that we did call 2,000 people and imagine that we obtained the same approval rating as before, 54%. Since we called 2,000 people, the new margin of error is about 2%, which reduces the confidence interval to 52%–56%. This confidence interval is more precise than the one with only 1,000 people, although the sample statistic we derived was the same (54%). However, since we must essentially double the number of observations in the sample to improve the margin of error in this way, many polls and surveys utilize samples of 1,000 randomly selected individuals from the population, with a margin of error of 3% at 95% confidence. You have likely seen methods statements such as this after reading opinion polls in the news. The use of probability samples with 1,000 observations with a 3% margin of error at 95% confidence is not arbitrary and is common in practice.

Researchers use several types of probability samples to represent populations that can be used to generate inferences between a sample and the population from which the sample was derived. For this discussion we will limit ourselves to only a few types that are commonly used, especially in survey research that deals with large populations of people: simple random samples, systematic samples, stratified random samples (which is what the WVS utilizes to generate probability samples for each country included in the survey), and cluster samples.

A **simple random sample** is the most basic type of probability sample, in which every potential observation in a population has an equal chance of being selected for the sample. Although this is the most basic form of probability sample, obtaining a true simple random sample is not as easy as it looks. First, a reliable list of all potential observations must be available so that all potential observations have an equal chance of being selected. For some populations, this may not be a challenge. For example, if the population is students on a college campus, the college likely has a reliable record of every person who is enrolled at the institution. However, there may be students who drop out or students whose records are not complete. Both scenarios complicate the process of generating a simple random sample. If the list contains dropouts, the sample ends up recruiting people who do not represent the population. Furthermore, if the list does not contain students whose records are not complete, individuals who should have an equal and independent chance of being selected cannot be part of the sample. For both problems, generating a true simple random sample that represents a population may not be possible. As the population size increases, the number of potential problems increases. Think about the population of cities or states or even countries. Generating a list of all potential observations for the population is a considerable challenge.

A second problem is that once a population is identified, a random selection method for inclusion in the simple random sample must be identified. To do this, most researchers utilize one of two methods. The first uses a set of random numbers. A list of random numbers is just that: it is a set of numbers that have been randomly generated, usually by a computer. To utilize random numbers for a sample, a researcher would number all of the potential observations in some way and then use the random numbers to identify which specific observations on the list to include in the sample until the desired sample size is obtained. A second method is to put all the names representing the observations into a receptacle of some kind (electronic or otherwise) and to select observations at random, one by one, for inclusion in the simple random sample, again until the desired sample size is obtained. This process would become tedious if the number of all potential observations in a population is large.

A **systematic sample** differs from a simple random sample in that it involves selecting observations at specific intervals from a list. Again, a list of all observations in the population is required. Whereas the simple random sample selects observations at random, a systematic sample selects an observation at every predetermined interval, say every 5th, 50th, or 500th observation. The interval is usually determined by taking the number of observations in the population and dividing it by the desired sample size. For example, if the number of observations in the population is 1,000 and the desired sample size is 100, the researcher would choose every 10th observation to include in the study (1,000/100 = 10). To ensure that the sample does not systematically exclude the first 9 observations in the list, a random start is required. For the 100-observation sample that uses every 10th observation, this would mean randomly selecting a number between 1 and 10 and beginning the selection at that number to ensure that every observation has an equal chance of being included in the study.

A **stratified random sample** is what the WVS utilizes to create a probability sample for each country in the survey.[3] The process of selecting a random stratified sample begins when observations from a population are grouped into predetermined categories of importance to the population. For the WVS, some of the categories used to stratify, or divide, the research populations are regions, districts, or census units. For the WVS, the population size or degree of urbanization within each category was also taken into account to ensure a proper stratified sample. The sample is stratified because all potential observations in the population were grouped into categories in advance to ensure that the resulting sample was proportionate to the predetermined categories. For example, if a country has two districts, with one containing 65% of the population and the other containing 35% of the population, the random stratified sample would deliberately contain 65% of its observations from the first district (selected through some random method within the district) and 35% from the second (again, selected through some random method within the district). In addition to producing a random probability sample, this method of sampling is also useful for studying subgroups in a general population.

---

3   You could visit the WVS methodology page on the WVS website to study how each country's sample was selected. From http://www.worldvaluessurvey.org/, select What We Do, and then Fieldwork and Sampling. http://www.worldvaluessurvey.org/WVSContents.jsp?CMSID=FieldworkSampling.

The final type of probability sample is the **cluster sample**, which is used when a complete list of all potential observations in a population is not available. To create a cluster sample, the population is divided by some meaningful characteristic, or cluster, such as state, region, district, or neighborhood. Once the clusters have been identified, a sample of clusters from all the clusters is drawn and the observations included in the eventual sample will include only observations that can be identified from the chosen clusters. This type of probability sample is useful when a list of all observations cannot be identified.

Nonprobability Samples

Probability samples are often considered superior to nonprobability samples because probability samples are deliberately designed to ensure that inferences between the samples and their populations are as accurate as possible. But in many cases obtaining a probability sample is not possible, especially for non–survey oriented research. As a result, **nonprobability samples**, in which every potential observation in the sample has an unknown probability of being included, are often drawn from the population. Because there is likely sample bias in nonprobability samples, making inferences between the nonprobability sample and the research population is sometimes difficult. Although it is still possible to make such inferences, it must be done carefully. There are several types of nonprobability samples; quota, convenience, purposive, and snowball samples are the most common.

A **quota sample** is derived when a researcher is guided by a particular characteristic within a population and deliberately chooses a sample based on that characteristic. The difference between a nonprobability quota sample and a stratified random sample (one of the probability samples) is that the selection method for the individual observations in the quota sample may not follow the rules of probability sampling. For example, take a researcher who wishes to interview 10 politicians in a legislature that is divided into two parties, Party A, which controls 60% of the legislative seats, and Party B, which controls 40%. To create a quota sample based on party, the researcher would deliberately interview 6 legislators from Party A and 4 legislators from Party B. A different researcher studying how gender influences the submission of amendments to bills in the same legislature might use the same method, but select a different sample. Using the quota method, he could choose his sample from the same population (the legislators) based on the legislature's gender composition. If the legislative body is 70% male and 30% female, the researcher would deliberately choose 7 males and 3 females to include in the 10-person sample. The quota method of selecting a sample is effective in ensuring that the sample contains variation on a particular characteristic that mirrors the variation in the research population, but the observations within each subgroup are not selected through random means.

Convenience samples are obtained when researchers study the cases to which they have the best access. Researchers who happen to speak Spanish might choose to include Spanish-speaking countries in their research samples simply because of their familiarity with Spanish. Scholars often utilize convenience sampling for such "convenient" reasons—including language skills, cultural affinity or background, or geographic proximity. The ambition of researchers who utilize convenience samples should be to remain objective and analytical, even if the observations in the study were chosen in a convenient manner.

Purposive samples are also common in political science. Researchers choose observations that they believe will return the strongest results for their hypotheses. A researcher who wants to understand something about ethnic conflict in the Middle East might select the countries that he identifies as having the most intense conflicts as a means to generate conclusions that would be generalizable to other countries that also experience conflicts.

A **snowball sample** is derived when a researcher studies an observation and learns from the inquiry itself that another observation might shed further light on the research question. The researcher had not intended to study the second observation when working with the first. For example, a researcher in public administration might choose to study a particular interest group and learn through interviews with representatives of the interest group that members from a second interest group might provide useful information as well. Snowball samples can be instrumental when a researcher is unclear about how to construct a sample, but the same reservations about generalization present in convenience and purposive samples are also present for snowball samples.

REVISITING THE DIFFERENT TYPES OF RESEARCH DESIGN

Now that we have an understanding of a study's unit of analysis and research population on the one hand and the different types of samples on the other hand, we can revisit the different types of research design to understand how these concepts are applied in actual research. Remember from earlier in the chapter that the particular categories of research design are quantitative versus qualitative research designs, experimental versus observational research designs, and comparative research designs.

Quantitative Versus Qualitative Research Design

The quantitative/qualitative divide is probably the most ubiquitous in political science. In fact, many researchers often describe their work as being either quantitative or qualitative in general. Several of the chapters that appear later in this book are also organized according to the quantitative/qualitative divide: Chapters 7, 8, and 9 are devoted to quantitative methods such as different types of descriptive statistics, bivariate analysis, and regression, whereas Chapter 10 covers qualitative research methods such as content analysis and process tracing.

Quantitative Research Designs

Quantitative research designs are sometimes called "large-n" analyses. The n in this context means number of observations for a particular unit of analysis. The unit of analysis can be individuals, policies, cities, or events—anything for which data can be collected on each observation for each of the variables in the analysis. The n in large-n studies must be large enough that reliable inferences from the sample and the research population can be made. For large-n research designs, probability samples are often used to represent a population.

Most studies that are based on quantitative designs utilize datasets that contain numerical representations of key variables for each observation. As a result, the datasets in quantitative research designs usually do not contain in-depth information about each observation. Rather, for each observation, each variable has a single numerical value associated with it. The benefit of quantitative research is the ability to identify statistical correlations among variables. When variables are shown to have significant relationships when paired together in large-n quantitative research, researchers expect similar relationships to be present for observations within the same research population that were not included in the study.

EXAMPLE FROM POLITICAL SCIENCE

Tausanovitch, Chris, and Christopher Warshaw. 2014. "Representation in Municipal Government." *American Political Science Review* 108 (3): 605–41.

The political science literature generally suggests that the policy preferences of citizens and the policy outcomes at the national and state levels of government in the United States are mostly in alignment. In other words, elected officials in national and state governments are often responsive to the ideological preferences of citizens who elected them. But what about local governments? Is the same relationship between citizen preferences and policy output found in national and state governments also present in local governments, specifically municipal governments? Furthermore, do some types of representative institutions—such as the presence of an elected mayor—also increase the connection between citizen preferences and municipal government output?

Tausanovitch and Warshaw attempt to answer these questions by gathering data on the policy preferences of citizens and the policy output of municipal governments in "large" cities and towns, which are defined as those with at least 20,000 citizens. Thus, the unit of analysis for the study is "cities" since the data used in the analysis are collected at the level of each city. The research population for the study, however, is specifically large cities and towns with at least 20,000 people; any findings generated by the study should be generalizable to this particular group. Furthermore, although the analysis included all large cities and towns in the United States for one moment in time, note that the collection of observations still comprises a sample from the population of large cities and town at all potential moments in time. The analysis can be used to make inferences from the sample to the population, cities, and towns with at least 20,000 citizens at other points in time or to other conceivable observations that have the same characteristics as the research population.

The main research hypotheses suggest that citizen preferences and certain types of institutions influence the policies produced by the municipal governments in the large cities and towns. To measure the first independent variable, labeled "policy conservatism," the researchers estimate citizens' ideal ideological positions in each large city and town by aggregating data from several national surveys and articulating them into a single data point. To measure the second independent variable, institutional differences, the researchers determine whether each large city or town had (1) an elected mayor, (2) some provision for direct democracy, (3) partisan elections, (4) term limits for elected officials, or (5) at-large elections for city councilors. Finally, the dependent variable, "policy outcomes," is measured in a number of different ways. The first is an estimate of liberal–conservative policy score for each large city and town. In addition, per capita expenditures, per capita taxes, and sales tax shares were used as dependent variables.

The results from the large-*n* data analysis (between 428 and 1,619 observations, depending on whether data were available or present for all variables) provide support for the researchers' first hypothesis: large cities and towns with more liberal populations tend to produce policies that are more liberal. Furthermore, large cities and towns with more liberal populations collect more taxes, have higher expenditures, and have lower sales taxes than large cities and towns that are more conservative. However, the predicted relationship between different types of institutions and policy output was not as supported. Some institutions were associated with greater levels of responsiveness, but this effect was not observed uniformly across the institutions. Rather, the analysis concludes that differences in municipal institutions in large cities and towns do not affect representation.

Since the research design included observations from cities and towns with more than 20,000 citizens, generalization to that particular group is possible. However, Tausanovitch and Warshaw note that it may not be possible to generalize these findings to "other contexts" (Tausanovitch and Warshaw 2014, 621), in other words, to other research populations. There may be something special about large cities and towns that make them unique compared with state and national governments on the one hand and compared with the local governments of smaller cities and towns on the other hand. This is why knowing both the unit of analysis and the research population of a study is important. It is first possible to generalize to the research population (large cities and towns) and then to think more broadly about other potential observations within the unit of analysis (cities and towns in general).

Qualitative Research Designs

Qualitative research designs are more difficult to define precisely than quantitative designs. Nonetheless, qualitative research usually involves the identification of one or more case studies that are used to understand how and why something happened the way it did. A **case study** involves an observation of some event or phenomenon in one place, either at one point in time or over multiple points in time. For example, a study about how marijuana was legalized in Uruguay could be classified as a case study. Another case study could involve the development of progressive policies in Uruguay over a 5-year period. Both are considered case studies because they investigate progressive policies in Uruguay alone, although the latter study considered several policies at the same time. Both studies could potentially bear the title "A Case Study on Policy Making in Uruguay."

This ambiguity in defining case study research has led to substantial controversy among researchers about the role case studies play in political science research. Nonetheless, case study research is crucial for social science. Case studies are highly descriptive and detailed. The term "case study" is sometimes analogous with qualitative analysis because a case study involves a deep understanding of what is being explained. Without thorough case studies, we would likely not understand how or why events unfold as they do. It is also possible to use the insight gleaned from case study work to determine which variables to eventually include in quantitative large-*n* analysis.

It is important to remember that in addition to producing rich information about a particular case, a central ambition of qualitative/case study research is to produce conclusions that might be generalized to a larger group of cases. Although it is admittedly harder to generalize from a single case study to a larger population because case studies form nonprobability samples (usually convenience or purposive samples), generalization is still an important part of qualitative research. What is important is to identify how the case study is representative of a larger group of cases. In other words, although there may be a single case under study, it should still be possible to identify a research population for a case study. Research conclusions would then be applicable to any other cases that belong to the research population. An example of this follows.

EXAMPLE FROM POLITICAL SCIENCE

Moore, Colin D. 2015. "Innovation without Reputation: How Bureaucrats Saved the Veteran's Health Care System." *Perspectives on Politics* 13 (2): 327–44.

This case study of the Veterans Health Administration (VA) in the United States is designed to explain how a state-run organization that is plagued with inefficiency and mismanagement can survive and even grow despite ongoing challenges. The VA is an unusual organization, given that the state directly administers health care to veterans, whereas most welfare-oriented programs in the United States utilize private entities for the provision of care. Some of the VA's resiliency stems from the country's need to serve a highly valued population (veterans), which created broad-based acceptance for the VA itself. But, as Moore argues, this alone cannot explain how the VA was able to survive. Rather, the case study highlights the role that "entrepreneurial bureaucrats" in the VA played "in forging partnerships with private interests and reframing the agency's policy failures as mandates for increased funding, discretion, and more generous benefits" (Moore 2015, 328).

Utilizing a wide variety of archives and libraries around the country, Moore was able to trace, over time, how entrepreneurial bureaucrats were able to implement managerial and organizational reform even when the VA was on the decline. One way this happens is through the "borrowing" of political capital and reputation of private actors as means of "collaborative state building" (Moore 2015, 330). After World War II, for example, VA leaders managed to secure partnerships with medical schools in large cities, which embedded the care of veterans in the larger nexus of medical facilities and helped increase the VA's reputation. Thus, the activities of entrepreneurial bureaucrats largely explain how the VA was able to sustain itself and even grow.

What applicability does this case study have for other observations within the study's research population? And what is the research population in the first place? Moore answers these questions toward the end of the article when he suggests that the VA is "not the only federal agency to show unusual resilience in the face of reputational failures" (Moore 2015, 336). Specifically, Moore mentions the Federal Emergency Management Agency as a case that might share striking similarities to what was observed in this case study of the VA. This reference to other possible cases within Moore's research population (federal agencies in decline that manage to survive despite their inefficiencies) suggests that the conclusions of Moore's detailed case study may be applicable to other cases.

Experimental Versus Observational Research Designs

Experimental Research Designs

Studies based on an experimental design are becoming more common in political science. Experiments have the same essential goal: to determine precisely how different values on an independent variable influence outcomes on a dependent variable in some real-world setting. Because they involve explicit controls, experiments are particularly effective in isolating the causal effect that variation in an independent variable has on a dependent variable. The idea of an experiment is to separate a group of subjects into at least two groups and to impose a treatment on one group but not the other. Medical experiments, especially ones involving pharmaceutical testing, often utilize this method: one group of participants (the treatment group) is given a particular medicine, whereas a second group (the control group) is not. The researchers' job is to determine what effect the medicine had on the treatment group by comparing the outcomes of the two groups after the treatment was given to the first group. If the treatment group responds differently than the control group, the treatment is likely the cause.

Thus, with an experimental design, a researcher controls which observations receive a particular treatment on an independent variable and which observations do not. For example, if a researcher wanted to understand whether exposure to a particular type of news (say, news with conservative bias) influences how respondents express opinions about a particular issue in international politics, he could devise an experimental design to test how exposure to conservatively biased news matters for how respondents change (or do not change) their opinions. First, the researcher could administer a pretest quiz to all participants in the study to gauge respondents' opinions about a particular international issue. Then the researcher could separate the participant group into two subgroups: one that would be given a series of conservatively biased news stories to watch on television (the treatment group) and one that would be given a children's program (or some other non–news oriented program) to watch (the control group). Then, after the first group watches the news programs, all participants could be given a second test that is similar to the first to gauge whether and how opinions about the international issue changed between the two tests. If the opinions in the first group change, and if the opinions in the second group stay the same, the researcher would have evidence suggesting that the independent variable (watching the conservatively biased news program) mattered for a change in the dependent variable, differences in opinions on the international issue. Since the researcher had control of the independent (or treatment) variable, this is an example of an experimental design. Experiments are particularly effective in establishing causality between a cause (the independent variable) and effect (the dependent variable) because any effect noted in the treatment group, but not in the control group, can likely be attributed to the treatment itself.

EXAMPLE FROM POLITICAL SCIENCE

Hock, Scott, Sarah Anderson, and Matthew Potoski. 2012. "Invitation Phone Calls Increase Attendance at Civic Meetings: Evidence from a Field Experiment." *Public Administration Review* 73 (2): 221–28.

How can public officials increase civic participation at important local political events? To answer this question, Hock, Anderson, and Potoski devised an experiment to show how personal phone call invitations can compel stakeholders, those with a vested interest in the system, to attend public meetings. The study was conducted in the downtown commercial district of Ames, Iowa. First, Hock, Anderson, and Potoski identified the district's 277 small business owners from listings in the local phone book. Then they randomly selected 108 of them to receive a personal phone call as an invitation to attend a specific civic meeting that had important agenda items for businesses. One item involved a small grant program to improve the appearance of nonresidential buildings and another involved a possible code change in the aesthetic criteria of storefronts. Based on the results of the study, the personal phone calls compelled more small business owners to attend the meeting: overall attendance was 8.3% for the treatment group (the group that received the invitation phone call) versus 4.7% for the control group (the group not contacted by the researchers). Based on this evidence, the researchers suggest that a relatively small investment on the part of politicians—making brief personal invitation phone calls—can result in greater civic participation for the stakeholders of important decisions.

How generalizable is this result? Do the results of the study imply that such phone calls can increase civic participation overall? The researchers are appropriately conservative with their conclusions. They suggest that although the study's findings may be applicable to other groups of people, they recognize that their study involved a highly specific research population: small business owners. Before we can generalize these findings to other groups, we must consider the fact that small business owners may have special characteristics that make them more likely to respond to phone call invitations. Thus, although the results are encouraging because they show how one relatively easy and inexpensive method of interaction can bolster civic participation, the researchers recognize that there may be limitations to the applicability of their findings because of how their research population was defined and suggest that future studies extend the parameters of the research design to include other groups of stakeholders.

Observational Research Designs

Contrast experimental designs with observational research designs, in which the researcher cannot control placement of values on the independent variable to the observations in the study. For most observational studies, researchers must work with the information they have at their disposal to assess how variation in an independent variable influences variation in a dependent variable. Many of the studies that have been used as examples in this book thus far (except for the previous example) were based on observational designs since the researchers who conducted the studies did not have control over the placement of values on the independent variable. For example, even when a researcher administers a survey to collect opinions about an issue (and hence collects the data herself), the analysis is still based on an observational design. For example, let's continue from the example offered for experimental studies in the previous section. Imagine that the research question is similar to the one explored previously and that a researcher wants to understand how regular consumption of conservatively biased news influences opinions about a particular international issue. In the previous section, an experimental design to answer the research question was described but now imagine that the researcher does not have the resources or inclination to conduct such an experiment. Rather, she decides to create a probability sample and administer a survey to ask respondents questions related to (1) the types of news programs that are watched on a regular basis and (2) opinions about a particular international issue. Once all the data are collected, she engages in quantitative analysis to understand how the variables are correlated with one another in the dataset. This, then, would be an observational study since the researcher could not manipulate the assignment of values to the independent variable.

EXAMPLE FROM POLITICAL SCIENCE

Dube, Arindrajit, Dube Oeindrila, and Oman García-Ponce. 2013. "Cross-Border Spillover: U.S. Gun Laws and Violence in Mexico." *American Political Science Review* **107 (3): 397–417.**

In 2004, the U.S. Federal Assault Weapons Ban expired. In Texas, Arizona, and New Mexico this meant that people could now buy military-style assault weapons and bring them across the border into Mexico. California, however, maintained its state-level ban on such arms and thus no assault weapons could be purchased. Dube, Oeindrila, and García-Ponce investigated whether and how this important institutional change—the expiration of the ban in Texas, Arizona, and New Mexico, but not California—affected violence by studying violent crime in the Mexican municipalities near the borders of all four states between 2002 and 2006. They found that violence (measured primarily as the number of gun-related homicides) increased by 60% in the Mexican municipalities near Texas, Arizona, and New Mexico compared with municipalities located further into Mexico, at least 100 miles away from the border with the United States. But such an increase in gun-related homicides was not observed in the Mexican municipalities near California, suggesting that access to military-style weapons in a particular area greatly increases gun-related deaths.

Furthermore, the researchers found that the nature of political competition among local officials also influenced the extent of gun-related violence. Here it is important to note the role that single-party dominance played in maintaining order in Mexico. One party, the Institutional Revolutionary Party (PRI), controlled all levels of Mexican government for decades until 2000, which led to a highly developed system of patronage among government, local officials, and gangs. This patronage, the giving and receiving of bribes to maintain order, may have kept violence at bay. But in 2000, the PRI lost the Mexican presidency to another political party, the National Action Party, and new types of competition emerged among local officials in the Mexican municipalities. Dube, Oeindrila, and García-Ponce thus suggest that where electoral competition among candidates of different parties was more intense, violence increased because "rising political competition reduced the ability of drug cartels to bribe PRI mayors in exchange for selective enforcement, fueling fighting with rival cartels and the state" (Dube, Oeindrila, and García-Ponce 2006, 398). Conversely, where there was less competition, violence was reduced because leaders in the drug cartels could utilize traditional forms of patronage to quell tensions. Thus, this study, based on an observational design, showed that the institutional change (the lifting of the assault weapons ban) precipitated an increase in gun-related violence in particular areas and that this effect was conditioned on the nature of electoral political competition in each municipality.

Comparative Studies

Comparative studies generally incorporate substantially fewer observations than large-*n* studies. The cases investigated in comparative studies are chosen deliberately and hence form a nonprobability sample. Given the difficulties of generalizing from nonprobability samples, it is important that comparative studies carefully identify the research population to which any potential conclusions apply, regardless of the number of observations in the sample.

For many researchers who use the comparative method, identifying whether a study involves a most similar or most different systems design is helpful. For most comparativists, these designs often involve the identification of geographical spaces like countries, states, regions, or cities that are either similar to one another (most similar systems design) or different from one another (most different systems design), which allows them to test hypotheses in different ways.

Most Similar Systems Design

The most similar systems design involves studies in which the cases included in the analysis are inherently similar to each other on a number of important dimensions. These similarities are said to be held constant since they do not vary among the cases. The similarities are thus controlled; they can be rejected as explanations for variation in the dependent variable. In other words, the important implication of a most similar systems design strategy is that the similarities among the cases cannot be used as independent variables to explain variation in a dependent variable.

The objective of a most similar systems design is to choose a research population in which the observations are similar to each other to determine whether variation in an independent variable is associated with variation in a dependent variable among the similar observations. For example, to understand how the ideological leaning of a government matters for defense spending in different countries with a most similar systems design, a researcher could choose a sample of countries that are inherently similar to one another so that the independent effect of ideology on defense spending can be assessed. Note that because the similarities among the countries do not vary among the observations, they cannot be used as the explanation for variation in the dependent variable. One most similar systems design could concentrate on only the democratic Spanish-speaking countries of South America with the reasoning that those countries are generally similar to one another in terms of identity, history, language, and culture. Any differences in defense spending, then, cannot be linked with the countries' identity, history, language, and culture since these are similar among the cases. What changes, then, is the ideological leaning of the governments. Another most similar systems design could investigate the same research question for European countries and deliberately concentrate on only East Central European countries that joined the European Union in 2004 and 2005 because they have much more in common with one another compared with countries in Western Europe or East Central European countries that did not join the European Union. The idea is that the research population chosen must contain a number of observations that have particular attributes in common so that those attributes can be rejected as potential independent variables for variation in the dependent variable. Any potential conclusions can then be generalized to other cases that share the similarity.

The number of observations that are included in a most similar systems design can range from low (generally between two and six) to high (several dozen or more). The number depends critically on the research population and whether a qualitative method (for a lower number of observations, or case studies) or a quantitative method (for a higher number of observations) is used to answer the research question. Some most similar systems designs are mixed, that is, they utilize both quantitative methods (involving as many observations that share the similarities as possible in statistical analysis) and qualitative methods (involving the presentation of one or more case studies that provide further evidence about the relationship between an independent and dependent variable) at the same time.

EXAMPLE FROM POLITICAL SCIENCE

Nepstad, Sharon Erickson. 2013. "Mutiny and Nonviolence in the Arab Spring: Exploring Military Defections and Loyalty in Egypt, Bahrain, and Syria." *Journal of Peace Research* 50 (3): 337–49.

Authoritarian rulers generally utilize repressive tactics through their police and military forces to retain power. However, during the Arab Spring, which began in 2010, there were several cases in which security forces defected and joined nonviolent opposition groups and movements. Why did this happen in some places, either fully, as in Egypt, or partially, as in Syria, but not at all in others, as in Bahrain? In this study, Nepstad attempts to understand the important differences of how security forces behaved during the uprisings in the Arab Spring by concentrating on these three specific cases. The differences in the behavior of the police and military forces—full defection, partial defection, or no defection—is the dependent variable for the analysis. The three cases studied, Egypt, Bahrain, and Syria, were included in the research design because they had certain commonalities that could not be used as explanations for differences in how security forces behaved during the uprisings. These commonalities are: (1) the size of the resistance movement, which for each country involved nonviolent

movements of tens of thousands of resisters; (2) similar periods of time in which the political rulers against whom the protests were directed had held power (each regime had been in power for 20 years or more when the Arab Spring began); and (3) similar ratings in terms of economic and political conditions of each country, including economic development and human rights abuses. These similarities allowed Nepstad to test how variables that do vary among the three cases matter for explaining variation in the degree to which security forces defected to join a nonviolent protest movement.

After presenting information about each of the three cases in this qualitative analysis, Nepstad concluded that two key independent variables explain variation in the dependent variable. First, she found that where there were economic and political incentives to remain loyal, security forces did not defect, and where there was economic or political uncertainty, defection was more likely. Second, the perception of how the international community might react to an uprising also matters. Where there was fear that there may have been sanctions or direct intervention against a ruler, military defection was more likely. But where there was a perception that the state would remain strong, the military remained loyal. Taken together, these variables explain why the military defected from the regime in Egypt: the military's actions were guided both by financial concerns since political instability threatened its livelihood and by a perception that continued conflict would propel the United States, which had been a long-standing ally, to withdraw its support. However, in Bahrain, the opposite was found: the military had too much to lose by defection and there was a perception among the security forces that the ruling family would retain power. In Syria, a different combination of factors led to yet a third outcome: some members of the military defected, whereas others did not. Nepstad notes that this third outcome might have something to do with the ethnic composition of the state and the fact that one minority population, the Alawite, controlled the military elite, whereas the rank-and-file were predominantly Sunni, who comprised about 75% of the overall population. This ethnic division meant that the Alawite military elite had different incentives to remain loyal than the Sunni conscripts: the Alawite had more to lose from defection because their fate was directly tied to the success of the Assad regime. Furthermore, the international community has been traditionally divided on Syria, which led to competing interests among the security forces as well.

This study thus showed that differences in the economic and political incentives faced by the security forces on the one hand and the perception of how the international community would react to repression on the other can serve to explain variation in defections during the Arab Spring. The most similar systems design was instrumental in this regard, since the similarities among the three cases explored through the analysis could not be used to explain variation in the dependent variable. How generalizable are these results? At the end of the article, Nepstad offers a number of hypotheses that could potentially be tested with other cases within the research population of authoritarian countries that experience significant uprisings. Future research should confirm whether the relationships between the independent and dependent variables still hold.

Most Different Systems Design

The logic of the most different systems design differs from that of the most similar systems design. For the most different systems design, something of interest is identified that is remarkably similar in radically different cases, in other words, cases in which a value on a dependent variable is the *same* form the sample. (This is the one instance in which the variables of interest should not vary!) The objective of the most different systems design is to identify one or more independent variables—whose values are also fixed—that are the same among the different cases. If a specific value of the independent variable can be identified and linked to a specific value of the dependent variable for all the different cases, the ways the cases are different can be discarded as potential independent variables. The research population is thus the set of cases in which the independent and dependent variables have the same values, regardless of the context in which the relationship exists. Any potential conclusions can then be generalized to those cases in which the independent and dependent variables are fixed in the same manner as those studied through the research.

EXAMPLE FROM POLITICAL SCIENCE

Skocpol, Theda. 1979. *States and Social Revolutions: A Comparative Analysis of France, Russia, and China.* New York: Cambridge University Press.

In this important book, Skocpol argued that although the French Revolution of 1789, the Chinese Revolution of 1911, and the Russian Revolution of 1917 were dramatically different in terms of their historical and social contexts, the three revolutions share important commonalities that explain why each society went through a complete social and political revolution when it did. The main commonality is the presence of a specific set of conditions that made social revolution more likely. First, the traditional state had come under crisis. The crisis could be the result of a number of factors, including a deteriorating economy, natural disasters, severe food shortages, and growing concerns about physical security. Skocpol suggests that these challenges broke down the entrenched power structures of military and administrative elites and compromised their ability to respond to problems effectively. Second, the role of the agricultural sector in voicing grievances against landlords during such challenging times was also important. Because of the reduced capacity of elites to respond effectively to challenges, new patterns of collusion among groups in society became possible. Taken together, these variables explain why the three revolutions under study involve both political and social change. Old political structures were replaced with new ones and new forms of social organization emerged.

Providing detailed accounts of the three main case studies to explain the casual linkages present at every step in her model of social revolutions, Skocpol concluded that each case of a full social revolution is associated with a similar pattern. The values for the independent variables (the breakdown of the state and presence of agrarian grievances against landlords) and dependent variable (complete social revolution) are similar for France in 1789, China in 1911, and Russia in 1917. Skocpol even takes this one step further and shows how other cases of revolution in other countries do not meet the full criteria for complete social revolutions and, hence, the revolutions present in those countries are not full social revolutions like the ones in France, China, and Russia.

Trying to Get the Best of Different Worlds: Mixed Methods Designs

No single research design is necessarily superior to another. Different types of information yield different types of conclusions. Thus, the research design that is chosen for a study should be based on what types of information are available and what is most appropriate for the answering of a research question. As mentioned previously, it has become somewhat common for researchers to combine different research designs in a single study to answer a research question as completely as possible. When this happens, a **mixed methods design** is created. For example, large-*n* quantitative studies that show how variables are correlated with one another are sometimes accompanied by some form of qualitative analysis that attempts to show how the relationships between the independent and dependent variables are present in different ways. Following is one example of such a study.

EXAMPLE FROM POLITICAL SCIENCE

Wallace, Sophia J., Chris Zepeda-Millán, and Michael Jones-Correa. 2014. "Spatial and Temporal Proximity: Examining the Effects of Protest on Political Attitudes." *American Journal of Political Science* **58 (2): 433–48.**

In their study of the effect of social movements on the development of political attitudes, Wallace, Zepeda-Millán, and Jones-Correa suggest that exposure to protests can create powerful cognitive effects in participants and that the size of the protests can influence people in different ways. Specifically, smaller protests can make participants feel more connected to an event, whereas larger protests may alienate participants and foster a feeling of inefficacy. To test the effect of the size of protests on specific political attitudes, such as political alienation and political efficacy, the researchers utilized the 2006 Latino National Survey (LNS). The LNS is based on a stratified random probability sample (stratified by state) and contains observations from thousands of people who self-identify as Latino or Hispanic in the United States. Using the respondents' addresses from the LNS, the researchers were able to add information to each observation about the size of local protests that were geographically proximate to where each person surveyed lived over a period of three and a half months in 2006.

Based on statistical analyses that investigated the relationship between the independent and dependent variables for the more than 7,000 people in the dataset, the findings from the study suggest that proximity to large marches (involving more than 10,000 people) resulted in a 3% decrease in the likelihood that people believe they have a say in government. Furthermore, a larger number of small protests (involving less than 10,000 people) near a person's home was associated with an 8% decrease in responses that people have little effect in government (Wallace, Zepeda-Millán, and Jones-Correa 2014, 442). This suggests that smaller protests and marches result in greater feelings of efficacy

and that larger protests and marches may unintentionally alienate participants.

In addition to the quantitative analysis that allowed the researchers to make such inferences from the sample to the research population, Wallace and her colleagues also engaged in qualitative analysis to further understand why the size of immigrant protests and the political attitudes of Latino and Hispanic people were related. This part of the research design included interviews with more than 100 activists and community organizers to help the researchers understand more about how different attributes concerning the protests themselves influence the political attitudes of the participants. Based on these interviews, the researchers learned that the larger protests occurred in locations where there were more divisions among the protesters themselves. These divisions were important in how protesters framed their positions, ranging from a "We Are America" integrationist frame to a more internationalist frame critical of the U.S. government. Larger protests were thus marked by a number of different frames, which may have influenced attitudes in a negative way. By contrast, protesters in the smaller events tended to adopt single frames that were more uniform and nonradical, which likely influenced participants' attitudes in a positive way. Thus, using a mixed methods design, the researchers were able to confirm their hypotheses and make inferences with their quantitative analysis, but they needed the qualitative analysis based on the interviews to provide further support for their overall theory about how issues are framed during protests and why those frames either negatively or positively impact participants' attitudes.

What Type of Data?

The last section in this chapter describes the different ways data can be categorized in research studies. This is linked to the subject of research design because the design will often designate how many contacts a researcher will have with the research population for a study. Terms like cross-section, pre–post, longitudinal, and panel to describe data are common in research.

Cross-section: One Contact with the Research Population at One Moment in Time

A **cross-section** is a "snapshot" of a population. A study that uses a cross-section of data involves information for a number of observations at one moment in time. Studies that are based on cross-sections of data are common in political science relative to the other types of information that researchers collect.

Pre–post: Two Contacts, Same Subject

A researcher has **pre–post data** when he or she collects data both before and after a particular event has occurred to measure the extent to which the event precipitated a change in a particular variable. Pre–post data are often used to gauge how a treatment of some kind (for experimental designs) or an institutional change (for observational designs) affects a variable. Data are collected at two points in time, with an expectation that something that happened between the two data points is going to cause a change in a dependent variable.

Panel: Multiple Contacts, Same Subjects

Panel data look a little like pre–post data, but rather than collecting data for only two points in time, panel data are collected for the same subjects over multiple points in time.

Longitudinal: Multiple Contacts, Different Subjects

Like panel data, **longitudinal data** are collected over multiple points in time, but for longitudinal data the observations are different. For example, the WVS contains longitudinal data because the survey respondents for each wave are different.

CONCLUSION

There are several types of research design from which to choose when determining how a research question will be answered. These designs generally fall into one of three possible categorizations: quantitative versus qualitative designs, experimental versus observational designs, and comparative designs. When designing a research study, the identification of the unit of analysis and research population is important. The unit of analysis is the general grouping of what is being studied, whereas the research population is the set of all observations within a particular unit of analysis with particular characteristics in common. Researchers must carefully choose the sample of information that will be used in a study. How the sample is selected impacts the potential generalizability of the research conclusions to observations within the research population that were not formally studied. Probability samples, most often used in quantitative large-*n* designs, are designed so that inferences from the sample to the research population can be made. Although it is harder to generalize from nonprobability samples, many researchers still aim to apply what was learned through qualitative research to other potential observations within the research population.

GLOSSARY

CASE STUDY An observation of some event or phenomenon in one place, either at one point in time or over multiple points in time.

CENTRAL LIMIT THEOREM The property through which a normal distribution (bell curve) is created when plotting a sample statistic, such as the average for a particular variable, for a large number of samples on a single line; the effect becomes more pronounced the larger the number of samples and the number of observations within each sample.

CLUSTER SAMPLE A probability sample that is used when a complete list of all potential observations in a population is not available; the population is divided by some meaningful characteristic, or cluster, and the observations that are included in the sample are those identified from the chosen clusters.

CONFIDENCE INTERVAL The interval of sample statistics that is expected to contain the true population parameter.

CONFIDENCE LEVEL The percentage of samples that can be expected to contain the true population parameter.

CONVENIENCE SAMPLE A non-probability sample in which observations are chosen because they are the ones to which a researcher has the best access.

CROSS-SECTION Data that are collected for one point in time for a group of observations.

EXPERIMENTAL DESIGN   A research design that allows a researcher to control the assignment of values on an independent variable (sometimes called a treatment) to test its effect on a dependent variable.

GENERALIZATION   The application of conclusions to observations that were not formally studied in a research project.

LONGITUDINAL DATA   Data collected over multiple points in time for different observations.

MARGIN OF ERROR   A measure of the precision of an estimate (using a sample) of the true population parameter.

MIXED METHODS DESIGN   A research design in which different types of research designs are included in a single study.

MOST DIFFERENT SYSTEMS DESIGN   A research design in which the observations included in the study differ from one another, but manifest the same value in the dependent variable under consideration.

MOST SIMILAR SYSTEMS DESIGN   A research design in which the observations included in a study are inherently similar to each other on a number of important dimensions so that variation in an independent variable can be used to explain variation in a dependent variable.

NONPROBABILITY SAMPLE   A type of sample in which every potential observation has an unknown probability of being included in the sample.

OBSERVATIONAL DESIGN   A type of research design in which the researcher does not have control over the assignment of values for an independent variable.

PANEL DATA   Data that are collected at multiple points in time for the same observations.

POPULATION PARAMETERS   Particular characteristics about the research population.

PRE-POST DATA   Data that are collected for the same observations both before and after a particular event has occurred to measure the extent to which the event precipitated a change in a particular variable.

PROBABILITY SAMPLE   A type of sample based on randomization.

PURPOSIVE SAMPLE   A nonprobability sample in which the observations are chosen because they are believed to provide the strongest results for a hypothesis.

QUALITATIVE RESEARCH DESIGN   A research design that uses the analysis of nonnumeric information for a small number of observations to produce a conclusion about how and why something happened in a particular way.

QUANTITATIVE RESEARCH DESIGN   A research design that uses numerical measures for a large number of observations in a sample to produce a conclusion about correlations between variables.

QUOTA SAMPLE A nonprobability sample in which a researcher is guided by a particular characteristic within a population and deliberately chooses a sample based on that characteristic.

RANDOMIZATION Each potential observation has an equal and independent chance of being included in the research study; used to generate probability samples.

RESEARCH DESIGN A plan that describes how a research question will be answered.

SAMPLE A microcosm of a larger population; a smaller group within a larger group.

SAMPLE BIAS The bias that occurs when a sample does not adequately reflect a population.

SAMPLE STATISTIC A specific piece of information derived from a sample.

SAMPLING ERROR The degree of error that is expected between a sample statistic and the true population parameter.

SIMPLE RANDOM SAMPLE The most basic type of probability sample in which every potential observation in a population has an equal chance of being selected for the sample.

SNOWBALL SAMPLE A nonprobability sample in which a researcher studies an observation and learns from the inquiry itself that another observation might shed further light on the research question.

STRATIFIED RANDOM SAMPLE A probability sample in which observations from a population are grouped into predetermined categories of importance to the population and then randomly selected by some means that ensures that the resulting sample is proportionate to the predetermined categories.

SYSTEMATIC SAMPLE A probability sample in which the observations included in the sample are chosen at predetermined intervals from a list.

EXERCISES

1. For the following analytical research questions, identify what you would do to create a hypothetical research study using different types of research design. For each question, identify a unit of analysis, a research population, which type of sample from the research population you would use to answer the question, and to whom or to what the conclusions to your hypothetical study could potentially apply.

   a. Quantitative design: How does personal income influence campaign donations to political parties?

    b. Qualitative design: How do extreme right-wing parties influence political discourse?

    c. Experimental design: How does watching morning news programs influence knowledge about local politics?

    d. Observational: How does globalization influence ethnic conflict?

    e. Comparative, most similar systems: How does the number of houses in a legislature influence government efficiency?

    f. Comparative, most different systems: How does the presence of civil war influence a country's possibility of economic growth?

2. Find one or more of the following articles through your institution's library and answer the questions below.

> Ziblatt, Daniel. 2008. "Does Landholding Inequality Block Democratization? A Test of the 'Bread and Democracy Thesis' and the Case of Prussia." *World Politics* 60 (4): 610–41.
>
> Brand, Laurie A. 2010. "Authoritarian States and Voting from Abroad: North African Experiences." *Comparative Politics* 43 (1): 81–99.
>
> Tilley, James, Geoffrey Evans, and Claire Mitchell. 2008. "Consociationalism and the Evolution of Political Cleavages in Northern Ireland." *British Journal of Political Science* 38 (4): 699–717.
>
> Gerber, Alan S., Gregory A. Huber, and Ebonya Washington. 2010. "Party Affiliation, Partisanship, and Political Beliefs: A Field Experiment." *American Political Science Review* 104 (4): 720–44.
>
> Kriner, Douglas, and Liam Schwartz. 2008. "Divided Government and Congressional Investigations." *Legislative Studies Quarterly* 33 (2): 295–321.
>
> Grossman, Guy, and Delia Baldassarri. 2012. "The Impact of Elections on Cooperation: Evidence from a Lab-in-the-Field Experiment in Uganda." *American Journal of Political Science* 56 (4): 964–85.
>
> Colgan, Jeff D. 2010. "Oil and Revolutionary Governments: Fuel for International Conflict." *International Organization* 64 (4): 661–94.

> What was the article's main research question?
>
> What was the unit of analysis for the study? What was the research population?
>
> Was the sample used in the study a probability or nonprobability sample? What specific type of sample was it?
>
> What kind of research design was used for the study: quantitative or qualitative, experimental or observational, or most similar systems or most different systems? Was a mixed methods design used?

What was the role of generalization in the study? Were the conclusions applied to observations not formally studied in the research? Were the data collected cross-sectional, pre–post, panel, or longitudinal?

PAPER PROGRESS

Research studies usually contain a brief section called Methods and data to explain the methods that were used to answer a research question. In this section, the research population, the sample of data, and the sources of information used in the study are usually presented. Write at least a few paragraphs to explain the methods you are using in your study, using the following information as a guide.

The design for the research study on political values and attitudes you are writing with this book is specific. Although the unit of analysis is "individuals," your research population is how you specified it in Chapter 3 when you wrote your analytical research question. Furthermore, your study involves a mixed methods research design that includes both quantitative and qualitative research. For the quantitative portion of your analysis, you will change the WVS's stratified random probability sample for the country you are studying so that only observations that represent your research population remain in the dataset (you will learn how to do this in Chapter 7). Furthermore, the data you will use were collected at one point in time, which means that you will analyze a cross-section of data for a particular year corresponding to a particular wave of surveys for a particular research population that you specified. You will conduct large-n statistical analysis on these data so that inferences to the research population can be made.

In addition, for the qualitative part of the design, you will conduct a small number of in-depth interviews with people who represent your research population. The place where you interview the participants in your study will be your single case for your case study, which will be explained in greater depth in Chapter 10. This project will be an illustrative case study and the interviews you conduct for the project will form a nonprobability sample from people who represent your research population. Specifically, you will construct a convenience sample since you will be interviewing people to whom you happen to have access on the day you conduct your interviews for your case study.

For our purposes then, your study involves a mixed methods design that combines (1) a quantitative large-n study based on a cross-section of data from a stratified random sample from the WVS that you will change to include only observations that represent your research population; and (2) a qualitative illustrative case study (see Chapter 10) based on a convenience sample of interviews at a place where you can interview participants who represent your research population. Include this information in a paragraph or two in the methods and data section of your paper. After completing the next chapter, you will also add information about your variables to this particular section.

COMING UP

Now that your study has a design, we can begin the process of collecting and analyzing data to test the hypotheses you have specified. We begin with concept measurement (Chapter 6) before moving on to quantitative data analysis (Chapters 7, 8, and 9) and qualitative data analysis (Chapter 10).

MORE ON MEASUREMENT

Consider the following conversation among three students. Each student has just finished presenting a research paper on political freedom in Asian countries at an undergraduate student conference.

> Student 1: I just finished presenting my paper on political freedom. I think the audience appreciated my streamlined approach, but one observer suggested that my decision to measure political freedom by assessing whether every eligible voter is allowed to vote, regardless of economic or social status, might be too narrow.
>
> Student 2: I presented a similar paper on political freedom earlier today at a different panel. I like your measure because it is straightforward, but I decided to define political freedom differently by investigating the barriers to entry in the political market. I wanted to see how permissive the political system is, in other words, how easy or difficult it is for opposition groups to form and influence the government.
>
> Student 3: I also presented a paper on political freedom. But I measured political freedom differently than both of you. Since political influence is often determined by economic resources, societies that have wide disparities between the rich and poor might not have as much political freedom because the rich have more influence than the poor. As a result, I decided to measure political freedom using an indicator that assesses the degree of income inequality in each society.

From the conversation, it is clear that each student is studying the same research topic: political freedom. Each student, however, has a different idea of how political freedom should be measured. Intuitively, we may have some basic perception of what political freedom is. For many people, political freedom has something to do with how free individuals are to influence their political system. But for use in research, different researchers will have different ideas about how to appropriately measure political freedom. An important part of the research process is **concept measurement**, the process through which concepts are precisely defined so that they can be used meaningfully in research.

Measuring Concepts

In the social sciences, finding general agreement between a term and a way to measure it is not always easy. For example, what is democracy? Would democracy be measured in the same way for all social scientists? For that matter, how should we measure political participation, international cooperation, ethnic conflict, or economic growth? These concepts can be measured in different ways. As a result, a lot of energy is put into making sure concepts are accurately and precisely defined in research. Most studies will include some text in the body of the paper that explains how concepts are measured in the research.

A **concept** is a general idea about something: war, ideology, development, representation, satisfaction, values, etc. A concept is not a tangible item that can be identified or counted on its own. To use concepts meaningfully in research, we must develop a definition for each term to study it empirically. To do this, we identify **indicators** for each concept, precise visible phenomena that can be directly measured. The process of identifying indicators for concepts is called **operationalization**. Keep in mind that the operational definition you choose for a concept may not capture the entirety of what the concept could mean. It is best to be as comprehensive as possible, but it is often the case, especially in quantitative research, that operational definitions involve narrow interpretations of an overall concept. Few perfect indicators for general concepts in the social sciences exist. Take the concept of political freedom from the above conversation among the students as an example. Each student thought of political freedom in a different way and, as a result, each identified a different operational definition for it. The first researcher thought of political freedom as the ability to vote. The second researcher thought of political freedom as the ability of opposition parties to form and to influence government. And the third researcher thought of political freedom differently from the first two and measured it as the degree of economic equality among citizens. Each researcher thus operationalized political freedom in a different way.

A concept's operational definition will create a precise measurement tool, an indicator, so that data can be collected and assessed. Once an acceptable indicator has been identified, variables that vary from case to case can be created. The variables allow us to analyze data scientifically. Remember that

TABLE 6.1:   MEASURING CONCEPTS

Concepts	Indicators	Variables
General ideas	Visible manifestations of a phenomenon	Numerical values that can change for each observation
Student 1: Political freedom	Accessibility of voting	Percentage of the adult population that is allowed to vote (ratio measurement)
Student 2: Political freedom	Opposition strength	Scale from 1 to 5 representing ability of opposition parties to form and influence government, from 1 = most restricted to 5 = least restricted (ordinal measurement)
Student 3: Political freedom	Economic inequality	Gini coefficient between 0 and 1 representing economic inequality; 0 represents pure economic equality (everyone possesses the same wealth) and 1 represents pure economic inequality (one person possesses all the wealth, whereas everyone else possesses nothing) (interval measurement)

variables can have different types of measurement too (see Chapter 2). The different levels of measurement are nominal, ordinal, interval, and ratio. The operationalization of a concept with an indicator will produce different types of variables (see Table 6.1).

ASSESSING THE BEST INDICATORS

As we have discussed, there are many different ways to define concepts in social science. Researchers must choose among many possible indicators for the concepts they wish to measure. Part of the research process involves justifying the reason for which a particular indicator was chosen. Why was one particular indicator better than an alternative? An assessment of the reliability and validity of the indicators we choose is critical to the social science research process. Reliability assesses the consistency of the results when using a particular indicator, whereas validity assesses the accuracy of the indicator in relation to a concept. When an indicator is both reliable and valid, the indicator is probably a good choice to use for measuring a concept.

Reliability

An indicator is said to be **reliable** if repeated use provides consistent results. For example, take two researchers who are working on a project to measure the extent of democratic development in individual countries in the Middle East. The researchers measure democratic development as the number of countries per year that make improvements to their democratic status using an elaborate coding scheme based on voter turnout, the stability of the electoral process, and the ability of opposition candidates to contest elections. Researcher A lists 10 countries and assigns each country a score based on the coding scheme. At the same time, Researcher B lists the same countries and also assigns a score to each based on the same coding scheme. If the scores for the 10 countries are the same for the two researchers, their indicator for democratic development is reliable because the research instrument, the coding scheme, produced the same results for two different researchers. If the scores from the two researchers differ for many of the countries, the indicator for democratic development is not reliable because the indicator did not produce similar results for the same set of observations.

Reliability may be compromised when indicators require a subjective interpretation of events. For example, take two researchers who wish to assess the amount of economic cooperation that exists among African nations. To measure economic cooperation, the researchers devise a coding scheme and assign a score for each country based on two separate indicators: the willingness of the country to engage in negotiations with other countries and the flexibility to change when problems arise. Since willingness and flexibility are also concepts, indicators for each must be identified. Many of the assessments for willingness or flexibility will likely involve subjective interpretations of events to assign scores and create variables. Consequently, there is some possibility that the two researchers will come to different conclusions about each country's final score on economic cooperation. If there is great disagreement on how the scores are assigned, the indicators for economic cooperation are not reliable. But if the amount of disagreement between the two researchers is small and the resultant scores for the countries they study are similar, the indicators of economic cooperation are reliable. This is called **intercoder reliability**, which is often used as a test to determine the degree of reliability for an indicator. The amount of reliability depends on how similar or different the two sets of scores are.

For survey research like the WVS, the reliability of an indicator (specifically, the use of a particular survey question to measure a concept) can be assessed in different ways. One common way is to ask respondents questions that are similar to each other. If respondents respond in consistent ways to similar questions, the indicators for the concept are most likely reliable. This is called the **split-half** method, which is often used in survey research. With this method, a researcher devises a set of similar indicators for a concept and collects data on each one. If the indicators are reliable, the resultant values on the indicators for a single observation should be highly correlated. If they are not correlated, then the indicators for the concept are likely not reliable.

Another way to test for reliability in survey research is called the **test–retest** method. After respondents have completed an initial round of surveys, the same respondents are asked to answer the same questions a second time to ensure that their answers remain consistent. Reliability is established when the answers from the two surveys are the same. If there are significant differences in the responses to the same questions, reliability is compromised. Although this is one traditional way of assessing reliability, researchers have often noted that the test–retest method has significant drawbacks. One drawback is that respondents can learn from their first experience taking a survey and utilize the time between the first and second surveys to think about their answer. For example, someone who has a relatively extreme reaction to an emotionally sensitive question on the first survey may moderate the answer on the second survey. This challenges the reliability of an indicator because the answers to the same question differed at different times.

An important element to establishing reliability in survey research is to ensure that the wording of the questions asked during the administration of the survey is clear. If the wording of a particular question is vague or confusing, respondents may not be able to answer the question honestly. This also compromises reliability. The clarity of questions is important to establish reliability. Keep this in mind as you consider the reliability of the questions you are working with in the WVS.

Validity

Validity evaluates how well a particular indicator matches the concept it is intended to measure. Here is an example. Take a researcher who wishes to understand something about the relationship between the education levels of U.S. senators and their views on abortion policy. To measure the education level of the senators, the researcher chooses to measure whether the senator attended parochial school at some point during K–12 education as an indicator for each senator's education level. The researcher measures this as a binary variable, assigning a value of 0 if a senator did not attend parochial school and 1 if the senator did.

Is this the best way to measure a senator's education level? Does attendance in parochial school match what most people might think of when they define education level? The answer is no. Education level, for most researchers, has more to do with the highest level of formal education attained by a person. Although attendance in parochial school does have something to do with education, using parochial school attendance is not valid as an indicator for education level.

Now consider the following. Assume the researcher changes focus and intends instead to study how parochial school attendance influences a senator's views on abortion policy. The indicator suggested in the previous example was a binary variable to measure whether a candidate had ever attended parochial school during his or her K–12 education. Again, any senator who had never attended parochial school would be assigned a 0 and any senator who had attended parochial school would be assigned a 1.

We now ask the same question to assess whether the indicator is valid for this new concept. In other words, is the indicator that simply asks whether a senator ever attended parochial school a good way to measure attendance in parochial school? If you believe the answer is yes, you would say that the indicator is valid. However, there may be some problems with this particular indicator. What if a senator attended parochial school for kindergarten but then attended public school for the remainder of his or her education? Is this senator the same as a senator who attended parochial school from kindergarten through the 12th grade? The coding scheme would assign both senators a 1, since both attended parochial school at some point during their education. In reality, however, these are two very different senators with regard to their parochial school attendance. The first attended parochial school for one year, the kindergarten year, whereas the second went for his or her entire precollege education. Although the indicator has **face validity** because it has something to do with attendance in parochial schools, it may be not the best we can possibly choose to measure parochial school attendance. Face validity is a way to question whether the chosen indicator has something to do with the concept that is being measured. The idea is to ensure that the indicator at the very least has something to do with the overall concept.

To increase validity, the researcher could utilize a different indicator, one that assesses the number of years, from kindergarten through 12th grade, that a senator attended parochial school. Rather than creating a binary variable, a variable with ratio measurement is constructed with a possible range of 0 to 13 or even 14, to count whether a student repeated a year. A score of 0 would indicate that a senator had never attended parochial school, whereas any other number would indicate the number of years that the senator attended parochial school. This indicator, it could be argued, has more **content validity** than the previous indicator because it contains more information and is more comprehensive.[1]

---

1 A good way to understand content validity is to think of indicators that measure political participation. Using voting to measure political participation, for example, may be somewhat valid, but its content validity is low since there are many other ways to participate in politics; voting is just one of them. If an indicator has content validity, it will provide the most comprehensive definition for the concept possible.

We are still not finished. Although the second indicator is arguably more valid than the first one, there may still be problems with it. It is important to think of all the possible variations of an indicator to determine whether the values placed on the observations in the dataset for the specific indicator match the truth of the concept you wish to measure as much as possible. If the indicator represents the intended definition of your concept as best as possible, then the indicator is valid. But if you can identify problems in how individual values might be assigned to actual observations, it is probably best to identify an alternate indicator if you can. An important part of the process of determining which indicators to use is vetting different indicators to determine which one will be the best to use in research. For example, someone might reason that the later years of K–12 education between the 9th and 12th grades, what is traditionally high school for most people, are what really matter for measuring parochial school attendance. This is especially true if the variable is going to be used to understand views on abortion policy. As a result, the researcher could think about devising a new indicator to measure the number of years from 9th through 12th grades that a senator attended parochial school. With this new indicator, the range of possible values is now restricted from 0 to 4 (0 = never attended, 1 = attended one year; 2 = attended two years, etc.). It is still a variable with ratio measurement, but the new variable has a narrower range.

Determining the best indicator for a concept is not easy. Each researcher must decide which indicator is the most valid for a concept. Some researchers might opt for the simple binary variable, some for the K–12 measure, and yet others for the high school–only measure. Most studies include some discussion as to why a particular indicator was chosen as the most valid for a concept.

For survey research like the WVS, the individual questions asked during the administration of the survey are the indicators for the concepts being measured. Unless you administer a survey yourself and have control over how individual survey questions are worded, you must rely on what is already available and assess how the questions, serving as indicators, are valid for the concepts you wish to measure. For example, say you want to understand how media consumption influences political participation for a certain group of people. To answer your research question, you must find a survey that asked respondents specific questions about both their media consumption and their levels of political participation. You must examine the questions asked during a particular survey to see whether any can serve as indicators for both concepts. For media consumption in the WVS, for example, respondents were given the following: "People learn what is going on in this country and the world from various sources. For each of the following sources, please indicate whether you use it to obtain information daily, weekly, monthly, less than monthly or never." The sources include a daily newspaper, printed magazines, television news, radio news, mobile phone, email, Internet, and talk with friends or colleagues as separate questions. Some of these choices, especially a daily newspaper, printed magazines, television news, and radio news, have face validity with regard to media consumption. These are all recognized media sources. It is unclear, however, whether using a mobile phone, email, Internet, and talk with friends or colleagues as an information source have face validity for media consumption. This is because using a mobile phone may serve as an information source, but not necessarily a media source. As a result, the face validity of the latter information sources may be low.

We could increase the content validity of an indicator for media consumption by combining the scores of several indicators together to create an overall index of media consumption. An **index** is a composite measure that combines scores from a number of individual items, like responses from several survey questions. For media consumption, you could combine the reading of daily newspapers and printed magazines with the watching of television news and listening of radio news to create an index for each respondent. A person who uses all the sources of media information daily would receive the highest score on the media consumption index, whereas a person who never uses the sources of media information would receive the lowest scores on the index. Because it combines information from several indicators, the index will be much more comprehensive than utilizing only one item from the information source list alone. As a result, the index will have more content validity than any one of the items included in the index. Each item has face validity, but creating a new composite measure to assess overall media consumption that takes into combined account how often a respondent reads a daily newspaper, reads a news magazine, watches television news, and listens to radio news has more content validity.

To measure political participation, the WVS likewise lists several ways that respondents can be involved with politics. One way is through voting. The WVS asks about the frequency with which respondents vote in either local or national elections: always, usually, or never. Another way to measure political participation is through participation in a number of "political actions" listed in the WVS, such as signing a petition, joining in boycotts, attending peaceful demonstrations, and joining strikes. Each one of these items has face validity. Combining several items in an index would increase an indicator's content validity. Indices that combine indicators as a means to promote content validity are common in political science analyses.

Establishing the validity of a measure requires the researcher to think carefully about all possible indicators for a concept and choose the one that best reflects what the concept means. In the next section we will see how creative some political scientists have been in the measurement of their concepts and how scholars have used questions in the WVS as indicators for the concepts they measured in their own work.

EXAMPLE FROM POLITICAL SCIENCE

Boix, Carles, and Frances Rosenbluth. 2014. "Bones of Contention: The Political Economy of Height Inequality." *American Political Science Review* 108 (1): 1–22.

In this innovative study, Boix and Rosenbluth make a case for using variance in human height within prehistoric communities as an indicator for the amount of inequality present in those communities. To understand how the argument is constructed, let's first understand what variance is. Variance, whose precise statistical definition is beyond the scope of this book, is a measure of the degree to which a range of values for a group is dispersed around the group's average. For example, say 20 people take a test. Once the test is scored, we calculate that the average score is 85%. But we also note that the lowest test score is 84% and the highest test score is 86%. Since the range of test scores is only between 84% and 86%, we know there is little variance among the individual test scores because each individual test score, of a possible 100 points, is between 84% and 86%. Now let's take a second group of 20 people in which the average is still 85%, but now the lowest test score is 70% and the highest test score is 100%. This signals that the variance is higher since the range is much wider, between 70% and 100%. The variance of a distribution of values tells us something about how much individual scores are dispersed around an average.

Boix and Rosenbluth suggest that communities in which the variance in human height is low (that is, where most people in a society have similar height) exhibit lower inequality among the people living in that community. Likewise, where there is greater variance in human height (where some people are significantly taller than others within the same community), there are higher levels of inequality among people living in the community. This is because, in addition to genetics,

height is strongly influenced by environmental factors, such as the nutritional quality of the food that people consume. People who have access to high-quality food will, on average, be taller than people who do not have access to high-quality food.

Boix and Rosenbluth thus utilize variance in human height within a community as an indicator for inequality because of how different communities function and how they are organized. For example, people who lived in hunting-and-gathering societies, in which there was often little social stratification, usually had access to a wide array of food sources and often enjoyed norms of sharing among individuals. Most individuals who lived in these communities likely consumed the same type and quantity of food and, as a result, the adult height of one individual compared with that of another should be similar. Thus, where there is little variance in height among the individuals in a community, there should be lower inequality among them. However, once people began to move away from the hunting-and-gathering way of life and developed techniques in agriculture and fishing that would allow them to settle into larger communities, new unforeseen patterns of human organization emerged. This had implications both for entire societies and for the individuals living within them. The societies that had access to the best soil or water and access to the most advanced farming or fishing techniques were the ones that could prosper; consequently, individuals in those societies should be taller than individuals in societies that did not have access to the best resources and farming and fishing techniques. Furthermore, some individuals within these new farming and fishing societies could specialize in ways that left them

CONTINUED

privileged compared with individuals who did not possess any natural or acquired skills. This, too, would leave the specialized individuals taller since, through new specialization, they would have access to better and higher quantities of food. Boix and Rosenbluth argue that this stratification among societies and the individuals within them is the source of inequality, which is why we can use the variance in height among individuals both within a single society and across societies as an indicator for inequality.

As a result of this argument, Boix and Rosenbluth suggest that measuring the length of the femur bone for a number of individuals within the same community and then calculating the variance among them for an entire community can serve as an indicator for inequality for each community. Since the femur bone is related to the height of an individual, lower variance in the femur bones among the individuals in a community indicates lower inequality; higher variance among the individuals in a community indicates higher inequality.

Boix and Rosenbluth recognize that this specific indicator may have questionable validity and take some time in their paper to justify it. First, they admit that political and military institutions can alter the degree of inequality among individuals in a society, which would affect a society's variance in human height. In addition, redistribution from the wealthy

(asset owners) to the poor (nonowners) can be a powerful tool in evening out potential height differences. Another issue is what the authors call "survivor bias" (Boix and Rosenbluth 2014, 5). Only the people who survived into adulthood are included as observations in their study, which means that people who died in childhood are not counted. Thus, it is possible that this measure of inequality misses a group of people who might have not have been as tall as the average individual in adulthood. Yet another challenge to validity is the role that genetics may play in determining height. We simply do not know the extent to which height is controlled by genetics or whether genetics play a greater role in some communities than in others. This, too, brings the validity of the indicator into question. Yet, despite these important concerns, the researchers defend their indicator, arguing for its validity to measure the extent to which inequality was present among individuals living in prehistoric societies for which little information about how they lived is available.

The use of height variance as an indicator for inequality in prehistoric communities is an interesting example of how creative political scientists can be in the crafting of innovative indicators for elusive concepts. The measure allows us to make statements about inequality in prehistorical contexts that would have been difficult to study otherwise.

EXAMPLES OF SCHOLARSHIP THAT UTILIZE INDICATORS FROM THE WORLD VALUES SURVEY TO MEASURE SOCIAL SCIENCE CONCEPTS

Cho, Youngho. 2013. "How Well Are Global Citizenries Informed about Democracy? Ascertaining the Breadth and Distribution of Their Democratic Enlightenment and Its Sources." *Political Studies* 63: 240–58.

This study evaluates how well informed citizens are about democracy across and within countries. To separate "essential" elements of democracy from "unessential" elements of democracy, Cho uses four particular questions from the WVS that ask respondents to rate on a scale from 1 to 10 how essential or

unessential certain characteristics are for democracy. To measure the essential elements of democracy, WVS questions concerning the use of popular elections and the provision of civil liberties as essential for democracy were used as indicators. To measure unessential elements of democracy, questions concerning military takeovers and religious interpretation of the law as essential for democracy were used as indicators. One of the main ambitions of the study was to determine which societies have the highest percentages of citizens who correctly identify free elections and civil liberties as essential characteristics of democracy while at the same time correctly identifying military takeovers and religious interpretation of the law as unessential characteristics of democracy. Using the fifth wave of WVS data from 49 countries, representing more than 69,000 people, the main conclusions suggest that only citizens in the West on the whole correctly differentiated the essential from the unessential characteristics of democracy. In contrast, citizens in the Middle East and South Asia were not as informed about democracy. Cho believes that this conclusion "suggests that democracy stands on the weak cognitive foundation of political culture despite decades and successive waves of global democratisation" (Cho 2013, 255).

Cho continues the study by inquiring whether there are independent variables that might explain individual variations in the number of "correct" responses to the four democracy-oriented questions. Survey respondents who answered all four questions correctly received a 4, survey respondents who answered only three questions correctly received a 3, and so on. Each respondent's score then became the dependent variable. For independent variables, Cho suggests that a number of questions from the WVS could serve as indicators for important concepts like modernization, social capital, and political learning. To measure modernization, the WVS questions about education level, family income, age, and biological sex were used as indicators. To measure social capital, the WVS questions about membership in civic organizations and interpersonal trust were used. Finally, to measure political learning, Cho used the WVS questions about political interest and media consumption. Data analysis provided strong support for the modernization and political learning independent variables, but only partial support for the social capital variables. Based on this, Cho concludes that increased economic and democratic development, more formal education and experiences with democracy, and democratic political environments are important for how enlightened citizens are about democracy.

This study thus demonstrates how individual questions in the WVS can be used to measure concepts like democratic enlightenment (for the dependent variable) and modernization, social capital, and political learning (for the independent variables). Furthermore, note that the dependent variable for democratic enlightenment is an index that combines several indicators together into a single measure.

Dorsch, Michael T. 2014. "Economic Development and Determinants of Environmental Concern." *Social Science Quarterly* **95 (4): 960–77.**

This study assesses the extent to which individuals in developed economies differ in their concern for the environment compared with individuals in underdeveloped economies. Dorsch takes a number of questions from the fifth wave of the WVS from 2005 to 2008 to create an indicator for the concept of environmental concern. These specific questions deal with the willingness of respondents to make economic sacrifices to preserve the environment. Specifically, the questions assess whether a respondent would be willing to give up some of his or her income, pay additional taxes, or forgo economic growth to prevent environmental pollution. Any respondent who answered yes to all three of these questions was coded with a 1. Any respondent who answered any single question with no was coded with a 0. This created a binary variable that was then used as the dependent variable. This indicator has more content validity than utilizing any single question alone as the variable. A respondent who was willing to give up some income, pay additional taxes, or forgo economic growth was considered distinct from someone who was not willing to make such economic sacrifices.

For independent variables, Dorsch takes questions about how various environmental issues of both local and global concern impact the respondents' lives. For issues of local concern, questions concerning beliefs

CONTINUED

about water quality, air pollution, and sanitation were used to create another binary variable: someone who felt that all three problems were "very serious" was coded with a 1. All other responses were coded as a 0. Again, this indicator has more content validity than utilizing any single question alone. For issues of global concern, questions concerning beliefs about the loss of plant and animal biodiversity, pollution of rivers, lakes, and oceans, and global warming were used to create yet another binary variable: someone who felt that these problems were all very serious was coded with a 1 and 0 otherwise.

Data analysis based on the WVS data for 40 countries, of which 25 were underdeveloped, suggest that concern for local issues was not related to environmental concern. Specifically, respondents who felt that issues of local concern were very serious were not willing to make economic sacrifices for the environment. Concern for global issues, however, was related to environmental concern. Respondents who felt that issues of global concern were very serious were more likely to respond that they would make economic sacrifices for the environment. The magnitude of this effect was much larger for respondents from advanced economies. Dorsch thus concludes that "the level of economic development matters for how this subjectively altruistic motivation affects the likelihood that respondents display concern for the environment" (Dorsch 2014, 970). Like the previous study, Dorsch's analysis shows how survey questions from the WVS can be used to create valid indicators for concepts like environmental concern, local concern, and global concern to see how they are correlated with each other.

Arwine, Alan, and Lawrence Mayer. 2014. "Tolerance and the Politics of Identity and the European Union." *Social Science Quarterly* 95 (3): 669–81.

This article's main purpose is to determine whether hostility toward out-groups is a product of events that happen in a country or whether hostility exists on its own. To test which statement is true, the authors assess whether there was any change in the degree of tolerance exhibited by respondents between two separate waves of the WVS for eight European Union countries. Between 2001 and 2006, two of the countries, France and the Netherlands, experienced threats from an unassimilated minority, which may have given people in those countries a reason to perceive a threat to their traditional way of life. Respondents from these two countries were thus expected to have lower levels of tolerance in 2006 compared with 2001. The other six countries included in the analysis, Austria, Italy, Spain, Switzerland, Sweden, and Belgium, did not experience the types of threats present in France and the Netherlands and hence were expected to have unchanged or higher levels of tolerance between 2001 and 2006.

To measure the concept of tolerance toward out-groups for their study, the authors use specific WVS questions that assess whether respondents have objections to (1) having immigrants and foreign workers as neighbors and/or (2) having people of a different race as neighbors. The researchers were interested in comparing the percentage of respondents in each country in 2001 that objected to having an immigrant or foreign worker or person of a different race as a neighbor with the percentage of respondents with the same objection in 2006. The results suggest that respondents in France and the Netherlands had stronger objections toward having immigrants or foreign workers or people of a different race as neighbors in 2006 compared with 2001. However, this effect was not noted in the other six countries, in which tolerance seemed to increase, although the effect was not as pronounced in Sweden and Italy. Since France and the Netherlands were the only two countries in the group to experience threats between 2001 and 2006 and were also the only two countries to experience an increase in intolerance during the same time period, the authors conclude that cultural tolerance toward out-groups is not something that occurs on its own.

Hu, Anning. 2015. "A Loosening Tray of Sand? Age, Period, and Cohort Effects on Generalized Trust in Reform-Era China, 1990–2007." *Social Science Research* 51: 233–46.

Generally, people in China have low confidence toward other people in their society. The main purpose of this study is to determine whether the large market-oriented social transitions that China has experienced over the past few decades had any effect on attitudes toward trustworthiness. On the one hand, the transition from communist egalitarianism to a system that produced increasing income inequality might have reduced trust, but on the other hand, the tendency to encourage interpersonal relationships through the development of new economies and markets might have increased trust. Furthermore, a number of other independent variables that might influence trust were added. One additional independent variable is age. Specifically, Hu suggests that people are expected to trust more as they age. A second independent variable is called a period effect, which measures the changes in the conditions in which people live. This concept captures the "horizontalization tendency" of interpersonal relationships that has been noted in Chinese society, which, Hu hypothesizes, may lead to more trust among people (Hu 2015, 235). The third independent variable is the generational cohort to which someone belongs. Given that China has experienced many significant historical events since the 1940s, it is possible that people who were in their formative years during different historical periods will have differing levels of trust toward others. Hu hypothesizes that people who

were in their formative stage during the most recent reform era (between 1990 and 2007) will have more trust than people who were in their formative stages at other times, specifically during Mao's era.

The dependent variable Hu uses is from the WVS for China for the four waves for which data exist (1990, 1995, 2001, and 2007). In this way, the study is based on longitudinal data. Specifically, the question that represents the indicator for the dependent variable is, "Generally speaking, would you say that most people can be trusted or that you can't be too careful in life?" to which the possible answers are 1 (most people can be trusted) or 0 (people cannot be too careful). The main independent variables used to explain differences in trust are age, a period effect, and the cohort to which a person belongs. Data analysis suggests that age is positively related to trust and that the historical period in which someone experienced their formative years is also important. Specifically, people who were in their formative years during the reform era have more trust than the people who were in their formative years during Mao's era. But Hu does not find support for the period effect hypothesis and instead notes a general decline in the level of trust overall. This result, Hu admits, is "pessimistic" and "implies that the phenomenal economic success in the Reform Era is not coupled with a commeasurable growth in people's confidence in the members of society" (Hu 2015, 241).

CONCLUSION

Concept measurement is extremely important in political science. Most of the concepts we work with in our field defy precise measurement and, as a result, we must identify visible indicators for them to create variables. The examples of scholarship presented in this chapter demonstrate how researchers in political science can be creative in how they craft indicators to measure the concepts they wish to use in their studies. Some indicators, however, are better than others, which is why an assessment of reliability and validity is necessary for any particular choice. Indicators should not be chosen arbitrarily. To the contrary, they should be vetted carefully against possible alternatives. For this reason, you must assess any indicator you choose for reliability and validity so that you remain as transparent as possible in your methods.

GLOSSARY

CONCEPT   A general idea about something.

CONCEPT MEASUREMENT   The process through which concepts are precisely defined so that they can be used meaningfully in research.

CONTENT VALIDITY   A type of validity to determine the comprehensiveness of a given indicator for the concept that is being measured.

FACE VALIDITY   A type of validity to determine whether a chosen indicator has something to do with the concept that is being measured.

INDEX   A composite measure that serves as an indicator for a concept that combines scores from a number of individual items, such as responses from several survey questions.

INDICATORS   Precise visible phenomena that can be directly measured.

INTERCODER RELIABILITY   Often used as a test to determine the degree of reliability for an indicator, this assesses the degree to which different coders arrive at the same result using the same indicator.

OPERATIONALIZATION   The process of identifying indicators for concepts.

RELIABLE   A property to assess whether repeated use of an indicator provides consistent results.

SPLIT-HALF METHOD (FOR RELIABILITY)   Used often in survey research, this is a means to assess the reliability of an indicator, whereby a researcher identifies similar indicators for a concept and then determines the degree to which the results from the different indicators are consistent.

TEST–RETEST METHOD (FOR RELIABILITY)   Used often in survey research, this is a means to assess the reliability of an indicator, whereby the same respondents are asked the same question at different points in time to determine whether the responses remain consistent.

VALIDITY   A property to evaluate how well a particular indicator matches the concept it is intended to measure.

EXERCISES

1. Think about the following concepts. Operationalize each one by identifying an indicator for it and write out the range of possible values the resultant variable could have. Does the variable you create with the indicator you chose have nominal, ordinal, interval, or ratio measurement? (Refer back to

Chapter 3 if necessary). Next, assess your indicator for reliability and validity.

> **a.** Economic development
> **b.** Political violence
> **c.** Globalization
> **d.** Political conservatism

2. Write a survey with questions designed to measure the concepts listed below. What kind of variables do the questions create? Compare the indicators you construct with the indicators that your friends or classmates construct. Distribute your survey to your classmates and offer to take their surveys. Based on the results, do you believe that your indicators are reliable and/or valid?

> **a.** Political knowledge
> **b.** Patriotism
> **c.** Religiosity
> **d.** Civic responsibility

PAPER PROGRESS

In Chapter 5, you specified a research design for the methods and data section of your paper on political attitudes and values. Use the information you have learned in this chapter to continue the work for this particular section by listing how you measure the concepts you are using for your study of political attitudes and values. Hopefully you see that the survey questions you identified in the WVS when you wrote your research question in Chapter 3 are indicators for a general concept. In some ways, the hard work in terms of concept measurement for your research has been done for you because the questions in the WVS are the indicators for your concepts.

Step 1: Create a table to display the progression from concept to indicator to variable.

You can create a table to display the information for how you measured your concepts. Use the online interface through the WVS to find out how the survey questions you are using as indicators for your concepts were asked and how the responses were ordered.[2] For example, if your depen-

---

2   As explained in Chapter 3, go to http://www.worldvaluessurvey.org/ and from the left side of the page, choose Data and Documentation, then Online Analysis, then the wave, the country, and finally the specific question to obtain information about how each question was asked and what the values mean. In the next chapter you will also be able to obtain this information through the dataset itself and determine exactly how the values assigned within a variable were ordered.

dent variable is views on responsibility, you would enter "views on re-sponsibility" as the concept, enter the specific question from the WVS as the indicator for the concept, and then provide the possible choices avail-able to respondents who created the variable.

Do this for your independent variables, too. For example, if you identified community trust as an independent variable, you probably chose V24 as your indicator for it. V24 asked, "Generally speaking, would you say that most people can be trusted or that you need to be very careful in dealing with people?" to measure community trust. There are only two possible responses to this question: "most people can be trusted" and "people can't be too careful." This means that the indicator for the concept of commu-nity trust is a question that measures whether someone believes that most people can be trusted or whether people cannot be too careful, and the result is a binary variable because respondents could choose from only two possible categories.

You would also use this part of your paper to explain how you trans-formed any variable with nominal measurement with more than two cat-egories into a binary variable. You decided how you would do this when you wrote your analytical research question in Chapter 3. You should have also used the binary independent variable to create one of your re-search hypotheses in Chapter 4. Remember that you have two possibili-ties for the transformation: (1) you can use only two of the several categories in the variable; or (2) you can condense the information from several categories to create new categories. Use the table and the methods and data section of your paper to explain how you created the binary variable.

Complete the table by including information for your second independent variable as well. For example, if you identified interest in politics as the concept for your independent variable, you probably chose V84 as an in-dicator for it. V84 asks, "How interested would you say you are in politics?" Thus, the question in the WVS is the indicator for the concept of interest in politics. The variable is measured on a scale from "very interested," to "somewhat interested," to "not very interested," to "not interested at all." Hence, the question results in a variable with ordinal measurement. Putting all this information in a table provides information for how you measured your concepts. See Table 6.2 for an example.

Step 2: Assess your indicators for reliability and validity

Your second task is to now assess the indicators you chose (the questions in the WVS) for reliability and validity. Are the questions reliable and

TABLE 6.2:   MEASURING CONCEPTS USING WVS SURVEY QUESTIONS

Concept	Indicator	Variable
DV: Views on responsibility	WVS question, V98: Placement of views on a scale for the two following statements: "Government should take more responsibility to ensure that everyone is provided for" versus "People should take more responsibility to provide for themselves"	Variable with ordinal measurement: 1 means complete agreement with the first statement; 10 means complete agreement with the second statement; numbers in between represent intermediate points of view
IV 1 (example 1, if your variable is binary on its own): Community trust	WVS question, V24: "Generally speaking, would you say that most people can be trusted or that you need to be very careful in dealing with people?"	Binary variable: Category 1, most people can be trusted; Category 2, people can't be too careful
IV 1 (example 2, if you need to create a binary variable from a variable with nominal measurement): Party choice	WVS question, V228: "If there were a national election tomorrow, for which party on this list would you vote?"	Variable with nominal measurement: Original categories: Don't know, I would not vote, Other, Republican, Democrat. Transformed binary variable: Category 1, Republican Category 2, Democrat
IV 2: Interest in politics	WVS question, V84: "How interested would you say you are in politics?"	Variable with ordinal measurement with four possible categories: very interested (1) somewhat interested (2) not very interested (3) not interested at all (4)

valid indicators of your concepts? In terms of reliability, you should ask whether the respondent could fully understand the question as written in the WVS and respond in a way that would be replicable if the same or a similar question was asked to the same respondent repeatedly over time. If the answer is yes, then the indicator you have chosen (the survey question in the WVS) is likely reliable.

In terms of validity, you must ask whether an indicator is the best way of measuring a concept you are using in your studies. Does the indicator have at least face validity, that is, does it have something to do with the overall concept? Does it have content validity? In truth, the content validity of many of the individual WVS questions that you are using as indicators may be low because a single survey question may not capture the entirety of a social science concept. You should ensure that at the very least there is face validity for the indicators you have chosen.

You should endeavor to choose the most reliable and valid indicators, but sometimes you must accept limitations, especially when you depend on data that have already been collected. You may find, for example, that you disagree with the way a particular question was worded, which might create confusion for a respondent and compromise the question's reliability. Or you may find that you are unsatisfied with some of the response choices available for a particular question, which may compromise validity because there was a better way to measure the concept. The best advice is to be honest about any limitations you discover and discuss them in the methods and data section. Although the excellent researchers who have been working on the WVS over the six waves for which data are available have likely refined how certain questions have been asked over time, the reality is that we cannot go back and change anything for any wave that has already been completed. Like many researchers who use already established data, we must make do with what we have.

COMING UP

In the next three chapters you will perform quantitative analysis on your variables, beginning with descriptive statistics and simple forms of data analysis, before moving on to ordinary least squares linear regression. With these techniques you will be able to assess whether you can support your research hypotheses with data from the WVS. We begin with an introduction to the Statistical Package for the Social Sciences and how to present descriptive statistics about your three variables.

CHAPTER 7

GETTING STARTED WITH SPSS AND DESCRIPTIVE STATISTICS

In the most generic sense, the word **data** means information. It is important to note that data can involve either quantitative or qualitative information. In the next three chapters you will begin to understand some basic forms of quantitative analysis.

Keep in mind as you progress through the next three chapters that the information provided is a relatively basic introduction to certain types of quantitative data analysis. Many researchers formally study quantitative data analysis for years before they begin to use statistical techniques in their own work. The goal of these chapters is to explain the logic of some simple forms of data analysis and to show you how to perform manipulations of the WVS data so that you can test the hypotheses you specified in Chapter 4. Students who choose to take additional classes in data analysis after this introduction will likely learn more complicated applications of statistics that are sometimes preferred by professional methodologists to what is covered in these chapters. Nonetheless, understanding these basic building blocks to data analysis is important. Once these basics are clear, expanding your own knowledge about data analysis techniques will be easier.

MEASUREMENT REVISITED

Before we continue, we must review the different types of measurement that were introduced in Chapter 3. The difference between variables with nominal measurement on the one hand and variables with ordinal, interval, or ratio

TABLE 7.1: DIFFERENT TYPES OF MEASUREMENT

The values of variables with *nominal* measurement observations are placed into discrete categories; the values themselves do not have meaning for understanding variation within the variable. A *binary* variable is a special type of variable with nominal measurement that contains only two categories.	The ordering of the values for variables with *ordinal*, *interval*, or *ratio* measurement has meaning for understanding variation in the variable.

measurement on the other is important in quantitative data analysis. Remember the information presented in Table 7.1:

First, consider variables with nominal measurement in the WVS. As demonstrated by the independent variable table in Chapter 3, there are many variables with nominal measurement in the WVS. For these variables, the values assigned to each category in the variable are often called codes in quantitative analysis. Take the question "Which party would you vote for if there were a national election tomorrow?" Each possible choice associated with this variable must have a code assigned to it so that a single code can be assigned to each individual observation (in this case, to each person responding to the survey) (see Table 7.2).

Note the codes for this variable. The first five choices list a series of possibilities for respondents who cannot or do not wish to select a particular political party. These are "no right to vote," "I would not vote," "I would cast a blank ballot," "none," and "other," denoted by the values 1 through 5. These specific codes were present for all countries covered in the WVS for this particular question. For the specific political parties in the United States, however, each individual party was given a particular code. The six-digit values seem strange because this particular question was asked of all respondents to the WVS worldwide, and

TABLE 7.2: SURVEY RESPONSES FOR "WHICH PARTY WOULD YOU VOTE FOR IF THERE WERE A NATIONAL ELECTION TOMORROW?" WVS US 2011

No right to vote	1
I would not vote	2
I would cast a blank ballot	3
None	4
Other	5
U.S.: Republican	840001
U.S.: Democrat	840002
U.S.: Independent	840003
U.S.: Libertarian	840004
U.S.: Reform Party	840005

TABLE 7.3:
ADDITIONAL RESPONSE CATEGORIES

Missing, not asked	−5
Not asked	−4
Not applicable	−3
No answer	−2
Don't know	−1

since every country has different political parties, each political party has a single specific code. Later in the chapter you will learn how to find these specific codes through the statistical package you will use to analyze your data.

It is also useful to mention that additional categories are present for every question posed in the WVS. There are categories for missing data, for questions that were not asked, or for questions that were not applicable. Furthermore, there are categories that gave respondents the possibility of not answering a question or stating that they did not have an answer to the question. The codes assigned to these categories are negative numbers in the WVS (see Table 7.3).

A variable representing the "most important aims of a country" also results in a variable with nominal measurement (Table 7.4). Each survey respondent was asked to pick from the following choices: a high level of economic growth (code = 1), making sure this country has strong defense forces (code = 2), seeing that people have more say about how things are done at their jobs and in their communities (code = 3), and trying to make our cities and countryside more beautiful (code = 4). Each aim requires a specific code.

Binary variables with only two values are also variables with nominal measurement. A good example from the WVS is the question about personal trust. The question is worded, "Generally speaking, would you say that most people can be trusted or that you need to be very careful in dealing with people?" The result is a variable with two codes: 1 represents "most people can be trusted" and 2 represents "need to be very careful."

Variables with ordinal, interval, and ratio measurement are different. With these variables, the ordering of the values in the variable matters for how we understand variation in the variable. For example, questions that ask respondents to place themselves on a scale form variables with ordinal measurement. The scale can have different ranges, depending on how the WVS ordered the possible responses to the questions. For example, in the WVS the question "How important is politics in your life?" has a range from 1 to 4, with 1 representing "very important" and 4 representing "not important at all" (see Table 7.5). The possible answers are categories, but unlike variables with nominal measurement, the numbering of the categories in a variable with ordinal measurement

TABLE 7.4:   BREAKDOWN OF VARIABLES WITH NOMINAL MEASUREMENT

	CONCEPT	INDICATOR	VARIABLE
Variables with nominal measurement			
	Party choice	Survey question: which party would you vote for if there were a national election tomorrow? (V228)	Each value represents a specific political party[1] 1 = No right to vote 2 = I would not vote 3 = I would cast a blank ballot 4 = None 5 = Other 840001 = Republican 840002 = Democrat 840003 = Independent 840004 = Libertarian 840005 = Reform Party
	Aims of country: first choice	Survey question: What is the most important aim for your country for next 10 years? (V60)	Each value represents a specific response: 1 = A high level of economic growth 2 = Making sure this country has strong defense forces 3 = Seeing that people have more say about how things are done at their jobs and in their communities 4 = Trying to make our cities and countryside more beautiful
	Personal trust	Survey question: Generally speaking, would you say that most people can be trusted or that you need to be very careful in dealing with people? (V24)	Each value represents a response to the survey question: 1 = Most people can be trusted 2 = Need to be very careful

contains meaning in how differences in values are understood. The question "What income group is your household in, counting all wages, salaries, pensions and other incomes?" also results in a variable with ordinal measurement. It has

---

1   As mentioned previously, note the codes for this variable. The numbers are strange because this particular question was asked of all respondents to the WVS worldwide, and since every country has different political parties, each country's political parties has specific codes assigned to it. The codes listed in Table 7.4 are the specific codes that were assigned to the parties in the United States.

TABLE 7.5:   BREAKDOWN OF VARIABLES WITH ORDINAL, INTERVAL, AND RATIO MEASUREMENT

	CONCEPT	INDICATOR	VARIABLE
Ordinal measure-ment (most common in WVS)	Importance of politics	Survey question: How important is politics in life? (V7)	Number representing a choice on a scale: 1 = Very important, 2 = Rather important, 3 = Not very important, 4 = Not at all important
	Income	Scale of income (V239)	Number representing a choice on a scale from 1 (lowest step) to 10 (10th step)
Interval measurement	Year of birth	Year of birth (V241)	Number representing year of birth
Ratio measurement	Age	Self-reported age (V242)	Number representing each respondent's age in years

a range from 1 to 10, with 1 representing the lowest wage group and 10 representing the highest. Many of the questions in the WVS result in variables with ordinal measurement because the questions ask respondents how strongly they agree or disagree with certain statements, how much confidence they have in particular institutions or agencies, or how important or not important certain aspects of the political, social, and economic world are in their lives.

When working with variables such as these, it is important to know how the variables are ordered and what the scales mean from one end of the scale to the other. The ordering of the values contained in the variable will directly influence how you interpret results.

Although questions that lead to variables with interval or ratio measurement are not common in the WVS, it is still important to understand how such variables are measured. As mentioned in Chapter 3, the best way to understand the difference between variables with interval or ratio measurement is to consider the two variables in the WVS related to a person's age: the year a respondent was born (V241) and a respondent's age in years (V242). The year a respondent was born results in a variable with interval measurement, whereas age in years results in a variable with ratio measurement.

The distinction between variables with nominal measurement on the one hand and variables with ordinal, interval, or ratio measurement on the other hand directly influences the statistical tests you can perform and the types of conclusions you can generate. It is also important to know how variables are coded so that you can interpret your results correctly.

SPSS

The next three chapters work with the Statistical Package for the Social Sciences, or SPSS, which is a popular program for students who are beginning to study quantitative data analysis. You will need access to a student "standard grad pack" version of SPSS to perform your own analyses.[2] The examples in this book use SPSS 22.[3] If you choose to purchase the program, download SPSS onto your computer. It is also possible that your college or university has a site license for SPSS on some of the common-use computers on your campus, has a way that you can utilize SPSS on your own computer using a remote server, or can allow temporary downloads of the program onto your computer. Check with the information technology department of your institution about different ways you can access and use SPSS before purchasing the program.

DATASETS AND CODEBOOKS

Quantitative data are usually presented in a spreadsheet. Information on a spreadsheet is organized into rows and columns. The spreadsheet is called a **dataset**. In most datasets, the columns represent variables and the rows represent observations.

Once you have access to SPSS, you will need to download the WVS dataset for the country and year you are analyzing. To download what you will need for your data analysis from the WVS, go to www.worldvaluessurvey.org. Then, from the left-hand menu on the WVS website:

1. Click on Data & Documentation.
2. Then, click on Documentation/Downloads.

You should see buttons for the six waves available in the WVS.

3. Click on Select Wave 6 (2010-2014).
4. Click on WV6_Official_Questionnaire_v5_SilatechMenaModule_English.doc.
   This will download the main questionnaire, which contains the questions asked during the administration of the survey for all countries. This is important because the questionnaire will show you exactly how the questions were asked of the survey respondents during the administration of the survey. The general questionnaire can serve as a **codebook** for understanding how the numbers are ordered for most of the questions in the WVS. A codebook is a list of codes and their meaning for

---

2   Several websites offer discounts for temporary access to SPSS. See, for example, http://onthehub. com/spss/. Be sure to select the Standard Grad Pack when purchasing your temporary access.

3   SPSS has recently released SPSS 23; the instructions provided throughout this book are applicable for both SPSS 22 and SPSS 23.

each variable in a dataset. Without this information to interpret the data, is impossible to understand what the values in a dataset mean. With some exceptions concerning the country-specific questions (such as "Which party would you vote for if there were a national election tomorrow?"), the questionnaire provides crucial information about every value contained in the dataset.

Once you have retrieved the questionnaire for wave 6 of the WVS, look at the right-hand side of the page. Under Integrated Documentation on the right-hand side:

5. Click on the country you wish to study.[4]

   Now you will need to download the WVS wave 6 dataset for the country you are studying. This will be in a zipped file under the Data Files for your specific country. In this chapter, the examples are derived from the U.S. 2011 WVS, but students who reside in other countries and have chosen that country to study for their research can choose the appropriate country from this list. Select the zipped file for the SPSS version. For example, for the 2011 data for the United States, the file is WV6_Data_United_States_2011_spss_v_2014_4_28.zip.

6. Click on WV6_Data_United_States_2011_spss_v_2014_4_28.zip.

   Once you click on the zipped file, you may need to provide some information about your institution and project. If this is the case, you will also need to indicate by checking a box that you have read the conditions for use of the WVS data before you can download any data files. The administrators of the WVS want to ensure that the data they have made available for the public are used for educational and nonprofit purposes. The data will most likely be downloaded to the downloads folder on your computer. Since the data are zipped, you will need to extract the data from the zipped file. This will open the .sav file that SPSS can read. To do this, click on the zipped file in your downloads folder and select extract all files. You will be asked to choose a destination for the unzipped file. Put the file where you know you will be able to find it, someplace like your desktop or a folder you have designated for the work you are doing for your research project. If you have SPSS downloaded onto your computer or if you are using a computer that already has SPSS on it,

---

4   If you do not see the country you wish to study on this list, it is not available for the sixth wave of WVS. You will need to select a previous wave to determine whether survey data for the country you wish to study are available for another point in time. You will also need to download the questionnaire for that wave of the survey.

selecting the saved unzipped file (which is now a .sav file) should open the dataset in SPSS. If this does not work, try opening SPSS first and then open the .sav file from the open menu in SPSS.

You should see now something similar to Figure 7.1.

This is the WVS dataset for the United States in 2011. Note that Data View is highlighted in the bottom left corner. This view displays the WVS's **raw data**, which is the data in their unaltered form. As mentioned earlier, we cannot interpret any of the values in the dataset until we have the codebook. You should be able to understand most of what these numbers mean from the questionnaire you downloaded earlier.

In addition to the questionnaire/codebook, there are two other ways to read the data in the dataset. One way is to use the Variable View of the dataset, which lists each variable by name. Clicking on the Values box for each variable will produce a small blue box. Clicking on that blue box will open a window that displays how each variable was coded. Note, however, that an abbreviated term for the variable is displayed in the window. The question "How

	V1	V2	V2A	V3	V4	V5	V6	V7	V8	V9
1	6	840	840	48	1	2	1	2	1	2
2	6	840	840	49	1	1	2	3	3	4
3	6	840	840	50	1	3	1	3	2	3
4	6	840	840	51	1	2	2	2	2	1
5	6	840	840	52	1	1	1	2	-2	1
6	6	840	840	53	1	1	2	1	1	2
7	6	840	840	54	2	1	1	3	2	2
8	6	840	840	55	1	2	2	2	2	2
9	6	840	840	56	1	1	2	2	1	2
10	6	840	840	57	1	1	2	3	1	2
11	6	840	840	58	1	1	1	2	2	4
12	6	840	840	59	1	-2	2	4	2	4
13	6	840	840	60	1	1	1	2	1	1
14	6	840	840	61	1	1	2	2	1	1
15	6	840	840	62	1	2	2	3	2	2
16	6	840	840	63	1	1	1	1	1	1
17	6	840	840	64	1	1	1	2	2	3
18	6	840	840	65	1	3	3	1	1	4
19	6	840	840	66	1	1	2	3	2	2
20	6	840	840	67	1	1	1	2	2	3
21	6	840	840	68	1	1	1	3	2	1
22	6	840	840	69	1	1	1	3	2	1

FIGURE 7.1:   WVS Dataset for U.S. 2011

important is politics in your life" is condensed to "important in life: politics" in the Variable View of the dataset. This is why having the questionnaire is helpful. The questionnaire contains all the information for the questions asked during the administration of the survey. Make sure that you have not misunderstood the abbreviation for a certain variable in the Variable View.

To understand the codes in the WVS dataset:

1. Ensure you are in Variable View.
2. Click on the white box under Values for the variable you are working with (V7 in the picture) and then click on the small blue box that appears.
3. See how the variable is coded.

In Figure 7.2 you can see that V7: Important in Life: Politics, is a variable with ordinal measurement that has a possible range of 1 to 4, with 1

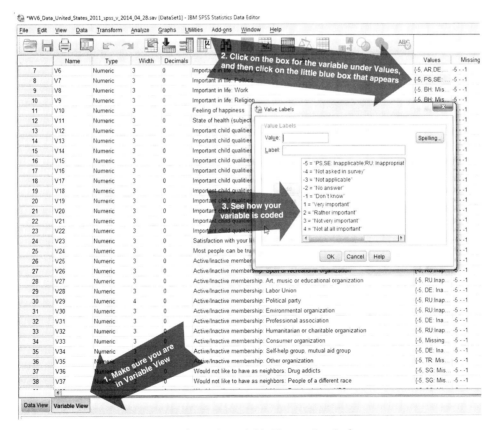

FIGURE 7.2: Using the Values Column in Variable View to See Codes

representing "very important" and 4 representing "not important at all." You should also see that there are special codes for categories representing categories such as "not applicable," "no answer," or "don't know." These codes are represented with negative numbers.

As you work with the illustrations provided in this chapter, look at how the large arrows in the pictures are numbered. This will tell you which manipulation you need to perform first, second, and so on as you work with SPSS. For example, in Figure 7.2, note that the first arrow is on the bottom left. It is denoted by the number 1. Make sure you are in Variable View before proceeding. From here, find the number 2 arrow, which is at the top of the picture. Using your mouse, click on the box under Values for the variable you are working with and then click on the small blue box that appears. This will open the next window, which shows you how each value is coded (number 3). You will see many illustrations like this as you work through the chapter. Study each picture carefully before beginning your own manipulations of the data to understand the order of arrows. These instructions are also provided in the text, with each number corresponding to the order of the commands.

Another way you can find information about how each variable was coded is to use the Variable icon in SPSS (Figure 7.3). This is another quick way to read the raw data.[5]

1. Click the Variables icon.
2. Click on the variable of interest (V7 in Figure 7.3).
3. See how the variable is coded.

Look through the data to find your three variables (your dependent variable and your two independent variables) and figure out exactly what the values in the dataset for your three variables represent. Note that every variable is also associated with a series of negative values that respondents could choose for special cases (such as not wanting to answer a question).

---

5   As mentioned previously, some of the codes for certain variables look different compared with the codes for the other variables across different countries in the WVS. This is because many questions involve country-specific responses, such as party choice, religion, ethnic group, or language spoken at home. The coders at the WVS gave each possible response a specific code for each country, but the precise codes for these country-specific variables are not listed in the questionnaire. Using the Variable View or the Variable icon to read the data is thus helpful because the codes for the country-specific variables in the WVS are provided through SPSS. From the Variable View or the Variable icon, scroll through the entire list of codes associated with the variable for the country you are working with so you can identify the codes for these country-specific variables; the countries are roughly listed in alphabetical order.

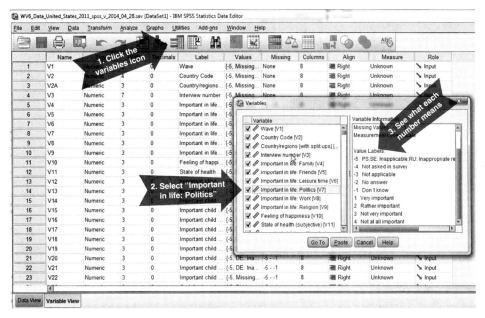

FIGURE 7.3: Using the Variables Icon to See Codes

Limiting the Data Based on the Research Population

In Chapter 3 you wrote a research question that specified one dependent variable and two independent variables. You also chose a specific research population so that you could study a particular subgroup based on a particular demographic characteristic within the overall population. Before continuing, you must limit your dataset so that only those observations that are contained within your research population remain in the dataset. For example, if you chose to study the millennial generation, you must remove all respondents over the age of 35 from the dataset. Likewise, if you chose to study females, you must remove the male respondents from the dataset. Any subsequent data manipulations will then include only the observations for your research population. For example, let's transform the dataset to include only women (Figure 7.4).

1. From the Data tab on the top bar, click on Select Cases. It will be toward the bottom of the list.
2. Select If condition is satisfied and select the If button. A new menu will open. You can enlarge the variable box by putting your cursor on the bottom left corner of the variable box and dragging it to the left. This will allow you to see the variable names more clearly.

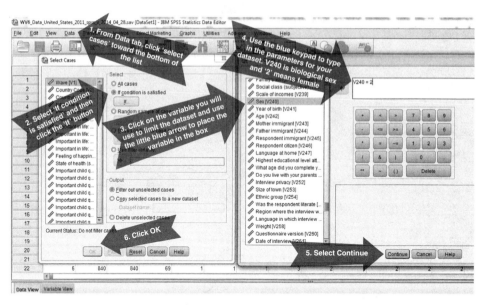

FIGURE 7.4:   Limiting Datasets to the Research Population

3. Click V240 (biological sex) from the list on the left-hand side and put it in the open box using the small blue arrow.

4. Once the variable number is in the bar, choose the parameters for the dataset's new research population. You will need to know how the variable you have in the bar is measured to do this properly. Refer to the Variable View of the dataset or the Variable command, as shown above, to obtain the specific codes for each variable. Since a value of 2 represents women for V240 (biological sex), you will need to enter = 2 after V240.

5. After entering the parameters, click Continue at the bottom of the Select Cases: If menu.

6. Click OK from the Select Cases menu.

You can choose any variable from the WVS to limit the dataset using the Select If menu. For example, if your research population is people who have some university-level education, you would select V248 (the highest education level attained by the respondent) and limit the dataset to observations with a value of 8 (some university-level education, without degree) or 9 (university-level education, with degree). To do this, choose V248 in the Select If menu and then enter ≥8. This will include only observations with an 8 or 9, people who have some university-level education, without degree, and people with university-level education, with degree. In contrast, if your research population is the millennial generation, you would choose V242 (age) and in the Select If menu enter ⩽35 because you want every future manipulation to be done only on respondents who are less than or equal to 35 years of age.

Once this process is complete, you will note that the dataset in the Data View now has diagonal slashes on some of the observations. If you were to scroll across to the variable that you used to change the dataset, you would see that a diagonal slash is now present for every observation that does not meet the specific condition you specified. In other words, SPSS will now remove all observations that have a slash for every future manipulation you perform (until you change the parameters of the "If condition is satisfied" menu). One way to check to ensure that you have limited the data successfully is to use the Data View in SPSS to look at the specific variable that you used to limit the data after you execute the transform command. If you limited the data correctly, the observations that represent your research population should *not* have a diagonal slash associated with them. Figure 7.5 shows a picture of the dataset taken after the data were limited to include only females (V240 = 2).

DESCRIPTIVE STATISTICS

In the beginning of the results section of a paper, it is common for a researcher to present basic information about the independent and dependent variables in a table called **descriptive statistics**. This information is usually displayed in a chart or table and discussed briefly in the text. The information allows the reader to understand something about the variation within each variable used in an analysis. Remember from Chapter 3 that variables must vary and that it is only through an assessment of variation that patterns between variables can be identified. Thus, it is important to know how values are distributed *within each variable* before working with the variables in data analysis. If a variable has a narrow range of values associated with it, the variable's ability to explain variation in another variable is restricted. This also impacts the generalizability of any findings you generate about the relationship between variables.

As mentioned previously in this chapter, it is useful to review the different types of levels of measurement for variables. You must know what kinds of variables you are working with before you can perform descriptive statistics on them. As discussed in earlier chapters and in the beginning of this chapter, there

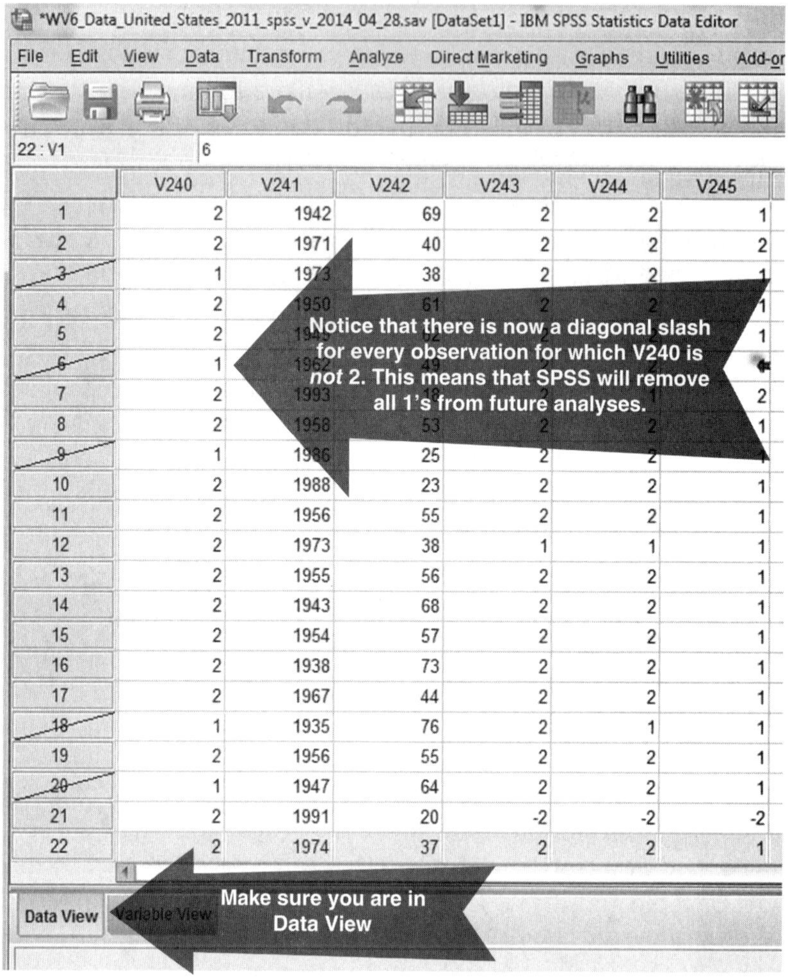

FIGURE 7.5:   Result of Data Being Limited to Include Only Women

is a central difference between variables with nominal measurement on the one hand and variables with ordinal, interval, and ratio measurement on the other. The distinction is important for the type of descriptive statistics you perform on the variables.

Descriptive Statistics for Variables with Nominal Measurement

V60 in the WVS asks the following question and assigned the following codes for each response.

People sometimes talk about what the aims of this country should be for the next 10 years. On this card are listed some of the goals which different people would give top priority. Would you please say which one of these you, yourself, consider the most important?

A high level of economic growth	1
Making sure this country has strong defense forces	2
Seeing that people have more say about how things are done at their jobs and in their communities	3
Trying to make our cities and countryside more beautiful	4

The best way to describe a variable with nominal measurement like this one is to provide a **frequency distribution** that lists the percentages for each code contained in the variable relative to the total number of observations in the dataset. In other words, for the descriptive statistics for this variable, we want to know what percentage of the respondents answered V60 with a 1 (a high level of economic growth), what percentage of the respondents answered V60 with a 2 (making sure this country has strong defense forces), and so on. In addition, a statistic called the **mode** is also useful. The mode is the value (or specific code) in the dataset that appears the most often relative to the other codes.

To generate a frequency distribution (Figure 7.6) and determine the mode for V60, return to the dataset in SPSS. (Note that the examples below include

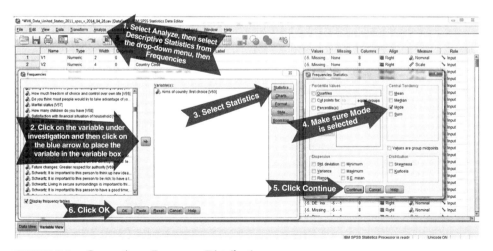

FIGURE 7.6:   Generating a Frequency Distribution

all the data from the U.S. 2011 survey. The data were not limited by a particular demographic characteristic).

1. From the top bar, select Analyze, and then look on the list to find Descriptive Statistics and then Frequencies. This will open a box with all the variables.
2. Find your variable and place it in the variable box by clicking on the variable and then on the small arrow between the variables and the variable box.
3. Click on the Statistics button.
4. A new menu opens. Make sure Mode is selected.
5. Click Continue.
6. Click OK from the frequencies menu.

This produces the information in Figure 7.7.

The table in Figure 7.7 is a frequency distribution. It shows that 68.6% of all of the respondents who answered the question believed that a high level of economic growth was the top priority for the United States. Making sure the country has a strong defense forces and seeing that people have more say about how things are done at their jobs and in their communities were almost equal, at 13.8% and 14.1%, respectively. Trying to make our cities and countryside

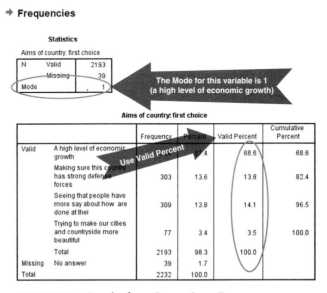

FIGURE 7.7: Results from Generating a Frequency Distribution

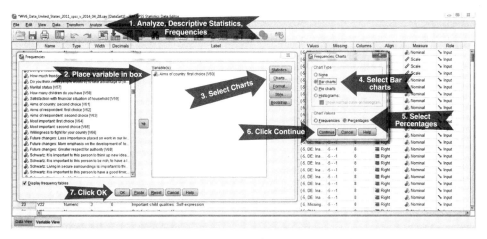

FIGURE 7.8: Producing a Visual Representation of Individual Variables

more beautiful was the least popular answer, with only 3.5%. Thus, from Figure 7.8 we can see that the values for V60 are not evenly distributed among the values because one response, a high level of economic growth, was clearly favored over the others. Thus, a high level of economic growth is the mode, which is shown above as well (the mode is "1," which represents a high level of economic growth).

Note, too, that the values reported in the paragraph above come from the valid percent column of the table. The valid percent column excludes information from respondents who did not supply a "positive" response to the survey question (for example, those who responded that they did not know or did not answer). This stands in contrast to the percent column, which includes information from all of the respondents, including those who did not answer the question. Since the statistical tests you will perform do not include information from respondents who did not answer the question, you should use the information from the valid percent column for your frequency distribution. But you should also look to see how many people did not answer a question by studying the percent column carefully. Discovering that a large number of respondents chose not to answer a question is an interesting finding to report.[6]

___

6   For example, a frequency distribution for V228 (which party would you vote for if there were a national election tomorrow?) for the United States in 2011 demonstrates that about 10% of the respondents responded that they would not vote and almost 27% responded that they did not know which party they would vote for. This means that more than one-third of the respondents did not choose a specific party, which is an interesting conclusion in itself.

It is also possible to produce a visual representation of individual variables, in the form of a bar chart or pie chart (Figure 7.8). These charts visually display the information for the valid percent column for V60. To do this in SPSS:

1. From Analyze, choose Descriptive Statistics, and then Frequencies.
2. Place the appropriate variable in the Variable box (note that SPSS will leave the most recently used variable in the Variable box).
3. Select Charts.
4. Select Bar charts (note that is also possible from this menu to choose Pie charts).
5. Select Percentages in this menu so that the results display the percentages for each value in the variable. This is preferable to displaying each value's frequency, which is the number of times each value is present in the dataset. Knowing that a certain value is present for 10% of respondents makes more intuitive sense than knowing that a certain value is present for 200 observations.

This will produce the bar chart in Figure 7.9. The benefit of using a bar chart is that we can visually grasp the frequency of each response in the dataset. It is

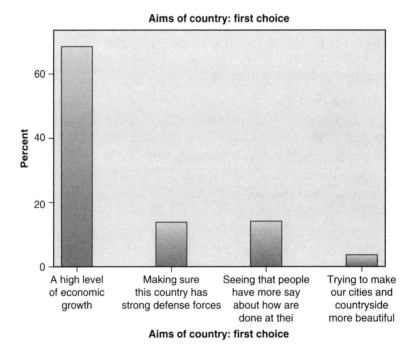

FIGURE 7.9: Bar Chart

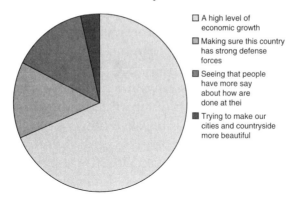

Aims of country: first choice

☐ A high level of
economic growth

☐ Making sure this country
has strong defense
forces

■ Seeing that people
have more say
about how are
done at thei

■ Trying to make our
cities and countryside
more beautiful

FIGURE 7.10: Pie Chart

also possible to produce a pie chart (Figure 7.10). Which type of chart you use is a matter of preference. (Use only one type of chart in your paper if you choose to include a visual display of your variables in your final report.)

Converting Variables with Nominal Measurement with More than Two Possible Categories into Binary Variables

As argued in Chapters 3 and 4, for the purposes of conducting statistical tests you will need to transform all independent variables with nominal measurement with more than two categories into binary variables. You have likely already decided how these variables will be transformed; the decision was made when you wrote your analytical research question and your first research hypothesis. Now you can use SPSS to transform the independent variable with nominal measurement with more than two categories into a binary variable. (Note, however, that if your variable with nominal measurement already has only two categories associated with it in the WVS (biological sex, for example), you will skip this step.)

As explained in previous chapters, there are two ways to transform a variable with nominal measurement with more than two categories into a binary variable. Both require you to make an important decision about which categories to include in the new variable. Again, you likely made the decision about how to change your first independent variable when you wrote your research question and hypotheses, but we revisit the choices that are available here so that you can know how to create binary variables with SPSS. The first way is to select only two categories associated with a particular variable to create a new variable. For example, for "Which party would you vote for if there were a national election tomorrow?" you may be interested in the difference between respondents who chose U.S.: Republican and respondents who chose U.S.: Democrat. This would exclude any individual who selected any other option, such as "Other" or "I don't know." The second way is to combine categories in the original variable to form new categories. For example, it is clear that the mode for the most important aims of the country: first choice (V60) is a high level of economic growth. One way to convert this variable into a binary variable is to recode all respondents who responded with a high level of economic growth as one value and then combine all other positive responses (making sure the country has strong defense forces, seeing that people have more say about how things are done, and trying to make out cities and countryside more beautiful) as a second value. The decision you make depends on what you believe is the most valid reflection for the concept you want to use in your analysis (party choice, aim of country, etc.).

To convert a variable with nominal measurement with more than two categories into a binary variable in SPSS (Figure 7.11), you must know how the WVS specifically coded the original variable. As noted earlier in the chapter, you can find out how your variables were coded using the Values column in the Variable View or the Variables icon in the SPSS Statistics Data Editor. Once you have the specific codes for each category, you can transform the variable into a binary variable. Two examples are provided below, one for selecting only two

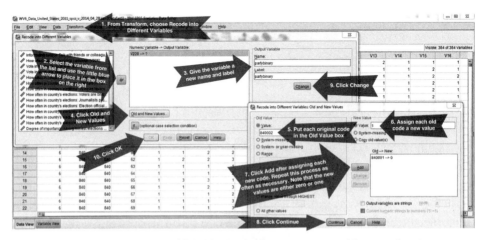

FIGURE 7.11: Converting a Variable with Nominal Measurement with More Than Two Categories into a Binary Variable

categories from a variable (party choice) and one for combining categories (aims of country: first choice).

Using only two categories from a variable: party choice:

1. From Transform on the top menu, select Recode into Different Variables.
2. In the Recode into Different Variables menu, place which party would you vote for if there were a national election tomorrow (V228) into the input variable box using the small blue arrow.
3. You will need to give this variable a new name and label in the Output Variable box. You could put something like "partybinary" in both boxes.
4. Click New and Old Values.
5. In the Recode into Different Variables: Old and New Values menu you will need to enter each original code for the variable in the Old Value box.
6. Add the new value for each original code in the New Value box. For partybinary, if the ambition is to compare U.S.: Republican with U.S.: Democrat, recode U.S.: Republican as 0 and U.S.: Democrat as 1. This requires you to know the specific codes for each category, which you can obtain with the Variable icon or in the Variable View of the dataset. Place 840001 (U.S.: Republican) as the old value and recode it as 0.
7. Click Add for each recoded category. Repeat the process for all the remaining values. Place 840002 (U.S.: Democrat) as the old value and recode it as 1.
8. Click Continue.
9. Click Change from the Recode into Different Variables menu.
10. Click OK.

Combining categories to form a new variable: aims of country: first choice (Figure 7.12):

1. From Transform on the top menu, select Recode into Different Variables.
2. In the Recode into Different Variables menu, place the aims of country: first choice (V60) into the input variable box using the small blue arrow.
3. You will need to give this variable a new name and label in the Output Variable box. You could put something like "aimsbinary" in both boxes to denote that the variable is now a binary variable.
4. Click New and Old Values.

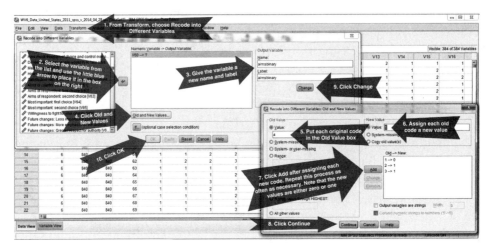

FIGURE 7.12: Combining Categories to Form a New Variable

5. In the Recode into Different Variables: Old and New Values menu you will need to enter each original code for the variable in the Old Value box.

6. Add the new value for each original code in the New Value box. For aims-binary, recode a high level of economic growth as 0.

7. Click Add for each recoded category. Repeat the process for all the remaining values. The 2's, 3's, and 4's from the original variable should all be recoded as 1 in the new variable.

8. Click Continue.

9. Click Change from the Recode into Different Variables menu.

10. Click OK.

Once you click OK, SPSS will take you to the statistics viewer, where you will see that the variable has been recoded (Figure 7.13). To ensure that the variable is recoded properly, generate a frequency distribution for the new variable to ensure that it is now a binary variable. If you recoded the new variable properly and you produce a visual chart along with your frequency distribution, your new variable should produce only two bars (for a bar chart) or two pie pieces (for a pie chart) for the variables you transformed. Note, too, that in Variable View, your new binary variable will appear at the bottom of the variable list. This is important because you will need to scroll down to the bottom of the list to find your new binary variable when you use it in SPSS.

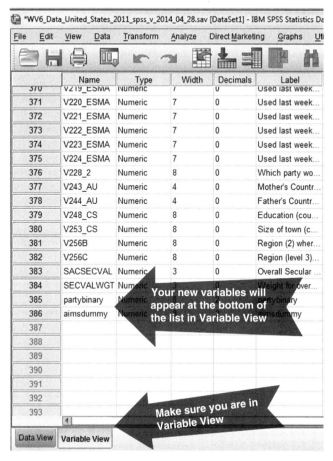

FIGURE 7.13: Result of Combining Categories to Form a New Variable

Descriptive Statistics for Variables with Ordinal, Interval, and Ratio Measurement

Part 1: For Variables with Ordinal Measurement When the Number of Categories is Low (Less than Five)

Many of the variables in the WVS have ordinal measurement with a range of values between 1 and 4. For example, respondents who answered V7: important in life: politics, were given four possible choices from which to choose: 1, very important; 2, somewhat important; 3, not important; or 4, not important at all. (Also remember that respondents could also opt to not answer a question or respond that they did not have an answer to the question.) For a variable with ordinal measurement that contains only a small number of possible responses like this one, it is useful to generate a frequency distribution and provide the mode to describe the variable (just as you do for variables with nominal measurement). This is the case for any variable with ordinal measurement when the number of categories is less than five.

For example, let's use a comparison between V4: important in life: family, and V7: important in life: politics, to show how descriptive statistics can provide valuable information about how values are distributed within a variable with ordinal measurement that has a small number of categories. Both variables have ordinal measurement on a scale from 1 to 4, with 1 representing very important and 4 representing not important at all. Figure 7.14 shows the frequency distributions for each variable.

The distribution of values for important in life: family is clearly different compared with the distribution of values for important in life: politics. According to these distributions, the overwhelming majority of respondents responded with 1 (very important) to the important in life: family question compared with the important in life: politics question, which has a more widespread distribution among the four categories. We can also tell from the bar

Frequency Table

Important in life: Family

		Frequency	Percent	Valid Percent	Cumulative Percent
Valid	Very important	2043	91.5	92.0	92.0
	Rather important	147	6.6	6.6	98.6
	Not very important	19	.9	.9	99.5
	Not at all important	12	.5	.5	100.0
	Total	2221	99.5	100.0	
Missing	No answer	11	.5		
Total		2232	100.0		

Important in life: Politics

		Frequency	Percent	Valid Percent	Cumulative Percent
Valid	Very important	270	12.1	12.2	12.2
	Rather important	954	42.7	43.2	55.5
	Not very important	746	33.4	33.8	89.3
	Not at all important	236	10.6	10.7	100.0
	Total	2206	98.8	100.0	
Missing	No answer	26	1.2		
Total		2232	100.0		

FIGURE 7.14: Frequency Distributions for Important in Life: Family and Important in Life: Politics]

charts (Figure 7.15) that the mode for important in life: family is "very important" (1), whereas the mode for important in life: politics is "rather important" (2). For variables with ordinal measurement such as these, frequency
distributions provide valuable information about how values are distributed
within a single variable. (You should also note that these frequency distributions tell us that using important in life: family would not be a useful independent variable because there is little variation in the variable. This is not the case,
however, with important in life: politics because the variable has more
variation.)

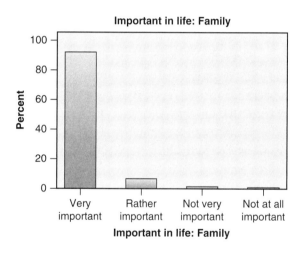

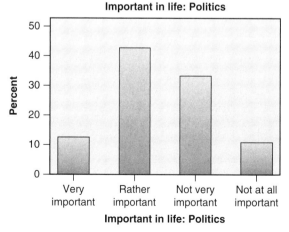

FIGURE 7.15: Bar Charts for Important in Life:
Family and Important in Life: Politics

Part 2: For Variables with Ordinal Measurement When the Number of Categories is High (Greater than or Equal to Five) and for Variables with Interval or Ratio Measurement

Variables with ordinal measurement that have more categories associated with them (five and above) and variables with interval or ratio measurement can be described in descriptive statistics differently than variables with nominal measurement or variables with ordinal measurement with a small number of categories. The information that can be provided for such variables is often called **summary statistics**, which generally includes a variable's minimum value, maximum value, mean (or average), and standard deviation.[7] Summary statistics provide valuable information about how each variable's values are distributed in a dataset. The **minimum value** is the lowest number represented among the respondents in a dataset, whereas the **maximum value** is the highest number represented among the respondents in the dataset. The **mean** is another word for average, which is the sum of all responses divided by the number of responses. In addition, a statistic called the **standard deviation** is helpful for understanding the degree to which responses are dispersed around a variable's mean. A small standard deviation indicates a narrow clustering of values around the variable mean; a large standard deviation indicates that the variable's values are more widely spread around the variable's mean. We will see how this works in an example.

Following are steps for generating summary statistics for a variable with ordinal measurement when the number of categories in the variable is greater than or equal to five (Figure 7.16) these steps are also appropriate for variables with interval and ratio measurement:

1. From Analyze, choose Descriptive Statistics, and select Descriptives from the pull-down menu.
2. Place your variable in the variable box by selecting it from the list and using the small blue arrow to the right of the variable box. For this example, satisfaction with life (V23) was used.
3. From here click on Options.

---

7   There is some controversy among statisticians and mathematicians about whether it is appropriate to utilize summary statistics for any variables with ordinal measurement. The book takes the point of view that the mean and standard deviation can provide useful information for variables with ordinal measurement when the number of categories in the variable is relatively high. Since many of the variables in the WVS, including your dependent variable, have this type of measurement (every dependent variable listed in Chapter 3 was measured on a scale from 1 to 10), we can provide the mean and standard deviation for them.

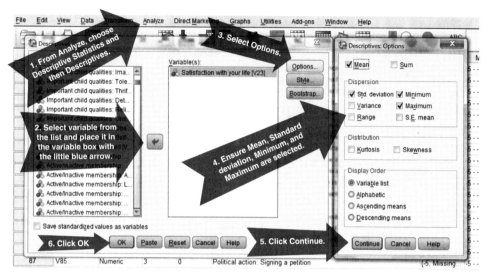

FIGURE 7.16:   Generating Summary Statistics for Variables with Ordinal Measurement

4. In the box that opens, select mean, standard deviation, minimum, and maximum (note that these options may already be selected).
5. Click Continue in the Descriptives: Options box.
6. Click OK in the Descriptives menu.

This should produce Figure 7.17.

Figure 7.17 shows us that the minimum is 1 and the maximum is 10 for life satisfaction, with a mean of 7.44 and a standard deviation of 1.862. The average of 7.44 suggests that life satisfaction among the American respondents is relatively high because the variable runs from 1 (completely dissatisfied) to 10 (completely satisfied). This is why knowing the meaning of the values from low to high is important; we must know how the values are ordered to interpret the average of 7.44 properly. The standard deviation of 1.862 also suggests that the data are somewhat dispersed around the mean. The standard deviation is based

Descriptive Statistics

	N	Minimum	Maximum	Mean	Std. Deviation
Satisfaction with your life	2216	1	10	7.44	1.862
Valid N (listwise)	2216				

FIGURE 7.17:   Descriptive Statistics for Satisfaction with Your Life

on the assumption that a variable's data are **normally distributed**, which means it should have certain properties relative to the mean of the variable. As mentioned in Chapter 5, the normal distribution is sometimes called a bell curve. If a variable is normally distributed, then roughly 68% of the observations for this variable should fall within one standard deviation on either side of the mean. In other words, if we add and subtract one standard deviation from the variable's mean value, we should obtain the range of values that encompasses 68% of the observations in the dataset. For the life satisfaction variable, this range is 7.44 – 1.862 = 5.578 and 7.44 + 1.862 = 9.302. This means that about 68% of the observations in this dataset should fall between 5.578 and 9.302 for life satisfaction. If we add another standard deviation to the 68% range, the range should contain about 95% of the observations and if we add yet another standard deviation, the range should contain about 99% of the observations. A high standard deviation means that a variable has a widespread distribution around a variable's mean. A low standard deviation means that the spread of the data is narrower around a variable's mean.

Keep in mind that the standard deviation is standardized to the units of the variable and that unless variables are measured in exactly the same way, comparing the standard deviation of one variable to another is not advised. A variable whose range has 10 possible values, such as life satisfaction, will produce a standard deviation in units relative to its range; a variable whose range is much greater will most likely have a higher standard deviation. For example, consider age (V242) in the WVS. Since it is a variable with ratio measurement, we can produce summary statistics for it. In Figure 7.18 we see that the lowest age among the respondents is 18, the highest is 93, and the average is almost 49. The standard deviation of 16.9 means that about 68% of the observations in the dataset are roughly between the ages of 32 and 66 (adding one more standard deviation would produce the range for about 95% of the observations, and one more after that, about 99%). It is not possible to compare the standard deviation of the life satisfaction variable (1.86) with the standard deviation of

Descriptive Statistics

	N	Minimum	Maximum	Mean	Std. Deviation
Age	2232	18	93	48.91	16.906
Valid N (listwise)	2232				

FIGURE 7.18: Descriptive Statistics; Age

TABLE 7.6: SUMMARY OF DESCRIPTIVE STATISTICS

Frequency distribution	Summary statistics (minimum value, maximum value, mean, and standard deviation)
Variables with nominal measurement Binary variables Variables with ordinal measurement when the number of categories is less than five	Variables with ordinal measurement when the number of categories is greater than or equal to five Variables with interval or ratio measurement

EXAMPLE FROM POLITICAL SCIENCE

Fox, Richard L., and Jennifer L. Lawless. 2014. "Uncovering the Origins of the Gender Gap in Political Ambition." *American Political Science Review* **108 (3): 499–519.**

It has long been noted that far fewer women serve as elected representatives in American political institutions than men. This article seeks to understand why there is such a "gender gap" in political ambition and to identify the origins of the gap in the first place. Theoretically, Fox and Lawless argue that parental encouragement, experiences with politics, participation in competitive activities, and the degree of personal self-confidence most likely matter in whether a young person expresses a preference for the desire to seek public office someday. Furthermore and importantly, demographic characteristics—specifically someone's biological sex—are also expected to matter.

Drawing on a survey administered to almost 4,000 high school and college students, the data analysis presented in the paper involved two key dependent variables. The first was a 4-point ambition scale measured at the ordinal level that indicated the extent to which a respondent would be interested in someday running for political office, from 1 (I would never run for office) to 4 (I definitely would like to run for office). The second was a binary variable to assess whether someone would be either open to or planning on running for office (1) or not (0). A number of demographic characteristics were included as independent variables to explain variation in the dependent variable. Among these were biological sex, race, political party affiliation, geographic region, estimated household income, and religion. Other independent variables were also explored as explanations for variation in the dependent variables. These independent variables were grouped into several categories, which included "family socialization," "political context," "competitive experiences," "self-confidence," and attitudes about "gender roles and

identity." Each category then contains a number of indicators that serve as independent variables. For example, for the general category of "family socialization" indicators to assess "parents encouraged a candidacy," "other family member encouraged a candidacy," "politicized household growing up," and "political activities with parents" were used as independent variables. For the category of "political context," indicators to assess "political discussion in classes," "political discussion with friends," "teacher encouraged a candidacy," "civic education in high school," and "time spent on political websites" were used as independent variables.

Table 7.7 is a descriptive statistics table that contains some of the variables that were used in the analysis. Note that percentages are listed for the variables with nominal measurement (such as party affiliation and race), whereas summary statistics are provided for the variables with ordinal or ratio measurement. Table 7.7 represents only a subset of what is contained in the article; refer to the tables in the article for the full content of the descriptive statistics for this study.

The information in Table 7.7 provides an excellent snapshot of what is contained in the dataset that represents almost 4,000 high school and college students. From this information, we can understand how each variable in the analysis was measured. In addition, it is possible to assess the amount of variation among the variables in the analysis. From Table 7.7, we can note that some variables have more variation than others. For example, contrast the variable Competitive experiences: "Leadership positions at school" with the variable Self-confidence: "Political traits index." The minimum value for leadership positions is 0 (no

CONTINUED

leadership positions), whereas the maximum is 15 (the highest number of leadership positions in the dataset). The mean of .90 and standard deviation of 1.90 for the variable tell us that most of the high school and college students in the dataset have held few leadership positions. We know this because the mean for the variable is close to the minimum value and the standard deviation is relatively low given the possible range of the variable (0–15). By contrast, the minimum value for the political traits index is 0 (no traits mentioned), whereas the maximum is 4 (all traits: confident, assertive, friendly, smart mentioned). The mean of 2.37 with a standard deviation of 1.14 tells us that the data in the dataset are more

dispersed among the possible values since the mean is closer to the middle of the possible range with a relatively high standard deviation. (Note, however, that is not possible to compare the standard deviations of the two variables directly with each other because the units for each are not the same.)

A table such as Table 7.7 is useful in quantitative analyses because (1) it clearly lists the variables used in an analysis and (2) it provides information about how the values associated with each variable are distributed. Most quantitative studies will include a table like this one before the results from data analysis are presented.

TABLE 7.7: SELECTED DESCRIPTIVE STATISTICS TAKEN FROM FOX AND LAWLESS, 2014

Descriptive statistics table for the full sample; selected variables taken from Fox and Lawless (2014). See the article for the full table.

Dependent Variable	Measurement level	Minimum value	Maximum value	Mean	Standard deviation		
Four-point ambition scale[8]	Ordinal, with four possible categories	1 (would never run for office)	4 (would definitely like to run for office)	2.22	.93		
Independent Variable	**Measurement level**	**Minimum value**	**Maximum value**	**Mean**	**Standard deviation**		
Party affiliation: Democrat Republican Independent Other/no affiliation[9]	Nominal, binary separated by female and male responses					Women 40% 9% 23% 27%	Men 38% 10% 26% 25%
Race: White Black Latino/Hispanic Other	Nominal, binary separated by female and male responses					Women 62% 12% 15% 11%	Men 62% 11% 17% 11%

---

8   Note that this variable has ordinal measurement with only four possible categories, yet the authors of the paper opted to provide summary statistics for the variable rather than providing a frequency distribution for it. Political scientists sometimes provide summary statistics for variables with ordinal measurement in this way.

9   The information provided here combines the frequencies for party affiliation and biological sex. This is possible since both party affiliation and biological sex are variables with nominal measurement. What this means is that 40% of women in the dataset identified as Democrat, 9% as Republican, and so on. This is also true for the following row, where information concerning race and biological sex is presented.

TABLE 7.7:   CONTINUED

Family social-ization: Politicized household growing up	Ratio, with 5 possible responses represent-ing number of de-scriptions that char-acterize household (the news is often on, parents sometimes yell at television when angry about politics, talking about politics at mealtimes, parents often talk about politics	0 (none present)	4 (all four present)	1.88	1.52		
Political con-text: Time spent on political websites	Ordinal, with 4 pos-sible categories	1 (rarely or never)	4 (every day)	1.89	1.02		
Competitive experiences: Leadership positions at school	Ratio, with 16 pos-sible values to repre-sent the number of leadership activities in which respondent participated	0 (no lead-ership activities)	15 (maximum number rep-resented in the dataset)	.90	1.90		
Self-confi-dence: Politi-cal traits index	Ratio, with 4 possible values to represent self-assessment of being: confidence, assertive, friendly, smart	0 (none of the traits present)	4 (all of the traits pres-ent)	2.37	1.14		
Gender roles and identity expression: Women's roles	Ratio, with 10 pos-sible values to repre-sent the number of statements about women's roles that respondent agrees with, such as "it is best when a mother stays home and takes care of the children rather than works" or "it's fine for girls to make the first move and ask someone they like out on a date"	3 (mini-mum number of statements that re-spondent agrees with)	12 (maximum number of statements that respon-dent agrees with)	6.3	1.66		

the age variable (16.9) because the units of each variable are not the same. You can compare standard deviations only when the units of the two variables are identical.

Descriptive statistics thus provide information about how the values for each variable are distributed within the variable itself. When computing descriptive statistics, it is important to know how a variable is measured. Provide a frequency distribution and identify the mode for variables with nominal measurement (including binary variables) and for variables with ordinal measurement when the number of categories associated with the variable is less than five. Compute summary statistics for variables with ordinal measurement when the number of categories associated with the variable is equal to or greater than five and for variables with interval or ratio measurement. This information is provided in Table 7.6.

CONCLUSION

This chapter provided a basic introduction to SPSS as a means to begin quantitative analysis on the data from the WVS. For many researchers, the first step in quantitative research is to compute descriptive statistics for the variables used in a study. Knowing what types of variables you are working with and knowing how they are measured before you begin are paramount.

Variables with nominal measurement and variables with ordinal measurement with a small number of categories (less than five) are described differently than variables with ordinal measurement with a larger number of categories (five or more) and variables with interval or ratio measurement. Frequency distributions that demonstrate how often a particular value appears relative to the other values for a variable in a dataset are extremely useful for variables with nominal measurement (including binary variables) and variables with ordinal measurement with a small number of categories. For these variables, it is also useful to identify the mode, which is the value in a given variable that appears the most relative to the others in the variable. In contrast, summary statistics that provide the minimum value, the maximum value, the mean, and the standard deviation help us understand how dispersed values are in variables with ordinal measurement with a larger number of categories or with variables with interval or ratio measurement. The standard deviation of a distribution is particularly valuable because it demonstrates how widespread the data are around a variable's mean.

Descriptive statistics are important. They provide information about how the data are dispersed for each variable used in an analysis. In other words, they show how much variation is contained within each of your variables. Researchers often provide this type of information in their papers in descriptive statistics tables before continuing with data analysis. A template that you can use for the descriptive statistics table you should produce to display the information for your three variables is provided in the Paper progress section.

GLOSSARY

CODEBOOK A list of codes and their meaning for each variable in a dataset.

DATA Information.

DATASET A spreadsheet containing quantitative data.

DESCRIPTIVE STATISTICS Information that is provided about each variable individually, for example, how values are distributed within a variable in a dataset.

FREQUENCY DISTRIBUTION Descriptive statistics that lists the percentages for each code or value contained in a variable, relative to the total number of observations in the dataset; usually the variable is one that has nominal measurement or has ordinal measurement with fewer than five categories.

MAXIMUM VALUE The highest number represented in a variable in a dataset.

MEAN Another word for average, which is the sum of all values for a variable divided by the number of observations.

MINIMUM VALUE The lowest number represented in a variable in a dataset.

MODE The value (or specific code) in the dataset that appears the most often relative to the other codes for the variable.

NORMALLY DISTRIBUTED A special type of distribution for a variable, in which roughly 68% of the observations for the variable should fall within one standard deviation on either side of the variable's mean (roughly 95% for two standard deviations and roughly 99% for three standard deviations); this particular distribution is often referred to as the bell curve.

RAW DATA Unaltered data in a spreadsheet; it is often necessary to have a codebook to understand what each numerical value in the dataset means.

STANDARD DEVIATION A statistic that demonstrates the degree to which values in a variable are dispersed around a variable's mean.

SUMMARY STATISTICS Descriptive statistics in which specific information concerning a variable's minimum value, maximum value, mean (or average), and standard deviation is provided for variables with ordinal measurement when the number of categories in the variable is equal to or greater than five and for variables with interval and ratio measurement.

EXERCISES

Before you can complete the exercises, you must have access to SPSS and download the WVS questionnaire and dataset for the wave and country you are studying through your research. The best advice is to go slow as you work with the data.
Descriptive statistics

The following variables have nominal measurement with only two categories (binary)
V13: Important child qualities: Hard work
V66: Willingness to fight for your country

> Limit the WVS dataset to include people who are 50 and older (age is V242).
> Use the Variables tool in SPSS to determine the codes for the categories associated with each varable.
> Generate a frequency distribution for each variable.
> What can you determine about the variation within each variable based on the results?

The following variables have nominal measurement with more than two categories
V80: Most serious problem in the world
V254: Ethnic group

> Limit the dataset to include only women (biological sex is V240).
> Use the Variables tool in SPSS to determine the codes for the categories associated with each varable.
> Generate a frequency distribution and identify the mode for each variable.
> Decide how to transform each variable into a binary variable. Defend the new variable you create as a valid reflection of the overall concept the new variable measures.
> Generate a frequency distribution for each new binary variable.
> What can you determine about the variation within each variable based on the results?

The following variables have ordinal measurement with a small number of categories (less than five)
V8: Important in life: work
V51: On the whole, men make better political leaders than women do

Limit the dataset to include only people with college-level education (highest educational level attained is V248).

Use the Variables tool in SPSS to determine the codes for the categories associated with each varable.

Generate a frequency distribution for each variable and identify the mode.

What can you determine about the the variation within each variable based on the results?

The following variables have ordinal measurement with a larger number of categories (five or more)

V74: It is important to this person to do something for the good of society

V140: Importance of democracy

V186: Worries: Government wiretapping

V201: Justifiable: Cheating on taxes if you have a chance

Use the Variables tool in SPSS to determine how the categories for each variable are ordered.

Generate summary statistics (minimum value, maximum value, mean, and standard deviation) for each variable.

What can you determine about the variation within each variable based on the results?

PAPER PROGRESS

Once you feel comfortable using SPSS in these exercises, you can generate descriptive statistics for the three variables you are using from the WVS for your research on political values and attitudes.

Step 1: Limit the WVS data to your research population.
The first step is to limit the WVS data so that only the observations that are contained within your research population are left in your new dataset. This is crucial: all data manipulations you perform should include only observations that represent your research population.

Step 2: If necessary, transform your variable with nominal measurement. Transform your independent variable with nominal measurement into a binary variable if the original variable you selected from Column A in Chapter 3 has more than two categories associated with it. Skip this step if your variable with nominal measurement already contains only two categories (such as biological sex).

Step 3: Generate descriptive statistics for your variables.

You are working with three variables: one dependent variable and two independent variables. First, generate summary statistics for your dependent variable since it has ordinal measurement on a scale from 1 to 10.

Next, generate descriptive statistics for your independent variables. Generate a frequency distribution for your first independent variable (which should now be a binary variable). What percentage of respondents fall into the first category and what percentage of respondents fall into the second?

For your second independent variable, depending on how it is measured, you will either (1) generate a frequency distribution and identify the mode (for an independent variable with ordinal measurement with a small number of categories (less than five)); or (2) provide summary statistics (for an independent variable with ordinal measurement with a larger number of categories (five or more) or for an independent variable with interval or ratio measurement).

After you generate your descriptive statistics, you can create a descriptive statistics table. Researchers often provide a descriptive statistics table that is placed in the beginning of the results section of a paper and then offer a paragraph or two to discuss it. How the information is presented depends on the type of variables in the analysis. See Table 7.8 for a general template of a table you could use to provide descriptive statistics in your papers. Table 7.8 uses variables from the United States' 2011 wave of the WVS. It provides a way to display the information for variables with every type of measurement discussed in this chapter.

The dependent variable in Table 7.8 (V131: the degree to which respondents believe that taxing the rich and redistributing to the poor is an essential characteristic for democracy) is presented first. Since it is a variable with ordinal measurement, information pertaining to its minimum value, maximum value, mean, and standard deviation is included. Its mean of 5.0 and standard deviation of 2.7 suggest that the data are widespread among the observations, since the range of the variable is between 1 and 10. It is a good idea, too, to include what the extreme values mean in the table (1 = not an essential characteristic of democracy, 10 = is an essential characteristic of democracy). This will help later when the results from data analysis are presented.

The independent variables are presented next. The first independent variable, biological sex (V240), is a binary variable, and hence only the percentages for each category are provided. From these numbers we can see that there is a roughly equal distribution of men and women in the data, although there are slightly more women than men represented here. The second independent variable, importance in life: politics (V7), is presented next. All four categories are presented here with the percentages from the percent valid column that SPSS produced.

The third independent variable, satisfaction with household financial situation (V59), is a variable with ordinal measurement with 10 possible categories, and hence, as for the dependent variable, its minimum value, maximum value, mean, and standard deviation are provided. Again, it is a good idea to include what the extreme values mean in the table (1 = completely dissatisfied, 10 = completely satisfied). Having a table such as this provides a good representation of what is contained in the dataset. A researcher could opt to provide bar or pie charts as visual representations for each variable as well.

TABLE 7.8: EXAMPLE OF A DESCRIPTIVE STATISTICS TABLE

Dependent Variable	Measurement level	Minimum value	Maximum value	Mean	Standard deviation				
V131: Democracy: Governments tax the rich and subsidize the poor	Ordinal, with 10 possible categories	1 (Not an essential characteristic of democracy)	10 (An essential characteristic of democracy)	5.0	2.7				
V240: Biological sex	Nominal, binary					Male 48.6%	Female 51.4%		
V7: Importance in life: politics	Ordinal, with 4 possible categories					Very important 12.2%	Somewhat important 43.2%	Not very important 33.8%	Not important at all 10.7%
Independent Variable	**Measurement level**	**Minimum value**	**Maximum value**	**Mean**	**Standard deviation**				
V59: Satisfaction with financial situation of household	Ordinal, with 10 possible categories	1 (Completely dissatisfied)	10 (Completely satisfied)	6.3	2.4				

Table 7.8 was created with four variables to show how the descriptive statistics for different types of variables can be presented. The table you produce will have only three variables in it because you are using one dependent variable and two independent variables for your analysis. The table you create should look similar to the top half of Table 7.8 for the dependent variable and the binary independent variable, since your dependent variable is measured from 1 to 10 and since you have a binary independent variable. However, the information you include for the bottom half of the table (for the second independent variable) depends crucially on the type of independent variable you are working with.

COMING UP

Descriptive statistics investigates the amount of variation in each individual variable. In the next two chapters, you will learn how to perform data analysis on your variables in SPSS. Data analysis investigates the nature of the relationship between the variables in a study. This is how you can test the hypotheses you specified in Chapter 4. Chapter 8 begins with an investigation of bivariate analysis, and Chapter 9 introduces regression.

BIVARIATE ANALYSIS

Descriptive statistics provide important information about each variable under investigation, one variable at a time. The next step in your quantitative analysis is to perform **data analysis**, which investigates the relationships between two or more of your variables.

As with the descriptive statistics you performed in the previous chapter, the form of the variables you are working with influences the type of analysis that can be done on them. We already know that your dependent variable has ordinal measurement because all of the possible dependent variables presented in Chapter 3 were associated with variables that have a possible range of 1 to 10. We also know how your independent variables are measured. If you selected your first independent variable from Column A in Chapter 3, one of your independent variables has nominal measurement. This variable should now be a binary variable. If you selected your second independent variable from Column B, one of your variables has ordinal, interval, or ratio measurement. The difference in the level of measurement between the two independent variables matters a great deal for the type of bivariate analysis you perform.

The rest of this chapter will cover bivariate analysis between one independent and one dependent variable. Specifically, you will learn how to do a difference of means test and compute a correlation coefficient using SPSS. The choice between the two analyses depends on the type of independent variable you are using.

BIVARIATE ANALYSIS BETWEEN AN INDEPENDENT BINARY VARIABLE AND A DEPENDENT VARIABLE WITH ORDINAL, INTERVAL, OR RATIO MEASUREMENT: THE DIFFERENCE OF MEANS TEST

When the two variables in bivariate analysis involve one independent binary variable and one dependent variable with ordinal, interval, or ratio measurement, a **difference of means test** can be performed to determine whether a relationship exists between the two variables.[1] The difference of means test involves (1) a comparison of the average value of the dependent variable for two groupings of the independent variable for a sample of data and (2) an evaluation of a test statistic that enables us to discern the likelihood that the difference in averages between the two groups is due to chance.

Consider, for example, a researcher who wishes to use the 2011 WVS data for the United States to evaluate the effect of biological sex (V240, the independent variable) on opinions as to whether it is ever justifiable to cheat on taxes when you have the chance (V201, the dependent variable). The researcher has developed a theory to explain why women are more likely than men to respond that cheating is never justifiable and has written a research hypothesis to suggest that women, on average, will score lower than men on the justifiability of cheating on taxes variable. (The range of the dependent variable is between 1, "never justifiable," and 10, "always justifiable"). Because the independent variable has binary measurement (male/female), the researcher can evaluate this hypothesis by conducting a difference of means test.

Of particular importance for the difference of means test is the null hypothesis. Remember from Chapter 4 that the null hypothesis stipulates that no relationship exists between the independent and dependent variables. In this case, the null hypothesis claims that no difference exists between men and women and their scores on the justifiability of cheating variable. In other words, if the null hypothesis is true, the average justifiability of cheating on taxes score for women and the average justifiability of cheating on taxes score for men should be equal to one another. As a result, the researcher writes the following as the null hypothesis:

> Null hypothesis: The average for women on the justifiability of cheating on taxes variable = the average for men on the justifiability of cheating on taxes variable.

But, given the theory and research hypothesis, the researcher has a different expectation. Specifically, she believes that the average justifiability of cheating on taxes score for women is lower than the average justifiability of cheating on taxes score for men. The expectation for this research hypothesis is as follows:

> Research hypothesis: The average for women on the justifiability of cheating on taxes variable < the average for men on the justifiability of cheating on taxes variable.

---

1   This test is also referred to as the *t* test.

Thus, the research hypothesis stipulates that there is a difference among women and men for this variable. In other words, the difference between the averages of the two groups (between women and men) should not be zero. Specifically, the average score for women should be lower than the average score for men for the dependent variable.

Calculating the averages between men and women for the dependent variable in the WVS sample and determining the mean difference between the two groups is not difficult. What is difficult is determining whether the result based on the sample of data can compel the researcher to reject the null hypothesis for the population from which the sample was derived.[2] The notion of statistical significance is of extreme importance here. Before any statistical manipulations can be performed, the significance level for the analysis must be set to determine the threshold at which the null hypothesis would be rejected. Most studies in the social sciences set the significance level of a hypothesis test at 5%. What this means is that there should be no greater than a 5% chance that a particular result was obtained from sampling error.[3] The statistical test produces a **p value** that is compared to the significance level. The p value is the *probability of observing a particular result when the null hypothesis is actually true for the population.*

If the p value is below the threshold of 5% ($p < .05$), the observed mean difference between the two groups is not likely due to chance. It was obtained because the null hypothesis is likely not true for the population. When this is the case, the result is said to be statistically significant. When a result is statistically significant, a second statistically significant result would likely be obtained if the same test were conducted on a similar sample from the population.

Thus, the difference of means test starts off with the assumption that the null hypothesis is actually true for the population from which a sample was taken. This is part of the reason that you had to specify a null hypothesis for each independent variable in Chapter 4. The purpose of the difference of means test is to determine the probability of obtaining a specific result in the WVS sample (for example, the mean difference between women and men on the justifiability of cheating on taxes variable in the WVS sample) if the null

---

2   The two bivariate tests introduced in this chapter work best when a probability sample is used. See Chapter 5. Probability samples are expected to represent the population as closely as possible, which suggests that the results from a probability sample can be reasonably applied to the population.

3   Some tests may use the 1% level ($p < .01$), as will be shown in the Examples from Political Science section at the end of the chapter, or even the .1% level ($p < .001$).

hypothesis for the population were indeed true. If the probability of getting such a result is high, that is, if the p value is greater than or equal to .05, the null hypothesis cannot be rejected. If the probability of getting such a result is low, that is, if the p value is less than .05, the null hypothesis can be rejected and the result is said to be statistically significant.

Let's continue with the researcher's example below to see this in practice. The independent variable, V240, is biological sex, a binary variable where 1 represents men and 2 represents women. The dependent variable, V201, is each person's response to the survey question regarding the justifiability of cheating on taxes when you have a chance. Again, it has a range from 1, "never justifiable," to 10, "always justifiable." The researcher's hypothesis posits that women are more likely, on average, to respond with lower scores on the variable, which means that the average justifiability for women should be lower than the average justifiability for men.

To perform a difference of means test (Figure 8.1):

1. From the Analyze tab, choose Compare Means from the pull-down menu and then select Independent Samples t test. Choose this option

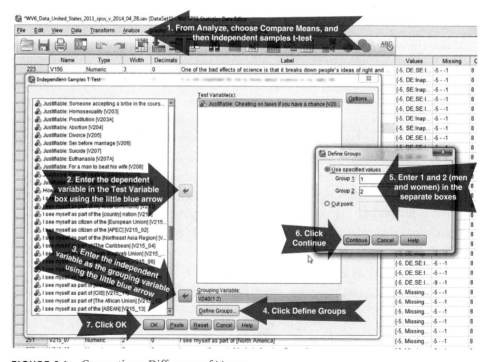

FIGURE 8.1: Computing a Difference of Means

because you wish to compare the averages of justifiability for cheating on taxes for independent groups, that is, the dependent variable's average for women and the dependent variable's average for men.

2. In the Independent Samples *t* test menu, enter Justifiability: Cheating on taxes when you have a chance (the dependent variable: V201) in the test variable box.

3. Next, enter biological sex (the independent variable: V240) as the grouping variable using the small blue arrow.

4. Click on Define Groups, the tab below the grouping variable.

5. In the Define Groups menu, enter 1 for Group 1 (for men) and 2 for Group 2 (for women). This is important because SPSS does not know which two values in the independent variable you wish to compare. The Define Groups menu allows you to select which groups are to be compared.

6. Click Continue from the Define Groups menu.

7. Click OK.

The difference of means test produces the following tables (Figure 8.2).

Figure 8.2 contains summary statistics for each subgroup, for men and for women. This information includes the number of observations, the mean of the dependent variable, and the standard deviation for each subgroup. The average score of the dependent variable for men is 1.95 and the average score of the dependent variable for women is 1.72. In other words, the two averages for the justifiability of cheating on taxes variable for the two groups are indeed different; specifically, women have a lower average score than men (which is what was suggested by the research hypothesis). Figure 8.2 also shows that the mean difference for the two groups is .225.

➤ **T-Test**

Group Statistics

	Sex	N	Mean	Std. Deviation	Std. Error Mean
Justifiable: Cheating on taxes if you have a chance	Male	1053	1.95	1.841	.057
	Female	1125	1.72	1.616	.048

Summary statistics for each group

Independent Samples Test

		Levene's Test for Equality of Variances		t-test for Equality of Means					95% Confidence Interval of the Difference	
		F	Sig.	t	df	Sig. (2-tailed)	Mean Difference	Std. Error Difference	Lower	Upper
taxes chance	Equal variances assumed	12.402	.000	3.039		.002	.225		.080	.371
	Equal variances not assumed			3.026	2095.968	.003	.225	.074	.079	.371

Use Equal variances not assumed

The Sig (2-tailed) is the p-value

Mean Difference between the two groups

FIGURE 8.2: Results from a Difference of Means Test: Biological Sex and the Justifiability of Cheating on Taxes When You Have a Chance

But is this particular result statistically significant, that is, is the .225 difference between women and men in the WVS sample enough to accept that the averages differ from one another in the general population too? Or could this result be due to chance? The information in Figure 8.2 is required to make this assessment. Use the second row of output labeled "Equal variances not assumed" to find the test statistics. The *p* value for this difference of means test is .003.[4] This *p* value suggests that in only 3 times of 1,000 would the researcher see a difference this large by chance if the null hypothesis were actually true in the general population. This probability is quite low. As a result, the null hypothesis that there is no relationship between biological sex and the justifiability of cheating on taxes can be rejected. In addition, since the average for women was lower than the average for men for the dependent variable, the researcher has evidence consistent with the research hypothesis.

Let's look at a second example. Take another researcher who wishes to use WVS data to determine whether a relationship exists between teaching children obedience as an important quality (measured by obedience being mentioned as one of the possible top 5 of 11 priorities that are important to teach children[5]) and the justifiability of claiming government benefits to which one is not entitled. In the WVS, teaching obedience as an important quality to teach children (V21) is already a binary variable because it contains only two categories to measure whether a respondent either (1) mentioned or (2) did not mention obedience as an important quality to teach children. As in the previous example, the variable to measure the justifiability of claiming government benefits to which one is not entitled (V198) is measured on a scale from 1 to 10, with 1 representing "never justifiable" and 10 representing "always justifiable." You should now understand that the null hypothesis stipulates that respondents who did not mention obedience as an important quality to teach children are expected to have the same average on the justifiability of claiming benefits to which one is not entitled as respondents who did mention obedience as an important quality to teach children. The research hypothesis is that respondents who mentioned obedience as an important quality to teach children will have a lower average on the justifiability of claiming government benefits to which one is not entitled compared with those who did not mention obedience as an important quality to teach children. A difference of means test

---

4   SPSS uses the term "Sig (2-tailed)" to denote the difference of means' *p* value.
5   The list of important qualities to teach children includes independence, hard work, feeling of responsibility, imagination, tolerance and respect for other people, thrift, determination and perseverance, religious faith, unselfishness, and self-expression.

T-Test

Group Statistics

	Important child qualities: Obedience	N	Mean	Std. Deviation	Std. Error Mean
Justifiable: Claiming government benefits to which you are not entitled	Mentioned	595	2.31	2.382	.098
	Not mentioned	1588	2.13	2.124	.053

Independent Samples Test

		Levene's Test for Equality of Variances		t-test for Equality of Means						
		F	Sig.	t	df	Sig. (2-tailed)	Mean Difference	Std. Error Difference	95% Confidence Interval of the Difference	
									Lower	Upper
Justifiable: Claiming government benefits to which you are not entitled	Equal variances assumed	15.322	.000	1.642	2181	.101	.173	.106	-.034	.381
	Equal variances not assumed			1.559	968.364	.119	.173	.111	-.045	.392

FIGURE 8.3: Results from a Difference of Means Test: Obedience as an Important Quality to Teach Children and Justifiability of Claiming Government Benefits to Which One Is Not Entitled

can determine whether the null hypothesis about the relationship between the two variables can be rejected. The results are displayed in Figure 8.3.

What do these results suggest? First, note that the respondents who mentioned obedience as an important child quality have a higher average (2.31) than the respondents who did not mention it (2.13), suggesting that people who mentioned obedience are actually more likely, on average, to respond that claiming government benefits to which one is not entitled is justified. This finding is exactly the opposite of what the researcher suggested in the research hypothesis. But is this result statistically significant? In other words, can the researcher use this specific result to reject the null hypothesis for the population? To answer this question, the p value of the mean difference (remember that in SPSS the p value is found in the Sig. (2-tailed) column) must be evaluated. The p value in Figure 8.3 is .119. This means that the researcher would expect to see a difference between the groups as large as the one obtained through the sample almost 12% of the time using different samples (like the WVS one) if the null hypothesis were true for the population. Since the p value is greater than .05, the null hypothesis cannot be rejected. The result is not statistically significant.

The difference of means test is a statistical technique that is effective in determining whether a single binary independent variable is significantly associated with variation in a dependent variable with ordinal, interval, or ratio measurement. It is a common test and an excellent starting point for evaluating hypotheses, especially since it involves the analysis of a p value to determine whether a particular result is statistically significant at a particular level (usually .05 in the social sciences) for the population from which a sample was derived. Next, we continue our discussion by investigating how to determine whether a bivariate association exists between two variables with ordinal, interval, or ratio measurement.

BIVARIATE ANALYSIS BETWEEN TWO VARIABLES WITH ORDINAL, INTERVAL, OR RATIO MEASUREMENT: THE CORRELATION COEFFICIENT

To understand whether a statistical relationship exists between two variables with ordinal, interval, or ratio measurement, SPSS can compute the **correlation coefficient** between the variables. The correlation coefficient is a single number that provides a measure for both the direction and the strength of the relationship between two variables with ordinal, interval, or ratio measurement. The correlation coefficient is based on a scatterplot of the two variables; it is the number that best summarizes the linear relationship between them. The correlation coefficient is always between –1 and +1. Numbers close to –1 imply an **inverse correlation** between two variables; numbers close to +1 imply a **positive correlation** between two variables. Numbers close to zero imply no correlation between two variables.

Positive Correlation, +1

In this example, the two variables are perfectly correlated; a one-unit increase in the independent variable is always associated with a one-unit increase in the dependent variable. The slope of the line in this case is +1 (Figure 8.4).

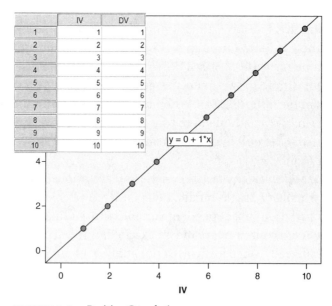

FIGURE 8.4: Positive Correlation

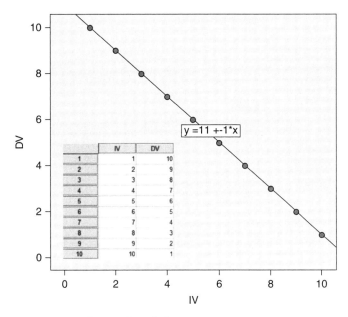

FIGURE 8.5: Inverse Correlation

Inverse Correlation, −1

In this example, the two variables are also perfectly correlated, but in this case, a one-unit increase in the independent variable is always associated with a one-unit decrease in the dependent variable. This means that there is an inverse relationship between the independent and dependent variables. The slope of the line is −1 (Figure 8.5).

No Correlation, 0

In this example, there is no linear correlation between the independent and dependent variables. There is no increase or decrease in the dependent variable for an increase or decrease in the independent variable. The result is that slope of the line is 0 (Figure 8.6).

The correlation coefficient is a powerful way to determine the relationship between variables with ordinal, interval, or ratio measurement. With a single number, the direction (positive number = positive association/negative number = inverse association) and the strength (closer to −1 or +1 = stronger association/closer to 0 = weaker association) of the relationship between two variables with ordinal, interval, or ratio measurement can be assessed. Keep in mind, however, that values of +1, −1, or 0 are rarely seen in the social sciences. Instead, the correlation coefficient usually falls somewhere in between and the

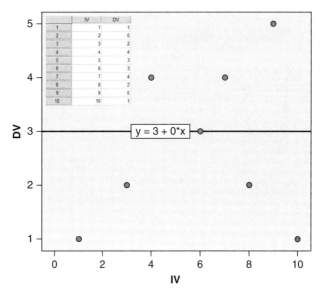

FIGURE 8.6: No Correlation

results must be interpreted. The precise definition of "large" for correlation coefficients is difficult to establish. There is no particular threshold above which a correlation coefficient is considered large, especially in the social sciences. For example, some researchers would argue that correlation coefficients greater than .30 imply strong correlations; others would prefer a correlation coefficient to be at least .40, or even higher, to warrant such a designation.

Like the difference of means test presented earlier in the chapter, SPSS computes a p value along with the correlation coefficient to evaluate whether the null hypothesis about the relationship between two variables can be rejected based on a sample of data. For this test, the null hypothesis posits that the correlation coefficient between the independent and dependent variables is 0, that is, that no relationship exists between the two variables.

Consider, for example, a researcher who wishes to understand how age is associated with attitudes concerning the importance of work. The research hypothesis is that as age increases, work becomes less important. In other words, older people will not put as much importance on work compared to younger people. Since age is a variable with ratio measurement and since important in life: work is a variable with ordinal measurement with 1 representing very important and 4 representing not important at all, the use of the correlation coefficient for this test is appropriate. Because of the research hypothesis, the researcher is expecting the correlation coefficient to be a positive number. As age increases, responses on the important in life: work variable are expected to

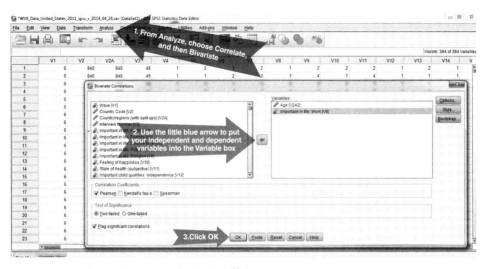

FIGURE 8.7: Computing a Correlation Coefficient

be higher numbers (indicating less importance) because of how the variable is measured in the WVS. To perform this test in SPSS, see Figure 8.7:

1. From Analyze, choose Correlate, and then Bivariate.
2. Find the independent variable and dependent variable you wish to correlate on the list, and then use the small blue arrow to place them into the Variables box.
3. Click OK.

This results in Figure 8.8.

The correlation coefficient between age and the variable for the importance of work is +.234. As expected given the research hypothesis, the results suggest

Correlations

Correlations

		Age	Important in life: Work
Age	Pearson Correlation		.234**
	Sig. (2-tailed)		.000
	N		2214
Important in life: Work	Pearson Correlation	.234**	1
	Sig. (2-tailed)	.000	
	N	2214	2214

** Correlation is significant at the 0.01 level (2-tailed).

FIGURE 8.8: Results from the Correlation Coefficient (Age and Importance of Work)

that as age increases, responses to the importance of work variable also increase (meaning work becomes less important). It also means that as age decreases, responses to the importance of work variable decrease (meaning work becomes more important). Thus, knowing how the variables are numbered is important for interpreting the results appropriately. But is this correlation coefficient statistically significant? To answer this question, the p value, which is the probability of obtaining a particular result due to chance when the null hypothesis is actually true for the population, must be evaluated. The test's p value, located directly below the correlation coefficient, is .000.[6] The p value of .000 tells the researcher that the probability of getting this particular correlation coefficient due to chance if the null hypothesis were actually true in the population is exceptionally low. Thus, since the p value is lower than .05, the researcher can reject the null hypothesis. In addition, since the correlation was positive (as values on age increase, values on the importance of work variable (moving toward less important) increase), the researcher has empirical evidence consistent with the research hypothesis.

Let's consider another researcher who wants to use the WVS data to test whether someone's age is related to opinions concerning the justifiability of divorce. The justifiability of divorce is a variable with ordinal measurement, where 1 represents that divorce is never justifiable and 10 represents that divorce is always justifiable. The research hypothesis is that as age increases, attitudes about the justifiability of divorce decrease (toward never justifiable). As a result, the researcher expects an inverse correlation between the two variables. Entering the new dependent variable into SPSS, she obtains the following results (Figure 8.9).

Correlations

Correlations

		Age	Justifiable: Divorce
Age	Pearson Correlation	1	-.006
	Sig. (2-tailed)		.798
	N	2232	2167
Justifiable: Divorce	Pearson Correlation	-.006	1
	Sig. (2-tailed)	.798	
	N	2167	2167

FIGURE 8.9: Results from the Correlation Coefficient (Age and the Justifiability of Divorce)

---

6   As before, the Sig. (2-tailed) in SPSS is the test's p value.

The results show that the correlation coefficient betweeen age and the justifiability of divorce is –.006. Although the negative coefficient implies an inverse correlation (as suggested in the research hypothesis), the researcher must examine the test's p value to determine whether this result is statistically significant. The p value of .798 suggests that the null hypothesis cannot be rejected. This high p value suggests that there is no correlation between age and the justifiability of divorce in the population from which the WVS sample was taken. The fact that the correlation coefficient is very close to zero in this example also supports this conclusion.

THE MAGNITUDE OF THE RESULT

For a difference of means test, the difference between the averages of the dependent variable for two groupings of the independent variable is produced. For the correlation coefficient, a measure between –1 and +1 to assess the direction and strength of the linear relationship between two variables is computed. The p value for both the difference of means and the correlation coefficient evaluates the likelihood of obtaining a result as large as the one obtained using the sample of data if the null hypothesis were true for the research population. If the p value is low enough, which for most social science researchers is below .05, the result is said to be statistically significant, which means that the null hypothesis about the relationship between the two variables in the analysis can be rejected.

But strict adherence to the p value of a test alone ignores the actual result of the test itself. A result can be statistically significant while still being quite small. This is why the magnitude of the result, relative to the units and range of the dependent variable, should be assessed alongside the test's p value.

Let's examine the results from different examples of both tests explored in this chapter to clarify this point. Consider Figure 8.10 for a difference of means

Group Statistics

	Sex	N	Mean	Std. Deviation	Std. Error Mean
Justifiable: Divorce	Male	1048	6.08	2.482	.077
	Female	1119	6.31	2.502	.075

Independent Samples Test

		Levene's Test for Equality of Variances		t-test for Equality of Means						95% Confidence Interval of the Difference	
		F	Sig.	t	df	Sig. (2-tailed)	Mean Difference	Std. Error Difference	Lower	Upper
Justifiable: Divorce	Equal variances assumed	1.206	.272	-2.120	2165	.034	-.227	.107	-.437	-.017
	Equal variances not assumed			-2.121	2157.836	.034	-.227	.107	-.437	-.017

FIGURE 8.10: Assessing the Magnitude of the Result for a Difference of Means Test (Biological Sex and the Justifiability of Divorce)

test. The independent variable is biological sex and the dependent variable is the justifiability of divorce (with 1 representing "never justifiable" and 10 representing "always justifiable").

The first table in Figure 8.10 shows that the average for men for the justifiability of divorce is 6.08 and the average for women is 6.31. The second table provides the mean difference between the two groups, which is –.227. The p value for the mean difference is .034, which is lower than .05, suggesting that this result is statistically significant. The null hypothesis that no difference exists between men and women on the justifiability of divorce in the population can be rejected. These results suggest that a significant difference exists between men and women in the general population for the justifiability of divorce variable. However, although this is the case, an important question must be asked: is –.227 between two groups a large result, given that the justifiability of divorce was measured on a scale from 1 to 10? Although the result is statistically significant, always consider the magnitude of the result and temper any results by mentioning the mean difference in the final report.

The same is true for the results obtained from correlation coefficients (Figure 8.11). For example, for the correlation coefficient presented below, age was used as the independent variable and the justifiability of abortion (from 1, "never justifiable," to 10, "always justifiable") was used as the dependent variable.

The correlation coefficient of –.059 is negative, which implies an inverse correlation between age and the justifiability of abortion. Specifically, for the respondents, as age increases, responses on the justifiability of abortion decrease, and as age decreases, responses on the justifiability of abortion increase. This result is also statistically significant at $p = .006$, suggesting that this result

Correlations

Correlations		Age	Justifiable: Abortion
Age	Pearson Correlation	1	-.059**
	Sig. (2-tailed)		.006
	N	2232	2167
Justifiable: Abortion	Pearson Correlation	-.059**	1
	Sig. (2-tailed)	.006	
	N	2167	2167

FIGURE 8.11: Assessing the Magnitude of the Result for a Correlation Coefficient (Age and the Justifiability of Abortion)

is not due to chance; in only 6 of 1,000 cases would we get a result this "large" by chance if the null hypothesis were true. Thus, based on the significance level, the null hypothesis can be rejected. The p value suggests that there is a significant correlation between age and responses to the justifiability of abortion question. Nonetheless, note the magnitude of the correlation coefficient, the actual number of the correlation coefficient itself. It is –.059, which is quite close to zero. Remember that a correlation coefficient of zero means that there is no correlation between the independent and dependent variables, and this correlation coefficient, although significant, is close to zero. This type of result can happen with correlation coefficients, especially when the number of observations in a dataset is large, as in large-n survey research. Thus, to repeat the point, it is important to ensure that you analyze not only whether a particular test statistic was significant, but also the magnitude of the result. At the very least, the magnitude of the result observed using quantitative data deserves mention in the discussion of the findings in your final report. Do not make grandiose claims about the relationships you find between your variables based only on the evaluation of the test's p value.

EXAMPLES FROM POLITICAL SCIENCE

Atkeson, Lonna Rae, and Cherie D. Maestas. 2010. "Race and the Formation of Attitudes: Responses to Hurricane Katrina." In *Understanding Public Opinion*. Eds. Barbara Norrander and Clyde Wilcox. Washington, DC: CQ Press.

In August 2005, Hurricane Katrina Katrina devastated much of New Orleans and other areas along the Gulf Coast. Cable news outlets attracted the attention of the American public both during and after the event by providing continual coverage of images of the storm and the subsequent plight of its victims. In the aftermath of the crisis, studies revealed that a disproportionate number of the hurricane's victims were black. Atkeson and Maestas argue that the "fact that the victims were predominantly of one racial identity has implications for attitude formation" (Atkeson and Maestas 2010, 105). Consequently, to evaluate hypotheses concerning how race influences general attitudes about the government's response to the crisis, a survey was randomly distributed to about 1,000 people in October and November 2005. Several survey questions were designed to capture agreement or disagreement with regard to specific attitudes as to why the government

was slow to respond to the crisis and distribute aid to victims. The results are provided in Table 8.1.

The first column of Table 8.1 lists the specific attitudes investigated in the study as presented to survey respondents. Each respondent was asked whether the particular attitude had an effect on the length of time it took for the victims of Hurricane Katrina to receive aid. The possible responses were between 1 (no effect) and 4 (great effect). The second column is the average score for the specific attitude for survey respondents who identified as black; the third column is the average score for the specific attitude for survey respondents who did not identify as black. The last column reports the difference in the two averages, or the difference of means between the two groups for each specific attitude. This last column shows that there are differences between blacks and nonblacks in terms of how they responded to the survey questions regarding why it took

CONTINUED

TABLE 8.1:   AVERAGE SCORES FOR ATTITUDES RELATED TO THE REASONS FOR WHICH THE GOVERNMENT TOOK A LONG TIME TO PROVIDE AID TO VICTIMS, BY RACE

	Black	Nonblack	Difference
The victims were mostly black.	3.16	1.99	1.17**
The victims were mostly poor.	3.42	2.34	1.08**
The area was too difficult to reach.	1.89	2.35	−.46**
Officials from Washington were too incompetent.	3.16	2.53	.63**
Officials from Washington were too inexperienced.	2.86	2.68	.18*
Lack of communication between levels of government.	3.35	3.50	−.15
State government failed to call for enough help.	3.29	3.11	.18

$*p \le .05, **p \le .01$.

Source: Atkeson and Maestas, 2010, 115.

a long time for authorities to respond to the victims of the crisis. Of particular note is that blacks were more likely than nonblacks to believe that the race and financial situation of the victims had a greater effect on the delayed response. For both questions, the average for blacks was higher than the average for nonblacks; the differences in means for the responses to these particular survey questions were 1.17 and 1.08, respectively. Concerning this point, it is important to note the direction of the difference when analyzing differences between groups: for example, for "the victims were mostly black" and "the victims were mostly poor," the average for blacks was higher than the average for nonblacks, whereas for "the area was too difficult to reach" the average for blacks was lower than the average for nonblacks.

Are the effects reported in Table 8.1, specifically the differences in the responses between blacks and nonblacks for these survey questions, statistically significant? That is, based on results from this sample, would we expect to find similar differences between blacks and nonblacks for these particular attitudes in the overall population? To answer this, we assess the last column of Table 8.1, in which the difference between the two groups for each survey question is

reported. The asterisks next to the differences reveal the level at which each test statistic, specifically the mean difference between the two groups for each survey question, was significant. For this study, one asterisk denotes that a test statistic was significant at .05, and two asterisks denote that a test statistic was significant at .01. A test statistic that is significant ($p < .01$) means that there is less than a 1% chance that a particular result was due to chance when the null hypothesis is true for the population. With this in mind, we see that the differences in means between blacks and nonblacks for the first four survey questions were significant at $p < .01$, whereas the fifth question, "officials from Washington were too inexperienced," was significant at $p < .05$. Furthermore, note that there are no asterisks next to "lack of communication between levels of government" and "state government failed to call for enough help," although there is still a mean difference, albeit small, between the two groups. The absence of asterisks for these test statistics means that the relationship between race and responses to these specific questions was not significant. Rather, blacks and nonblacks are likely to have similar responses for these particular questions in the population.

Schroedel, Jean Reith. 2000. *Is the Fetus a Person? A Comparison of Policies across the Fifty States.* Ithaca, NY: Cornell University Press.

This book attempts to understand why the individual states within the United States differ greatly in terms of their "fetal policies," which include abortion policies, policies about how pregnant women who use drugs are treated, and policies about how individuals who commit acts of violence against pregnant women are prosecuted. An important part of the analysis involves the creation of a valid classification scheme in terms of how restrictive or permissive abortion laws are in each state. The classification scheme is based on the "restrictiveness of abortion bans, partial birth and postviability bans, other limitations on adult women's access to abortion, and finally, restrictions applicable only to minors"

(Schrodel 2000, 97). Based on these factors, each state received a score ranging from 0, representing highly permissive abortional laws, to 34, representing highly restrictive abortion laws.[7]

Later in the book, Schroedel uses her classification scheme as an independent variable to understand how the restrictiveness of abortion is related to a series of variables concerning women's status in society. Because the variables in the analysis have ordinal, interval, or ratio measurement, Schrodel is able to compute a correlation coefficient for each pairing of variables for the 50 U.S. states. Some of these correlations and the p values associated with them are listed in Table 8.2.

TABLE 8.2: CORRELATIONS BETWEEN WOMEN'S STATUS VARIABLES AND EACH STATE'S RESTRICTIVENESS OF ABORTION LAWS

Measures of women's status	Correlation coefficient	p value
Percentage of women in state legislature	−.266	.114
Percentage of women with four years of college	−.397**	.004
Percentage of women in the workforce	+.007	.961
Percentage of women in managerial and professional occupations	−.390**	.005
Percentage of businesses owned by women	−.309*	.029
Percentage of women in poverty	+.257	.071

*$p < .05$, **$p < .01$
Taken from Schroedel (2000, 153).

Let's study these correlations to understand what they mean. First, some of the correlations have a positive sign, whereas others have a negative sign. Remember that a positive sign means that as the first variable increases, the second also increases. A negative sign means that as the first variable increases, the second variable decreases. Thus, the correlation coefficients with a positive sign imply that as the restrictiveness of abortion in a state increases (remember that the restrictiveness of abortion variable runs from low restrictiveness to high restrictiveness), the percentage of women in the workforce and the percentage of women living in poverty in a state also increase. The correlation coefficients with a

negative sign imply that as the restrictiveness of abortion in a state increases, the percentage of women in the state legislature, of women with four years of college, of women in managerial and professional occupations, and of businesses owned by women decreases.

Next, note the size of the correlation coefficients. One correlation coefficient is small: the correlation coefficient between the restrictiveness of abortion laws and women in the workforce is .007. Since this number is very close to 0, there is effectively no correlation between the variables. However, other correlation coefficients are larger. For example, the correlation coefficient between the restrictiveness of abortion laws

---

7   The range of possible scores for the classification scheme was between 0 and 34; the actual range was between 1 (for Hawaii and Oregon) and 23 (for Louisiana).

and the percentage of women with four years of college is −.397 and that between the restrictiveness of abortion laws and the percentage of women in managerial and professional occupations is −.390.

Finally, note the significance levels for each of the correlation coefficients. The correlation coefficient for the percentage of women in the workforce is highly insignificant ($p = .961$); note, however, that the correlation coefficient was close to zero (.007). But several of the other correlation coefficients are indeed significant, at $p < .05$ or even $p < .01$. Note the asterisks next to the correlation

coefficients. As mentioned previously, the use of asterisks is common when such results are reported: they denote the level at which a test statistic is significant. In this example (and also in the previous example), one asterisk means that the correlation coefficient is significant at the .05 level (percentage of businesses owned by women); two asterisks mean that the correlation coefficient is significant at the .01 level (percentage of women with four years of college and percentage of women in managerial and professional occupations). The absence of an asterisk denotes that a correlation coefficient is not significant.

CONCLUSION

In this chapter, you learned two forms of bivariate analysis: a difference of means and correlation coefficient. Compute a difference of means when you want to test whether a binary independent variable is associated with a dependent variable with ordinal, interval, or ratio measurement; compute a correlation coefficient when you want to test whether two variables with ordinal, interval, or ratio measurement are associated with one another. When performing these tests, you should first study the results to determine whether they are consistent with your research hypothesis. Next, evaluate each test's p value to determine whether the null hypothesis concerning the relationship between the variables in the population can be rejected. Remember that the p value is the probability of observing a particular result with a sample when the null hypothesis is actually true for the population. When a p-value is lower than .05, you can reject the null hypothesis. However, even when you are able to reject a null hypothesis based on the results from a statistical test, it is always a good idea to evaluate the magnitude of the result you obtain. A result can be statistically significant, but very small at the same time. Use caution in how you interpret your results.

You will use the two forms of bivariate analysis you learned in this chapter for your study on political attitudes and values because your dependent variable has ordinal measurement. This is why you had to choose a particular topic in Chapter 1 and a particular dependent variable in Chapter 3; each dependent variable related to each topic has ordinal measurement on a scale from 1 to 10. It is not possible to use the tests you have learned in this chapter for dependent variables that have nominal measurement. Although there are bivariate statistical techniques that can be used for a dependent variable with nominal measurement, they were not covered here. One possible test that is somewhat common is **cross-tabulation**, which assesses the relationship between two variables with nominal measurement. You must always know the level of measurement for each variable in your analysis to perform the appropriate statistical test.

It is also important to remember that behind most statistical tests, there is a hypothesis that was derived from a causal theory that explained why two or more variables should be related to each other. There should be a reason for including variables in a statistical analysis; otherwise, you might make erroneous conclusions about the nature of the relationship between variables. Many statistical correlations exist among variables, but remember the important adage that correlation is not causation. Some correlations are in fact spurious: we can show that variables are correlated, but in truth the relationship between them is not causal. Just because two variables are shown to be correlated does not mean that they are causally related to one another. Thus, use caution in how you interpret your results. Always return to the conditions of causality before making any causal claims. Even when two variables are shown to have a statistical correlation to one another, it is possible, for example, that the correlation is caused by the presence of a third, unincluded variable that in reality causes variation in both the independent and the dependent variables. This is why theory should drive the choice of the variables we include in our hypotheses and why theory development and causal reasoning are paramount for any research project.

The analyses explained in this chapter are only the beginning. But this is a tremendous start. Understanding how these analyses work forms a solid basis for other types of statistical inquiry, such as ordinary least squares linear regression, which is covered in the next chapter. Once a student understands the basics in descriptive statistics and data analysis, further analysis becomes much easier.

GLOSSARY

CORRELATION COEFFICIENT   A single number between –1 and +1 that best summarizes the linear relationship between two variables with ordinal, interval, or ratio measurement.

CROSS-TABULATION   A statistical analysis to assess the relationship between two variables with nominal measurement.

DATA ANALYSIS   Investigates the relationships between two or more variables.

DIFFERENCE OF MEANS TEST A statistical test involving one binary independent variable and one variable with ordinal, interval, or ratio measurement that compares the average value of the dependent variable for two groupings of the independent variable.

INVERSE CORRELATION A correlation in which as one variable increases, a second variable decreases.

p VALUE The probability of observing a particular result when the null hypothesis is true for the population.

POSITIVE CORRELATION A correlation in which as one variable increases, a second variable also increases.

EXERCISES

Working with SPSS and the WVS, complete the exercises below.

Difference of means test:

1. A. For the country and wave you are working with, transform V238: Social class into a binary variable, combining the categories 1 (upper class) and 2 (upper middle class) into a single category (0) and the categories 3 (lower middle class), 4 (working class), and 5 (lower class) into a second category (1). Then use the new binary variable as the independent variable to assess its effect on V95: Self-positioning in political scale in a difference of means test. (Note that the new variable you create will be listed at the bottom of the variable list in Variable View.) What do the results tell you?

   B. Use V19: Important child qualities: Religious faith as the independent variable (remember to check how the numbers are ordered for this variable) and use it to assess its effect on V137: Democracy: The state makes people's incomes equal in a difference of means test. What do the results tell you?

   Correlation coefficient:

2. A. Determine the correlation coefficient between V131: Democracy: Governments tax the rich and subsidize the poor and V198: Justifiable: Claiming government benefits to which you are not entitled. What do the results tell you? Make sure you understand the ordering of the values on each variable's scale before interpreting the results.

   B. Determine the correlation coefficient between V95: Self-positioning in political scale and V138: Democracy: People obey their rulers. What do the results tell you? Again, make sure you understand the ordering of the values on each variable's scale before interpreting the results.

PAPER PROGRESS

By this point you should have (1) limited the WVS to your research population, (2) transformed any variables with nominal measurement with more than two categories into a binary variable, and (3) generated descriptive statistics for each of your variables (of which there are three: two independent variables and one dependent variable).

Now you can perform bivariate analysis to determine whether your hypotheses are empirically supported with the WVS sample for a particular country. Start with the difference of means test between your variable with nominal measurement (which should now be a binary variable) and your dependent variable. Once you perform the analysis, interpret the results. Was the mean difference of the dependent variable for the two groupings of your independent variable consistent with your hypothesis? Furthermore, based on the *p* value SPSS generated, were you able to reject the null hypothesis that stipulated that there was no relationship between your binary independent variable and the dependent variable in the population from which the WVS sample was derived? Furthermore, even if you could reject the null hypothesis based on the *p* value, what was the magnitude of the result? Was it large or small?

To present the results of the difference of means test, in the results section of your eventual paper you could write a summary statement, being explicit about each group and its associated average for the dependent variable (based on groupings in the independent variable). Include whether the *p* value for the difference of means was significant. For example,

> The difference of means for *the dependent variable* based on *the independent variable* showed that *the first group of the independent variable* had an average of *value*, whereas *the second group of the independent variable* had an average of *value*. The mean difference of *mean difference* between the two groups was significant (or insignificant) at *p* < *.05*.
> Or
> The difference of means for *whether taxing the rich and subsidizing the poor is an essential characteristic of democracy* based on *biological sex* showed that *males* had an average of *4.76*, whereas *females* had an average of *5.16*. The mean difference of *–.401* between the two groups was *significant* at *p* < *.05*.

Once you finish your difference of means test, use SPSS to calculate the correlation coefficient between your second independent variable (the one with ordinal, interval, or ratio measurement) and your dependent variable. Once you obtain the results, study them carefully. What was the correlation between the variables? Was it consistent with your research hypothesis? Furthermore, what was the *p* value for the test? Does the *p* value generated by the test for the sample allow you to reject the null hypothesis about the relationship between the two variables in the population? And even if you could reject the null hypothesis based on the *p* value, what was the magnitude of the result? Was the correlation coefficient large or small?

In the results section of your eventual paper, statements that demonstrate the correlation and whether it was significant are helpful. For example,

> The correlation between *the independent variable* and *the dependent variable* was a *positive (or inverse)* one at *value*, which was *significant (or insignificant)* at $p < .05$.
> Or
> The correlation between *satisfaction with financial situation of household* and *the degree to which a respondent believed that it is an essential characteristic of democracy to tax the rich and subsidize the poor* was an inverse one at *−.145*, which was significant at $p < .05$.

COMING UP

This chapter introduced data analysis and showed you how to determine whether two variables are correlated in a sample of data. In Chapter 11 you will be given more information about how to discuss your findings more clearly in the results section of your eventual research paper. In the next chapter we continue our discussion of data analysis, with single-variable and multivariate ordinal least squares linear regression.

CHAPTER 9

INTRODUCTION TO REGRESSION

In the previous chapter, you learned how to determine whether a relationship exists bewteen two variables through a difference of means test or correlation coefficient. Another statistical tool to determine the degree of association between variables is **regression analysis**.

Regression analysis can be used in different ways. For many researchers, regression analysis is used to test hypotheses by providing evidence that variation in an independent variable explains variation in a dependent variable. Other researchers use regression analysis to make predictions about the value a dependent variable would take based on particular values of one or more independent variables. Regression analysis is flexible in this way and has become a powerful tool for both explanation and prediction for researchers across many disciplines.

ORDINARY LEAST SQUARES LINEAR REGRESSION

Regression analysis utilizes a sample of data to produce estimates of a dependent variable based on the values of one or more independent variables. **Ordinary least squares linear regression** (called linear regression in this chapter) is the simplest type of regression analysis. Like the difference of means test and the correlation coefficient covered in the last chapter, linear regression requires a dependent variable that has ordinal, interval, or ratio measurement with a relatively large distribution of values. Ordinal variables whose range is from only 1 to 4, like many of the variables in the WVS, are not well suited as dependent variables in linear regression. For linear regression to work properly, the dependent variable should have a larger range. This is why you were required to choose one of the possible dependent variables listed in Chapter 3. Each of those variables has a range of 1 to 10, which makes your particular choice more suited as a dependent variable for linear regression.[1]

Single Variable Linear Regression Between One Independent Variable and One Dependent Variable

Let's work with a simple example of regression analysis before returning to the WVS data to see how regression works in practice. Take a professor who is going to administer a political science test to her students in one week. She wants to know whether certain independent variables contribute to either higher or lower scores on the test. Believing study time to be an important variable, she writes a theory to explain why study time should be related to test scores and derives a research hypothesis that study time is positively related to test scores. Specifically, she believes that as the number of hours that a student studies increases, that student's grade on the test will also increase. This hypothesis stands in constrast to the null hypothesis, which is that study time is not related to test grades. The following week, the students take the test. As the students turn the test in, the professor asks the students to report how many hours were spent studying for it, and after the tests have been graded, the professor creates a dataset with the information she collected (Figure 9.1).

How can single-variable linear regression help the professor understand the relationship between the number of hours each student studied for the test and each student's final test grade? First, let's write out the regression equation that is used to produce the estimates for the dependent variable.[2]

We can take the following equation apart, piece by piece, to undestand what each term means.

$$y_i = \alpha + \beta x_i$$

First, note the lowercase i's after some of the terms, which in regular language is translated "for any student i." The i denotes that all the information for every observation of a given variable is at the level of an individual student.

y_i is the value of the dependent variable for each student i (the test grade for any single observation in the dataset) given a particular value of an independent variable.

---

1   Some methodologists suggest that linear regression is technically not appropriate for dependent variables measured at an ordinal level (whereby the distance between values may not be absolute, as is the case for the opinion-oriented variables in the WVS). Nonetheless, when the number of values within the dependent variable is large enough, linear regression will generally produce accurate results.

2   Scholars sometimes call such equations a model.

	gradeontest	hoursstudied
1	95	10
2	60	0
3	100	20
4	75	5
5	80	7
6	60	3
7	92	8
8	95	15
9	85	12
10	70	2
11	95	20
12	75	7
13	80	5
14	60	5
15	55	0
16	70	12
17	93	15
18	88	10
19	75	8
20	96	10
21	100	15
22	72	7
23	68	2
24	89	7
25	80	8
26	70	5
27	95	12
28	85	10
29	100	20
30	75	5

FIGURE 9.1: Regression Analysis
Data, Study Hours and Test Grades

α is the **constant**, which is the value of the dependent variable when the independent variable is zero. Sometimes this is called the y-intercept. The constant in this equation is the predicted test grade received when a student studies zero hours.

β is the **unstandardized beta coefficient**, or what we will call "coefficient" in this chapter. The coefficient in linear regression (not to be confused with the correlation coefficient covered in the last chapter) is the slope of the line that best describes the relationship between the independent and dependent variables. In the case of the professor, the coefficient is the best fitting line that describes the linear relationship between the number of hours studied and the test grade for each student. In practical terms, the coefficient is the number of units by which a dependent variable is expected to change when the independent variable increases by one unit. In other words, the coefficient is the number of points by which a test grade is expected to change (since the exam score is in points) for a one-unit (one-hour) increase in study time. If the coefficient is a positive number, the test grade is expected to increase for each hour studied; if the coefficient is a negative number, the test grade is expected to decrease. Thus, both the sign and the size of the coefficient are important. The sign of the coefficient indicates the direction of the change and the size of the coefficient indicates how much of a change is expected in the dependent variable for a one-unit increase in the independent variable. Note that if the coefficient for an independent variable is 0, then no relationship exists between the independent and dependent variables. There is no change in the dependent variable for a one-unit change in the independent variable.

x_i is the value of the independent variable for each student i (the number of hours studied that corresponds to the test grade for any single observation (student in this case) in the dataset).

For the professor, then, the equation can be rewritten as follows:

Exam grade for student$_i$ = α + β (Number of hours studied for student$_i$)

The professor's hypothesis is that the number of study hours positively impacts her students' exam grades. Ordinary least squares linear regression can help the professor determine whether this hypothesis is supported with data. To perform a single-variable linear regression (single variable because only one independent variable is used) between the number of hours studied and a student's final test grade in SPSS, do the following (Figure 9.2):

1. From Analyze choose Regression and then Linear (the second on the list). This will open the Linear Regression window.
2. Place the dependent variable in the top line by selecting it from the variable list and using the small blue arrow to place it in the box.
3. Then select the single independent variable from the variable list and use the small blue arrow to place it in the independent variable box.
4. Click Statistics.
5. Check the Confidence Intervals Level box. Leave the setting at 95%.
6. Check the Descriptives box.
7. Click Continue.
8. Click OK.

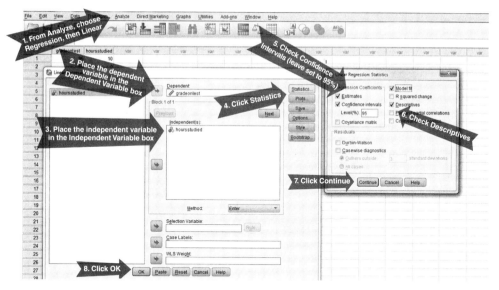

FIGURE 9.2:   Performing A Single-Variable Linear Regression, Hours Studied and Test Scores

SPSS will generate a number of tables. For our purposes right now, we will look at three of them: descriptive statistics (Figure 9.3), model summary (Figure 9.4), and coefficients (Figure 9.5).[3]

What do these statistics tell us? What should we look for in these tables? First, let's examine the coefficients table (the third listed here, and the last that is displayed in the SPSS output, Figure 9.5.

The first piece of information to consider is the constant. Remember that the constant is the value of the dependent variable when the independent variable is zero, that is, when a student studies zero hours. Thus, the coefficients table tells us that when a student has not studied at all (zero hours), the associated test grade is 63.2 points. (It is never a good plan to study zero hours for a test!)

Next, we should examine the statistics concerning the independent variable's coefficient under the unstandardized coefficients columns. Three key pieces of information—what we will call the three S's—are important. The three S's are the sign, size, and significance of each independent variable's coefficient. The first S is the coefficient's *sign* for each independent variable. A coefficient's sign reveals the direction of the relationship between the independent and dependent variables. The professor's hypothesis was that as study time

---

3   SPSS provides a number of tables in the output; some tables (such as variables entered/removed and ANOVA) were removed for this presentation.

Regression

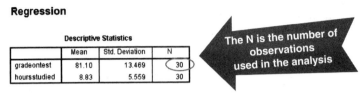

FIGURE 9.3:   Results from a Single-Variable Linear Regression, Hours Studied and Test Scores: Descriptive Statistics

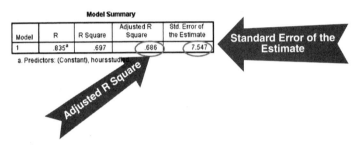

FIGURE 9.4:   Results from a Single Variable Linear Regression, Hours Studied and Test Scores: Model Summary

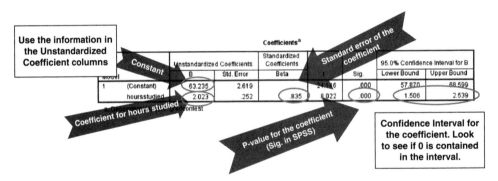

FIGURE 9.5:   Results from a Single Variable Linear Regression, Hours Studied and Test Scores: Coefficients

increases, grades increase as well. Because increased values of the independent variable are expected to lead to increased values of the dependent variable, it is expected that the coefficient has a positive sign. If the professor had expected that increased study time decreases grades, she would have instead expected an inverse relationship and hence a negative sign for the coefficient. The sign of the coefficient is important because it tells us whether the data support the predicted direction of your research hypothesis.

The second S is the *size*, or magnitude, of an independent variable's coefficient. The coefficient tells us how much of an increase (positive coefficient) or decrease (negative coefficient) there is in a dependent variable for every one-unit increase in an independent variable. Thus, a larger coefficient will indicate that a one-unit increase in the independent variable has a larger impact on a dependent variable, whereas a smaller coefficient has a smaller impact, relative to the units of the dependent variable. (Remember that the coefficient's units are the same as the units of the dependent variable.) Since the coefficient is 2.023 (make sure you use the information in the unstandardized coefficients column), a test score is expected to increase by a little more than 2 points for every additional hour of study time. Thus, if studying zero hours results in a score of about 63 points, each additional hour will increase the grade by a little more than 2 points. So if a student studies only one hour for the test, the expected test score is about 65 points (constant + 1 coefficient). If a student studies two hours, the expected test score is about 67 points (constant + 2 coefficients). We start with the constant because that is the expected test score when the number of hours is zero and then add one coefficient for each one-unit (one-hour) increase in study time.

We can see these statistics graphically in Figure 9.6, where the independent and dependent variables are represented on a scatterplot. For single-variable linear regression between two variables like this one, the regression line,

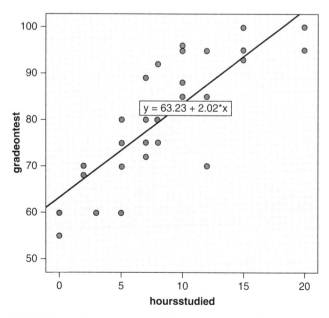

FIGURE 9.6: Independent and Dependent Variables on a Scatterplot

sometimes called the "best fitting line," is the slope that best represents the linear relationship between the independent and dependent variables. In technical terms, in linear regression the best fitting line is the one that minimizes the sum of squared vertical residuals (or deviations between the actual and predicted values of the dependent variable) for each observation in the dataset. In other words, linear regression takes all of the residuals and squares them (squaring the differences emphasizes larger deviations and deemphasizes smaller ones) and draws the specific regression line that minimizes the overall sum of the squared residuals.

From the scatterplot we can see how the constant is the value of Y when X is zero. The regression line will cross the Y axis at $X = 0$ when Y is somewhere between 60 and 70 (specifically, we know from the coefficients table that this value is about 63). The coefficient, or slope, of the regression line is 2.02, which means that as the number of study hours increases by one unit (one study hour), a student's test score is expected to increase by a little more than two points. Note that the coefficient is always represented by the units of the dependent variable, in this case, points on the test.

There is one point of caution in using an independent variable's coefficient to create predicted values of the dependent variable. Although it is technically possible to create a predicted value of the dependent variable for any value of an independent variable, doing so is not advised. It is not possible, for example, to study a negative number of hours. Consequently, in this case, negative numbers should never be used as values for the independent variable to predict a test grade. In addtion, it would be unrealistic for someone to study more than a certain threshold of hours for a single test, say more than 20 hours (which is the highest value of hours studied in the dataset). For this reason, you are strongly advised to use only reasonable values of an independent variable when making predictions for a dependent variable.

Finally, the *significance* of an independent variable's coefficient is extremely important. Remember that the information the professor collected is based on a sample. Although she may have collected information on all her students in a particular class, the sample still represents a larger population of students who take tests. The idea is to see whether the information used in the professor's sample can explain how the number of study hours influences test grades in other but similar contexts. Thus, since the information the professor collected is based on a sample, in theory, the statistics generated by regression analysis can reveal whether the coefficient for an independent variable is statistically significant, that is, not likely due to chance. Thus, in this way, the p value that was crucial to understanding the significance of test statistics in the previous chapter is still relevant here. For most social scientists, if the p value for an independent variable's coefficient is lower than .05, the null hypothesis that posits that the coefficient in the population is actually zero can be rejected. When an independent variable's regression coefficient is zero, no relationship exists between the independent and dependent variables because the best fitting line to describe the relationship between the two variables is flat.

Is the coefficient for the hours studied independent variable statistically significant? To determine the statistical significance of an independent variable's coefficient, look for the Sig. value (p value) for the hours studied coefficient, located in the coefficients table. From the coefficients table we see that the p value for the coefficient for the number of hours studied is .001. Since .001 is lower than .05, the professor can reject the null hypothesis. These results suggest that a significant relationship exists between the number of hours studied and the test grade. The p value tells us that it would be highly unlikely to obtain a coefficient as large as this one if in the overall population the coefficient's true value were zero. Given the p value of .001, this would happen only once in 1,000 samples.

In addition to the constant and coefficient, the coefficients table also reports the **standard error of the coefficient**, which measures how precisely the regression model estimates the coefficient's value for the population. From the coefficients table, we see that the standard error for the coefficient for hours studied is .382. The standard error of the coefficient is important because it is used as part of the formula that determines each coefficient's p value. It is also used to estimate a range of values in which the true population coefficient is likely to fall. This range is the **confidence interval** produced by the regression model. In the coefficients table the lower bound of the confidence interval is 1.211, whereas the upper bound is 2.975. Since SPSS calculated the confidence interval with 95% confidence, this range of values is likely to contain the true population coefficient. This does not mean that we are 95% confident that the true population coefficient is within the range of the confidence interval. Rather, we are confident that we will construct a confidence interval that will contain the true population parameter 95% of the time when using a sample like this one.

In addition to these specific statistics, the SPSS output provides a table labeled "model summary." There are two important pieces of information in this table: adjusted R^2 (R squared) and the standard error of the estimate, both of which are discussed here.

R^2 (R squared) is often used by researchers to understand the extent to which the inclusion of one or more independent variables explains variation in a dependent variable. Specifically, R^2 is the percentage of variation in the dependent variable that is explained by the independent variable(s) included in the analysis. R^2 is usually presented as a number between 0 and 1, but you could simply multiply this number by 100 to get the percentage of variation in the dependent variable that is explained by the inclusion of one or more independent variables. The adjusted R^2 for the professor's single-variable linear regression between hours studied and test grades is .686. What this means is that that almost 69% of the variation in test grades is explained by the inclusion of the hours studied variable.

There is a good deal of controversy among statisticians about how to use R^2 appropriately. Some researchers note that R^2 is usually a low number, which might imply that most analyses are incomplete because R^2 tells us how comprehensively we have explained variation in the dependent variable. Many variables contribute to different values on a dependent variable. Leaving out independent variables that explain variation in the dependent variable is called **omitted variable bias**. For this reason, researchers sometimes use regression analysis simply to determine whether and how one or more independent variables matter for variation in the dependent variable. In this case, researchers put more emphasis on the examination of the sign, size, and significance of each coefficient than on the value of R^2.

When reporting the value for R^2 in your anaylses, you should use the value for the **adjusted R^2**. This is advised because R^2 always increases with the addition of each independent variable; it never decreases when additional variables are added. As a result, R^2 will increase even when we add an independent variable that does not actually impact variation in the dependent variable. The value for adjusted R^2 thus takes the number of independent variables in the regression equation into account, which is why for single-variable regression the values for R^2 and adjusted R^2 are similar numbers. The values between R^2 and adjusted R^2 diverge as more independent variables are added to the regression equation.

The second number highlighted in the model summary is the **standard error of the estimate**. This is not to be confused with the standard error of each independent variable's coefficient described earlier. The standard error of the estimate is a measure of the accuracy of the predictions made by the regression line. It is a summary statistic that gives us an impression of how far off the predictions are from the observed values in the dataset by providing the average distance of each actual observation to its corresponding prediction on the regression line. Remember that the regression equation produces an estimated value of the dependent variable based on a configuration of independent variables. As a result, there is some error that is expected between the actual value and the predicted value of the dependent varaible for given values of the independent variable. If the prediction for the value of a dependent variable matches what was observed in the sample of data, then the error for that prediction will be small. But if prediction for the value of a dependent variable is far off from what was actually observed in the dataset, then the error for that prediction will be large. The standard error of the estimate is the average of all these errors. Overall, the standard error of the estimate gets smaller when the observed values in the dataset are closer to the regression line and bigger when the observed values in the dataset are farther away from the regression line. Thus, the standard error of the estimate reported in the coefficients table is a single value that averages all the deviations.

In the coefficients table, the standard error of the estimate is 7.129. Since the standard error is reported in the units of the dependent variable, the average deviation between the predicted and actual values on the regression line is a little more than seven test points.

Now that we have understood what some of the statistics in the regression model mean, let's continue with the professor's example. Based on her first single-variable linear regression, she has evidence that the number of hours studied is positively associated with test grades, but she now wants to change the independent variable. She has another theory that explains why a student's interest in the subject matter also matters for test scores. Based on this theory, the professor's second research hypothesis is that students who were more interested in political science before the test are more likely to get a high score on the test than students who were less interested in political science before the test. Consequently, in addition to asking the students in class how many hours were spent studying, the professor also asks each student to report his or her interest level in political science, which is then added to her dataset (Figure 9.7). Specifically, the professor asked each student to rate his or her interest in political science on a scale from 1 to 4, like many of the variables in the WVS, whereby 1 represents "very interested," 2 represents "somewhat interested," 3 represents "not very interested," and 4 represents "not interested at all."

Let's conduct a single-variable regression to see how interest in political science influences a student's test grade. To do this, simply substitute the hoursstudied variable with interestinsubject variable in the linear regression menu in SPSS. Doing so produces the tables in Figure 9.8; again we concentrate on descriptive statistics (which tells us the number of observations that were used in the analysis), the model summary (which tells us the adjusted R^2), and the

	gradeontest	hoursstudied	interestinsubject
1	95	10	1
2	60	0	4
3	100	20	1
4	75	5	4
5	80	7	1
6	60	3	1
7	92	8	3
8	95	15	2
9	85	12	2
10	70	2	4
11	95	20	2
12	75	7	4
13	80	5	2
14	60	5	4
15	55	0	3
16	70	12	1
17	93	15	1
18	88	10	2
19	75	8	2
20	96	10	2
21	100	15	2
22	72	7	1
23	68	2	2
24	89	7	2
25	80	8	3
26	70	5	2
27	95	12	1
28	85	10	4
29	100	20	1
30	75	5	1

FIGURE 9.7: Regression Analysis Data, Interest in Subject Added

coefficients table, which lists the constant and the information about the independent variable's coefficient.

First, let's look at the statistics in the coefficients table to determine whether student interest in the test's subject significantly influences test grades. First, note the constant. It is 91.194. Technically, this means that a student's grade on the test is 91.194 when the interest in the subject is 0. But use great caution when interpreting the constant; the constant in this particular example is not interpretable. The constant is the expected value of Y when X is 0, but in our example, a value of 0 has no substantive meaning. Why? Because the variable interestinsubject has no zero. Like many variables in the WVS, it is measured on an ordinal scale from 1 to 4. There was no possibility for a respondent to choose zero. As a result, we cannot interpret the constant as it is

Regression

Descriptive Statistics

	Mean	Std. Deviation	N
gradeontest	81.10	13.469	30
interestinsubject	2.17	1.117	30

Model Summary

Model	R	R Square	Adjusted R Square	Std. Error of the Estimate
1	.386ᵃ	.149	.119	12.643

a. Predictors: (Constant), interestinsubject

Coefficientsᵃ

Model		Unstandardized Coefficients		Standardized Coefficients	t	Sig.	95.0% Confidence Interval for B	
		B	Std. Error	Beta			Lower Bound	Upper Bound
1	(Constant)	91.194	5.106		17.859	.000	80.734	101.655
	interestinsubject	-4.659	2.102	-.386	-2.216	.035	-8.965	-.353

a. Dependent Variable: gradeontest

FIGURE 9.8:   Results from a Single Variable Regression, Interest in Subject and Test Scores

presented in the coefficients table.[4] Since many variables in the WVS are constructed in this way, it is possible that you will not be able to interpret the constant on its own.

Now let's evaluate the three S's for the new variable's coefficient. First we look at the sign. It is negative, which means an inverse relationship exists between the independent and dependent variables. What this means is that for a one-unit increase in the independent variable, there is a decrease in the test score. However, to interpret this correctly, we must consider how the original varable was coded. Remember that lower numbers represent more interest in political science and higher numbers represent less interest. This means that as a student becomes less interested in the subject (moving from (1) very interested to (2) somewhat interested, or from (2) somewhat interested to (3) not very interested, or from (3) not very interested to (4) not interested at all), test scores are expected to decrease. The negative sign means that the relationship

---

4   Another way to think about this problem in interpreting the constant is to imagine that we had used age as an independent variable in this analysis. The minimum value for age in the WVS is 18. If you had run a regression analysis for how age impacts a dependent variable, the constant would tell you what the expected value of that dependent variable would be when age is equal to zero. Clearly, for age the constant would not have substantive meaning (unless you have a truly exceptional newborn!). But if the independent variable in a single-variable linear regression equation did have a range that included zero with substantive meaning, we could interpret the constant in a meaningful way: it would be the predicted value of the dependent variable when the independent variable is zero.

between the variables is inverse, but it is important to know how the variables are measured to interpret this result correctly. The negative sign for the coefficient means that students who had less interest in political science have decreased test scores.

Next, we consider the size of the coefficient. The coefficient is –4.659, which means that for a one-unit increase in the interest level (becoming less interested), a test score is expected to decrease by 4.659 points. Again, be careful how you use values in the independent variable to create predictions of the dependent variable. Since the independent variable only had four possible values contained in it, it is not advised to create predictions beyond the 1–4 range.

Finally, we must determine whether the result is significant. We see from the p value (Sig. for SPSS) of .035 that the coefficient for interest in subject is significant. Since this value is lower than .05, we can say that a student's interest level in political science before the test was taken is significantly related to test scores and that this relationship is not likely due to chance. Thus, the null hypothesis that interest in political science is not related to test grades in the population can be rejected. Another way to confirm this result is to look at the 95% confidence interval for the interest in subject independent variable. The lower bound is –8.965 and the upper bound is –.353. Since the range does not contain a possible coefficient of 0, we can say that interest in political science is statistically significant.

Armed with these statistics, the professor has some evidence that test scores are associated with two independent variables—the number of hours studied and the level of interest each student had in political science before the test was taken—that she included as individual independent variables in two separate single-variable regression equations. But now she thinks about how important class attendance is and devises a third theory about why class attendance matters for test scores. From this new theory the professor derives a third research hypothesis to suggest that attending class is also positively related to test scores. She looks at her class roll and devises a binary variable to measure whether the students included in her dataset attended all classes or missed any classes. Any student who attended all classes received a score of 1, and any student who missed a class before the test received a score of zero. The professor then adds this last variable to the dataset (Figure 9.9).

The professor now runs a third single-variable linear regression equation to determine whether attending class is related to test scores. Figure 9.10 below displays the results.

Before we interpret these results, let's think about how the attendance variable was measured. The professor decided to code the variable as a binary

	gradeontest	hoursstudied	interestinsubject	attendancebinary
1	95	10	1	1
2	60	0	4	0
3	100	20	1	1
4	75	5	4	0
5	80	7	1	1
6	60	3	1	0
7	92	8	3	1
8	95	15	2	1
9	85	12	2	0
10	70	2	4	1
11	95	20	2	1
12	75	7	2	1
13	80	5	2	1
14	60	5	4	0
15	55	0	3	0
16	70	12	1	0
17	93	15	1	1
18	88	10	2	0
19	75	8	2	1
20	96	10	2	1
21	100	15	3	0
22	72	7	1	0
23	68	2	2	0
24	89	7	2	1
25	80	8	3	0
26	70	5	2	0
27	95	12	1	1
28	85	10	4	1
29	100	20	1	1
30	75	5	1	1

FIGURE 9.9: Regression Analysis Data, Attendance Added

Descriptive Statistics

	Mean	Std. Deviation	N
gradeontest	81.10	13.469	30
attendancebinary	.57	.504	30

Model Summary

Model	R	R Square	Adjusted R Square	Std. Error of the Estimate
1	.565[a]	.320	.295	11.306

a. Predictors: (Constant), attendancebinary

Coefficients[a]

Model		Unstandardized Coefficients		Standardized Coefficients	t	Sig.	95.0% Confidence Interval for B	
		B	Std. Error	Beta			Lower Bound	Upper Bound
1	(Constant)	72.538	3.136		23.133	.000	66.115	78.962
	attendancebinary	15.109	4.166	.565	3.627	.001	6.576	23.641

a. Dependent Variable: gradeontest

FIGURE 9.10: Results from a Single Variable Regression, Attendance and Test Scores

variable, with zero representing students who missed at least one class and 1 representing students who attended all classes. Since the variable includes zero (in other words, the zero has substantive meaning because it represents the category for students who missed at least one class), we can interpret the constant meaningfully in this single-variable linear regression. Since the constant is the expected value of the dependent variable when the independent variable is zero, the constant of 72.5 is the expected test score for students who missed at least one class. Now, remember that the sign and size of the coefficient represent the change in the dependent variable for a one-unit change in the independent variable. For this example, the one-unit change is going from students who missed at least one class ($X = 0$) to students who missed no classes at all ($X = 1$). Since the coefficient is +15.109, we must add one coefficient to the constant to get the predicted test score for students who attended all classes. Thus, for students who missed at least one class, the predicted test score is 72.5 (the constant); for students who attended all classes, the predicted test score is about 87.5 points (= the constant 72.5 + one coefficient 15). This result is also significant, since the p value of the attendancebinary variable is .001. In addition, the 95% confidence interval is 6.576 and 23.641. Since the p value for this coefficient is less than .05 and since the confidence interval does not contain a coefficient of 0, the professor can reject the null hypothesis that class attendance is not related to test scores. On the contrary, the results here show that the attendance variable is strongly associated with student scores on the test. Another way to interpret this result is to say that there is about a 15-point difference between the two categories, between those who attended all classes and those who missed one or more classes.

Multivariate Linear Regression Between Several Independent Variables and One Dependent Variable

One of the most useful benefits of regression analysis is that we can include several independent variables in a regression equation at the same time. Here the notion of control is important. Multiple regression can tell us which of the included independent variables is the most significant for explaining variation in the dependent variable, controlling for all the other independent variables in the equation. What this means is that we can assess the independent effect of each independent variable on the dependent variable while assuming that the other independent variables are held constant. This is the statistical equivalent of studying two individuals who are exactly the same on every variable in the equation, but differ on the independent variable in question.

Now the professor who is interested in understanding which variables are most important for explaining variation in test scores can include all three independent variables in the same regression equation. The results will tell her which of the three variables is the most significant in explaining variation in test scores, holding the other two variables constant. She writes the following equation:

$$y_i = \alpha + (\beta 1 \times x1_i) + (\beta 2 \times x2_i) + (\beta 3 \times x3_i)$$

where $x1$, $x2$, and $x3$ are the three independent variables and $\beta 1$, $\beta 2$, and $\beta 3$ are the individual coefficients associated with each independent variable. $x1$ is the number of hours studied, $x2$ is the student's interest level in the subject, and $x3$ is the binary variable that captures whether a student missed a class or attended all classes. Until now, we have examined how each independent variable, on its own, influences variation in test scores in single-variable linear regression equations. In separate analyses, each variable was shown to have a significant effect on the dependent variable. With multiple regression we can include all three independent variables at the same time to see whether any of the relationships between the independent variables and test scores still hold. Thus, the equation becomes

test score$_i$ =

$\alpha + (\beta 1 \times$ number of hours studied$_i) + (\beta 2 \times$ level of interest in subject$_i) +$ $(\beta 3 \times$ attendance binary$_i)$

To perform multivariate linear regression in SPSS, we simply repeat the same steps that we used for single-variable linear regression, but now include all three independent variables in the independent variable box (Figure 9.11).

1. From Analyze choose Regression and then Linear.
2. Place the dependent variable in the dependent variable box.
3. Rather than entering a single variable in the independent variable box, enter all the variables we wish to include in the regression equation.
4. Click on Statistics.
5. Check Confidence Intervals Levels box. Leave the setting at 95%.
6. Check Descriptives.
7. Click Continue.
8. Click OK.

Study the tables in Figure 9.12 carefully. Look at what happened. Although each variable was significant when included in a single variable regression equation, only two of the variables are significant when all three are included in the same regression equation.

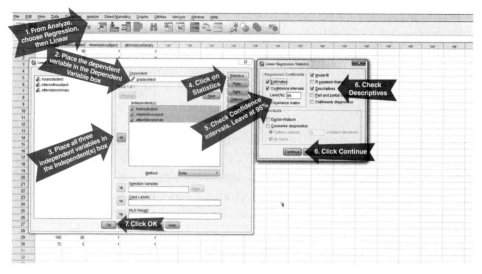

FIGURE 9.11: Performing a Multivariate Linear Regression

Regression

Descriptive Statistics

	Mean	Std. Deviation	N
gradeontest	81.10	13.469	30
hoursstudied	8.83	5.559	30
interestinsubject	2.13	1.074	30
attendancebinary	.57	.504	30

Model Summary

Model	R	R Square	Adjusted R Square	Std. Error of the Estimate
1	.879[a]	.772	.746	6.791

a. Predictors: (Constant), attendancebinary, interestinsubject, hoursstudied

Coefficients[a]

Model		Unstandardized Coefficients B	Unstandardized Coefficients Std. Error	Standardized Coefficients Beta	t	Sig.	95.0% Confidence Interval for B Lower Bound	95.0% Confidence Interval for B Upper Bound
1	(Constant)	58.959	4.516		13.054	.000	49.676	68.243
	hoursstudied	1.809	.261	.747	6.920	.000	1.272	2.346
	interestinsubject	.768	1.300	.061	.590	.560	-1.905	3.441
	attendancebinary	7.982	2.730	.299	2.924	.007	2.370	13.593

a. Dependent Variable: gradeontest

FIGURE 9.12: Results from a Multivariate Linear Regression, Three Independent Variables and Test Scores

First, look at the constant. It is 58.959. Technically, this is the predicted test score when all the independent variables are zero. However, as discussed previously, the second independent variable (interest in subject) does not have a zero associated with it. As a result, we cannot meaningfully interpret this constant. A discussion of the constant is appropriate only when it has substantive meaning.

Next, let's examine the three S's for each independent variable included in the equation.

First, the sign of the coefficient for hours studied is positive. The size of the coefficient is 1.809 points on the test. Holding a student's interest level in political science and his or her attendance constant, a one-hour increase in study time is associated with an increase of 1.809 points on the test. The p value for the coefficient for hours studied is .000, which is significant because .000 is lower than .05.

The sign of the coefficient for interest in subject is positive. (Note that the sign changed from when it was included on its own in single-variable regression). The size of the coefficient is .768 points on the test. Holding a student's number of hours studied and his or her attandance constant, a one-unit increase in the interest in subject variable (as someone becomes less interested in the subject) is associated with an increase of .387 points on the test. However, the p value for the coefficient for interest in subject is .560, which is not significant because .560 is higher than .05.

The sign for the attendance binary variable is positive. The size of the coefficient is 7.982 points on the test. Holding a student's number of hours studied and interest in subject constant, the difference between missing one or more classes and not missing any classes is 7.982 points on the test. The p value for the coefficient for the attendance binary variable is .007, which is significant because .007 is lower than .05.

Thus, when all three variables are included in the regression equation, only two of them are significant for understanding variation in test scores. Although each of the three independent variables achieved significance when included in separate single-variable regressions, the interest in politics variable failed to achieve significance when included in the multiple-variable regression equation. This means that the hypotheses concerning study time and class attendance have more explanatory power than interest in subject. Thus, we see the benefit of multivariate regression. We can use multivariate regression to identify the variables that explain the most variation in the dependent variable. Many researchers use this approach when there are competing hypotheses for a particular dependent variable. The idea is to find which hypothesis has the most explanatory power (see Chapter 4). This is not to say that the interest in political science is not important, but the results from the analysis above do suggest that study time and attending class are the most significant factors explaining variation in students' test scores.

In addition, note that the adjusted R^2 is .746. This means that almost 75% of the variation in test scores is explained by the inclusion of these three variables.

Using Data from the World Values Survey

Let's work with an example from the WVS. Take a researcher who wants to understand variation in self-placement on the left/right political scale using particular demographic characteristics as independent variables. Self-placement on the left/right political scale is measured on an ordinal scale from 1 to 10, with 1 representing the political left and 10 representing the political right. The first independent variable is education level, V248. This variable, which has nominal measurement in the WVS, was transformed into a binary variable to capture whether someone had attended or completed university (the 1 category) or not (the 0 category).[5] The second independent variable is the number of children, V58, which is a variable with ratio measurement. The research specifies the following hypotheses:

> $X1$: education level, nominal measurement. Transformed into a binary variable. The 0 category contains respondents who have not attended or completed university. The 1 category contains respondents who have either attended or completed university.
>
>> Null hypothesis: No relationship exists between education level and self-placement on the left/right political scale.
>> Research hypothesis: Respondents who have not attended or completed university are more likely to identify with the political right than respondents who did attend or complete university.
>
> $X2$: number of children, ratio level measurement. 0 = no children, 1 = one child, 2 = two children and so on, up until 7 = seven children.
>
>> Null hypothesis: No difference exists between the number of children and scores on the left/right political scale.
>> Hypothesis 2: Respondents who have a higher number of children are more likely to identify with the political right than respondents who have a lower number of children.

---

5   The education level variable was taken from V248, the highest education level attained. Values of 1 through 7 became the 0 category, whereas values of 8 and 9 became the 1 category.

Figures 9.13–9.15 provides the results from three models: the first with the education level binary variable; the second with the number of children variable; and the third with both independent variables included.

Model 1

Self-placement on left/right scale$_i$ = α + (β1 $^\times$ education level$_i$)

Before you read any further, try to interpret the results. What does the constant tell us? What was the coefficient for the education level independent variable? Was it significant?

The constant for this equation is 5.918. Since this single-variable regression equation includes only one independent variable and since the value 0 has real meaning (representing respondents who have not attended or completed university), we can interpret the constant. In this case, this is the predicted self-placement on the left/right scale for people who have not attended university.

The sign of the coefficient for education level is negative. This means that as we move from the 0 category (less education) to the 1 category (more education), placement on the left/right political scale decreases (toward the political left). The size of the coefficient is .204, which means that as we move from respondents who have not attended or complete university to respondents who have attended or completed university, placement on the left/right political scale deceases by .204, which is 5.918 – .204 = 5.714. Thus, the predicted value

Descriptive Statistics

	Mean	Std. Deviation	N
Self positioning in political scale	5.80	2.047	2162
educationbinary	.5883	.49225	2162

Model Summary

Model	R	R Square	Adjusted R Square	Std. Error of the Estimate
1	.049ᵃ	.002	.002	2.045

a. Predictors: (Constant), educationbinary

Coefficientsᵃ

Model		Unstandardized Coefficients		Standardized Coefficients	t	Sig.	95.0% Confidence Interval for B	
		B	Std. Error	Beta			Lower Bound	Upper Bound
1	(Constant)	5.918	.069		86.353	.000	5.784	6.052
	educationbinary	-.204	.089	-.049	-2.285	.022	-.379	-.029

a. Dependent Variable: Self positioning in political scale

FIGURE 9.13: Results from a Single Variable Regression, Education Level and Self-Placement on the Left/Right Scale

for respondents who have not attended or completed university is 5.918, and the predicted value for respondents who have attended or completed university is 5.714. Overall, this means that respondents who have not attended or completed university are more likely to self-identify with the political right than respondents who did attend or complete university, who are more likely to self-identify with the political left.

But is this significant? From the coefficients table we see that the coefficient for this variable is .022, which is significant at the .05 level. This tells us the likelihood that achieving this particular result is not caused by chance, which means the null hypothesis can be rejected. In addition, the confidence interval does not contain a coefficient of 0.

Although the coefficient for education level is significant in this equation, the difference between 5.918 (for the 0 category) and 5.714 (for the 1 category) may not seem like much. This is why the size of the coefficient is important. In addition, note that the upper bound of the confidence interval is somewhat close to 0. Keep this in mind as we continue with this example.

Model 2

Self-placement on left/right scale$_i$ = α + ($\beta 2$ $^\times$ number of children$_i$)

Model 2 now includes the number of children as an independent variable. The results from this regression analysis are provided in Figure 9.14. Again,

Descriptive Statistics

	Mean	Std. Deviation	N
Self positioning in political scale	5.80	2.048	2157
How many children do you have	1.75	1.606	2157

Model Summary

Model	R	R Square	Adjusted R Square	Std. Error of the Estimate
1	.131[a]	.017	.017	2.031

a. Predictors: (Constant), How many children do you have

Coefficients[a]

Model		Unstandardized Coefficients		Standardized Coefficients	t	Sig.	95.0% Confidence Interval for B	
		B	Std. Error	Beta			Lower Bound	Upper Bound
1	(Constant)	5.506	.065		85.072	.000	5.379	5.633
	How many children do you have	.167	.027	.131	6.143	.000	.114	.221

a. Dependent Variable: Self positioning in political scale

FIGURE 9.14: Results of a Single Variable Regression Model, Number of Children and Self-Placement on the Left/Right Scale

before you read any further, try to interpret the results. What does the constant tell us? What was the coefficient for the independent variable that measured a respondent's number of children? Was the coefficient significant?

The constant in this equation was 5.506. Since 0 was included in this variable in the WVS, indicating that a respondent has no children, we can interpret the constant. Specifically, the predicted value of the self-placement on the left/right scale for someone who has no children is 5.506.

Next, the sign of the coefficient for the number of children is positive. This means that as the number of children increases, self-placement on the left/right scale also increases (toward the political right). The size of the coefficient is .167, which means that we can add .167 to the constant for every additional child to determine the predicted self-placement on the left/right scale. We can do this for any number of children between zero and seven. (Again, remember that it is not advised to use values outside the range of the independent variable to make predictions of the dependent variable. It does not make sense to use negative numbers or numbers higher than seven for this variable.)

And is this coefficient significant? The *p* value for the number of children is .000, which means that the variable is significant at the .05 level. This suggests that the relationship between the number of children and self-placement on the left/right scale is not likely chance, which means that the null hypothesis that the number of children does not influene left/right ideological placement can be rejected. In addition, the confidence interval does not contain a coefficient of 0.

What happens now when we add both independent variables in a multivariate regression equation?

Model 3

Placement on left/right scale$_i$ = α + ($\beta1$ $^\times$ education level$_i$) + ($\beta2$ $^\times$ number of children$_i$)

By now you should be adept at reading these tables. What do the statistics in the coefficients table tell us (Figure 9.15)?

First, look at the constant. Because both independent variables had a zero value with substantive meaning (education level = 0 means a respondent did not attend or complete university and number of children = 0 means a respondent did not have children), we can interpret this constant. It is 5.602. This means that the predicted self-placement on the right/left scale for someone who did not attend or complete university and who does not have children is 5.602. (Remember, however, that you would not be able to interpret this constant if any of your independent variables did not have a zero with substantive meaning.)

Descriptive Statistics

	Mean	Std. Deviation	N
Self positioning in political scale	5.80	2.048	2157
educationbinary	.5892	.49209	2157
How many children do you have	1.75	1.606	2157

Model Summary

Model	R	R Square	Adjusted R Square	Std. Error of the Estimate
1	.136[a]	.018	.018	2.030

a. Predictors: (Constant), How many children do you have, educationbinary

Coefficients[a]

Model		Unstandardized Coefficients B	Std. Error	Standardized Coefficients Beta	t	Sig.	95.0% Confidence Interval for B Lower Bound	Upper Bound
1	(Constant)	5.602	.087		64.348	.000	5.431	5.773
	educationbinary	-.147	.089	-.035	-1.648	.100	-.323	.028
	How many children do you have	.162	.027	.127	5.914	.000	.108	.216

a. Dependent Variable: Self positioning in political scale

FIGURE 9.15: Results from a Multivariate Regression, Two Independent Variables and Self-Placement on the Left/Right Scale

Second, we look at the signs of the two coefficients, one for each independent variable. The coefficient for the education level independent variable is negative, whereas the coefficient for the number of children independent variable is positive. This remains consistent with the results when each variable was included on its own in Models 1 and 2. Next, look at the size of the coefficients. The coefficient for education level is –.147, whereas the coefficient for the number of children is +.162. The magnitude of the result for education is not large since the only meaningful comparison is between the 0 (high school education or less) and 1 (some college or more) categories. Although the coefficient for the number of children is only slightly larger than the coefficient for education level, the magnitude of the effect for the number of children is somewhat greater, especially since eight categories were included in the original variable (0 = no children up to 7 = seven children). This means that the predicted value of someone who has seven children is more than an entire point higher on the left/right scale than the value of someone who has no children.

What about the significance of these variables? From the coefficients table we see that the p value for the coefficient for education level is .100, whereas the p value for the coefficient for the number of children is .000. Thus, the coefficient for the number of children is significant and the coefficient for education level is not. In addition, the confidence level for education contains the possibility of a 0 coefficient, whereas the confidence level for the number of children does not. This means that the number of children variable has more explanatory power than the education variable for explaining variation in the left/right scale. This result is not entirely surprising, given the very small size of the coefficient for education level, both when it was included on its own in a single-variable regression equation and when it was included alongside number of children. Although it was significant on its own, it lost significance when included with another variable with greater explanatory power. Again, this is the benefit of using multivariate regression: it allows us to test which of several independent variables is the most significant for explaining a particular outcome.

EXAMPLE FROM POLITICAL SCIENCE

Kenny, Paul D. 2015. "The Origins of Patronage Politics: State Building, Centrifugalism, and Decolonization." *British Journal of Political Science* 45 (1): 141–71.

Although political corruption is damaging to the economic and political health of a country, patronage politics is a relatively common feature around the globe. Why does patronage exist and why do some countries experience more of it than others? Using a mixed methods approach to incorporate qualitative hypothesis-confirming case studies (see Chapter 10) with a most similar system design that presents the results from several linear regression models, Kenny traces the origins of modern political patronage within a particular research population: former British colonies. His argument involves a key independent variable to explain why some former British colonies currently have different levels of patronage within them: the type of rule, direct or indirect, that Britain utilized to provide governance to the colonies before they achieved independence. Where there was direct rule, British authorities maintained political control and ruled through a centralized administration. Where there was indirect rule, native elites held significant power in different locations within a single colony and were able to maintain control and extract benefits from the British authorities who ruled through them. Kenny suggests that the type of rule used during the colonial period matters for modern-day patronage because where colonies were ruled directly, Britain was able to consolidate power and any political spoils were allocated directly from a single political center. As a result, the amount of patronage in such places should be less in the modern day since only one center of power should currently distribute patronage. However, where colonies were ruled indirectly, there were centrifugal forces that pulled power away from the center and transferred it to local elites who claimed legitimacy and demanded benefits from central leaders, leading to a greater proliferation of patronage. As a result, in the modern day, patronage should be higher in locations where a colony was governed by indirect rule because of the increased number of demands being made to the state from subnational units.

Kenny also includes the extent of economic development in each colony in 1950 as a second independent variable. Previous studies have found that where there is greater economic development, corruption is lower, and where there is less economic development, corruption is higher. Hence, Kenny also includes economic development as an independent variable.

To construct the empirical test, Kenny created a dataset using information pertaining to former British colonies. A variable to measure the first independent variable, the extent of direct rule, was borrowed from another study. The variable was made by combining information about the proportion of court cases that were decided by colonial courts, rather than native ones, and the size of the British police force in the colony. To measure economic development, the second independent variable was the logged gross domestic

CONTINUED

product (GDP) per capita in each colony in 1950. Finally, for the dependent variable of patronage Kenny took data from the World Bank's Worldwide Governance Indicators to measure modern-day levels of corruption, which was used as a proxy for patronage.[6] Because the primary interest was to determine whether the form of rule and the degree of economic development matter for explaining differences in modern-day patronage, Kenny averaged the scores for the World Bank's corruption measure between 1996 and 2010 for each country.

The World Bank's indicator for corruption, the dependent variable, is measured on an interval scale from –2.5 to +2.5 (moving from low levels of corruption (–2.5) to high levels of corruption (+2.5)). As a result, Kenny was able use ordinary least squares linear regression to determine whether and how the two independent variables are correlated with the dependent variable. The results are given in Table 9.1.[7]

First, note how the data are presented in three separate models. In Model 1, only direct rule was used as an independent variable; in Model 2, only the logged GDP per capita in 1950 was used as an independent variable; and in Model 3, both independent variables were used at the same time. Starting with Model 1, we see that the

coefficient for direct rule is negative. This means that for a one-unit change in the independent variable (moving from indirect to direct rule), corruption decreases (remember that corruption was measured from –2.5 to +2.5, from low to high corruption). Also, note that there are three asterisks next to the coefficient. This means that the coefficient was significant at a particular p level. The p levels used in the analysis are displayed at the bottom of Table 9.1: *** means that the coefficient's p value was below .01, ** means that the coefficient's p value was below .05, and * means that the coefficient's p value was below .10. Remember that the p value represents the probability of obtaining a particular result due to chance when the null hypothesis (that no relationship exists between the type of rule used in a colony and its current level of corruption) is true. Thus, the three asterisks next to coefficient indicates that the p value for the direct rule independent variable was below .01. As a result, Kenny can reject the null hypothesis that the type of rule is not related to corruption. To the contrary, the regression table shows that the type of rule Britain used for its colonies is significant in explaining differences in modern-day corruption and that, as colonies move from indirect to direct rule, corruption decreases.

TABLE 9.1: ANALYSIS OF MODELS 1–3

Ordinary least squares regression for corruption, taken from Kenny 2015

Independent variable	Model 1 β (Std. error)	Model 2 β (Std. error)	Model 3 β (Std. error)
Direct rule	–1.085*** (0.204)		–1.250*** (0.422)
Log gross domestic product per capita in 1950		–0.563*** (0.251)	0.233 (0.343)
N	32	22	22
Adj. R^2	.47	.47	.40

***$p \leq .01$, **$p \leq .05$, *$p \leq .10$.

---

6   In the World Bank's Worldwide Governance Indicators the data for "control of corruption" is measured from –2.5 to +2.5, where –2.5 represents no control of corruption and +2.5 represents great control of corruption. To make +2.5 represent higher corruption, Kenny reversed the ordering of the values.

7   Note that Table 9.1 represents only the first 3 models that Kenny presented in the article; several additional independent variables, such as precolonial development, precolonial population density, and settler population, were also offered to test their effect on the dependent variable. In all, 10 models were presented. To keep the presentation in this chapter as straightforward as possible, only the first 3 models are included here.

Note, too, that the coefficient for the logged GDP per capita independent variable in Model 2 (–0.563) is also negative. The negative coefficient suggests that as the logged GDP per capita in each colony in 1950 increases, the level of each country's current corruption decreases. The coefficient also has three asterisks next to it, which means that the *p* value for this variable was lower than .01. Thus, like the type of rule used in the colonies, in single-variable regression the logged GDP per capita in 1950 is also highly significant.

Model 3 includes both independent variables at the same time. In this model we see that the direct rule independent variable retains its sign, size (the coefficient's size actually increases slightly from Model 1 to Model 3), and significance (the *p* value must be below .01). However, note that the economic variable not only changes sign and size (relative to Model 2) but also loses significance when controlling for direct rule. These results suggest that the direct rule independent variable has more explanatory power than the economic independent variable. Controlling for the logged GDP per capita in each colony in 1950, differences in direct rule are significantly associated with the amount of corruption present in modern British postcolonial states. However, controlling for the type of rule that was used in a colony, the logged GDP per capita in 1950 is not significant. This demonstrates the power of regression analysis: it can tell us which of several independent variables is most significant for explaining variation in a dependent variable.

CONCLUSION

Keep in mind that this chapter has only provided the most basic introduction on how to perform and interpret the results from basic linear regression models. Most regression analyses are complicated, involve many variables, and require the researcher to understand the nature of the variables contained in the dataset for the statistical technique to work properly and be interpreted correctly. In addition, there are a number of important assumptions that must be satisfied by the data when using regression analysis. If these assumptions are violated, the results from regression can be problematic. Although it is beyond the scope of this book to cover each assumption, we can highlight a few as we conclude this section. One assumption is that the relationship between the independent and dependent variables is linear. Remember that the regression line in the ordinary least squares linear regression equation is a straight line. If the relationship between the independent and dependent variables is not linear, the estimates from the ordinary least squares regression equation will not be accurate.

Another assumption is that the independent variables in the analysis are not too similar to one another. Including two similar independent variables in the same equation produces a problem called **multicollinearity**. When two independent variables are highly correlated with each other, it is difficult to determine which of the two has more explanatory power. Hence, when you have multicollinearity in your model, it is advised that you remove one of the similar independent variables.

In addition, it is important to include enough observations in your analysis for the statistics of linear regression to work properly. A good rule of thumb is to include at least 10 observations for every independent variable you include in your analysis. This is why the professor example included 30 students; when three independent variables were included, at least 30 observations were necessary. Also, note that the regression analysis presented in the political science example involved 32 and 22 observations for equations that incuded only two independent variables (see the N at the bottom of the table). Regression cannot work properly unless a minimum number of observations are included.

Finally, for our purposes it was incumbent that the dependent variable have ordinal, interval, or ratio measurement. There are ways to use regression for dependent variables with nominal measurement, but those analyses are beyond the scope of this book. For binary dependent variables, for example, many researchers use **logistic regression** analysis, which generates predicted probabilities of an observation falling in either of the two categories of the binary dependent variable for a given array of independent variables. The interpretation of the coefficients from logistic analysis is more complicated than the interpretation of coefficients from linear regression analysis, however. Be aware that methodologists are continually finding new ways to study different types of variables through regression analysis. What you have learned here is just the beginning. Nonetheless, understanding the logic of ordinary least squares regression analysis and how to interpret regression results will prepare you well for futher study.

GLOSSARY

ADJUSTED R^2   A value of R^2 that takes the number of independent variables in the regression equation into account.

CONFIDENCE INTERVAL (FOR REGRESSION)   A range of values in which the true population coefficient is likely to fall.

CONSTANT   The predicted value of the dependent variable when the independent variable is zero.

LOGISTIC REGRESSION   A type of regression that uses a binary variable as a dependent variable that generates predicted probabilities of an observation falling in either of the two categories of the binary dependent variable for a given array of independent variables.

MULTICOLLINEARITY   When two independent variables are highly correlated with each other.

OMITTED VARIABLE BIAS   Leaving out independent variables that explain variation in the dependent variable.

ORDINARY LEAST SQUARES LINEAR REGRESSION   A type of regression analysis that requires a dependent variable with ordinal, interval, or ratio measurement and a relatively widespread distribution of values.

R^2   The percentage of variation in the dependent variable that is explained by the independent variable(s) included in the analysis.

REGRESSION ANALYSIS   Utilizes a sample of data to determine how variables are correlated or to produce estimates of a dependent variable based on the values of one or more independent variables.

STANDARD ERROR OF THE ESTIMATE   A measure of the accuracy of the predictions made by the regression line in the units of the dependent variable.

STANDARD ERROR OF THE COEFFICIENT   A measure of how precisely the regression model estimates the coefficient's value for the population.

UNSTANDARDIZED BETA COEFFICIENT   The slope of the line that best describes the relationship between the independent and dependent variables.

EXERCISES

Continue to use SPSS and the WVS dataset for the wave and country you are studying through your research to complete the following exercises.

Single-variable linear regression:

1. Use the following variables to run single-variable linear regression equations:

   Dependent: V198: Justifiable: Claiming government benefits to which you are not entitled.
   Independent: V131: Democracy: Governments tax the rich and subsidize the poor
   What does the regression analysis tell you? Is the constant interpretable? Examine the sign, size, and significance of the coefficient.

   Dependent: V138: Democracy: People obey their rulers.
   Independent: V95: Self-positioning in political scale.
   What does the regression analysis tell you? Is the constant interpretable? Examine the sign, size, and significance of the coefficient.

Multivariate linear regression

2. Perform a multiple-variable regression analysis with the following variables:

Independent 1: V59: Satisfaction with financial situation of household.
Independent 2: V84: Interest in politics.
Independent 3: V107: How much you trust: People of another nationality.
Dependent: V141: How democratically is this country being governed today?
What does the regression analysis tell you? Is the constant interpretable? Examine the sign, size, and significance of each coefficient. Which independent variable has the most explanatory power?

PAPER PROGRESS

In the last chapter you performed two forms of bivariate analysis to assess the relationships between your independent and dependent variables. Now use SPSS to continue your data analysis using ordinary least squares linear regression.

Step 1: Perform two single-variable linear regression models.
It is a good idea to perform single-variable regression analyses before including all your variables in a multiple regression model. It is instructive to know the sign, size, and significance of each independent variable on its own before including the variables together in a single equation. Since you have two independent variables, begin by doing two single-variable regression analyses: the first analysis will be between your variable with nominal measurement (the binary variable) and the dependent variable; the second will be between your variable with ordinal, interval, or ratio measurement and the dependent variable. Use caution in interpreting the sign, size, and significance of the coefficients in each model. Determine whether the null hypothesis associated with each independent variable can be rejected based on the results.

Step 2: Perform one multivariate linear regression model with your two independent variables.
Once the two single-variable regression analyses are complete, create a multiple regression equation that incorporates both independent variables in the same model. Use what you have learned to interpret the results and determine whether your hypotheses are supported. Based on the output, you should be able to answer the following questions:

Given your hypotheses, were the signs of the coefficients in the predicted direction?

What was the size of the coefficients? Controlling for the other variables in the equation, what is the change in the dependent variable for a one-unit change in each independent variable? Interpret the results carefully, given that one of your independent variables has only two possible values associated with it, whereas the second is measured with ordinal, interval, or ratio measurement.

Finally, were the coefficients for the independent variables significant? Was one significant but the other was not? Can the null hypothesis for either independent variable be rejected?

Step 3: Create a table to display your results.

In your paper you will continue your results and discussion section from the previous two chapters with your results from linear regression. To present your results, you should create a streamlined table to display the important information from the SPSS output. One such table, using the same variables from the paper progress section of Chapter 7, is below (Table 9.2). You can use the exact format of this table for your own information. The example used biological sex and satisfaction with financial situation of household as independent variables for explaining variation in respondents' opinions about whether taxing the rich and subsidizing the poor are essential characteristics of democracy.

Table 9.2 is similar to the political science example about former British colonies that was discussed previously. Multiple models are presented. Model 1 includes only the first independent variable for whether respondents believed that governments taxing the rich and subsidizing the poor is essential for

TABLE 9.2: EXAMPLE OF A TABLE FOR DISPLAYING RESULTS FROM REGRESSION ANALYSIS

Ordinary Least Squares Regression for Essential Characteristics of Democracy: Tax Rich and Subsidize Poor

Independent variable	Model 1 β (Std. error)	Model 2 β (Std. error)	Model 3 β (Std. error)
Biological sex	.401* (.116)		.433* (.115)
Satisfaction with financial situation of household		−.163* (.024)	−.166* (.024)
Constant	4.356	5.994	5.360
N	2,165	2,161	2,161
Adj. R^2	.005	.02	.026

*$p \leq .05$.

democracy. Table 9.2 provides the information associated with this variable's unstandardized beta coefficient (β) and the coefficient's standard error, which is also in the coefficients table. In essence, Model 1 is a single-variable linear regression equation with only biological sex included as the independent variable and the dependent variable. Model 2 then provides the results from the single-variable linear regression equation for the second independent variable, satisfaction with financial situation of household. Finally, Model 3 includes both independent variables together in a multiple-variable linear regression analysis. This is the equation that shows us whether one independent variable is significant while controlling for the other. This part of Table 9.2 is usually of greatest interest to the reader. Some researchers will include tables with several models in their results, even 10 or more. The number of equations a researcher presents often depends on the number of independent variables that were used in the research. Since your projects utilized two independent variables, your table should have three data columns: one for each single-variable regression equation and one to incorporate both variables in a single equation.

You may have noted, too, that the coefficients in Table 9.2 have an asterisk next to them. As mentioned previously, researchers often use an asterisk to let a reader know which of the independent variable coefficients are significant at a particular level. The level of significance is often placed after the table itself, as seen in the example. In this case, an asterisk is associated with a p value of .05 or less, which is the general standard for p values in social science research. Note that in Table 9.2, both independent variables are significant in the single-variable regression models and in the multivariate regression model. This means that the p value associated with the coefficients for both independent variables in the three models was lower than .05. The absence of an asterisk would mean that the p value for a coefficient was not significant, in other words, greater than or equal to .05. Using asterisks in this way is common among researchers in political science to denote when a variable is significant in a regression analysis.

At the end of your table, you should include the constant, the N (number of observations), and the adjusted R^2 (adj. R^2). This is standard practice when political scientists present the results of their regression analyses. The N is in the descriptive statistics table and the adjusted R^2 is in the model summary table. Note that the number of observations can change from model to model; this simply denotes that data are not present for all possible variables for all possible observations in a given model.

Once you create your table and fill it with information, you will need to discuss your results, which is discussed more fully in Chapter 10.

COMING UP

Now that you have completed some quantitative analysis for your study and have created tables to present your results, the next step is to move on to qualitative analysis. You can use qualitative information to further study the relationships between and among your variables.

QUALITATIVE ANALYSIS THROUGH CASE STUDIES

Quantitative analysis utilizes numeric data to test hypotheses about the relationships between or among numeric variables. By contrast, qualitative analysis uses a researcher's interpretation of nonnumeric data to reach conclusions about a particular topic. Unlike quantitative analysis, qualitative analysis tends to be highly complex and open ended. There is no straightforward p value in qualitative research to help you determine whether a result is significant. Rather, when performing qualitative analysis a researcher must find meaning in different forms of information, such as the transcripts from interviews or focus groups, notes from observation, or the study of primary or secondary documents.

CASE STUDIES

For many researchers in political science, qualitative research is often captured by the general term case study.[1] As explained in Chapter 5, a case study case involves a study of an event or phenomenon in one place or at one time. It is a thorough investigation of a particular phenomenon in a bounded context. A case study subject can be as broad as a country or government or as specific as an individual or single policy. It may involve a process, a law, a group, or a movement. It can be any social phenomenon that a researcher identifies as important for analysis. The researcher defines the parameters of both the object

---

1   The typology of qualitative research that is presented in this chapter is relatively simple. In practice, the field of qualitative research is extensive and many typologies for different types of qualitative work exist in the literature. For example, for some researchers, especially in other disciplines, case studies represent one method among many to answer questions through qualitative research.

of investigation and the time period under which the phenomenon is studied for his or her definition of the case study.

The rest of this chapter is designed to help you develop a case study. How to perform case studies will be presented in four steps: (1) determining what is to be studied; (2) gathering information; (3) analyzing what was collected through content analysis; and (4) writing the case study.

HOW TO CONDUCT CASE STUDIES: STEP 1, DETERMINING WHAT IS TO BE STUDIED

The first step in conducting a case study is to choose a case. Here, the lessons from previous chapters apply: how each case is chosen will impact the potential generalizability of the overall study. Cases in case studies are chosen in a nonrandom fashion. As a result, the cases involved in a case study form a non-probability sample of a research population. This means that the generalizability of a case study's findings is tricky. Nonetheless, with a careful research design, generalizability is still possible and, for many researchers in political science, desirable. How generalizable a case study's findings are to other cases is called **external validity**. Researchers who engage in case study research often provide some explanation in their final reports to demonstrate the extent to which they believe a case study's findings are externally valid. (But do not confuse external validity in case study research with the face validity or content validity of an indicator when measuring a concept—see Chapter 6).

Methodologists from different disciplines define case studies in different ways, and you should be aware that significant disagreement exists, even among qualitative specialists in political science, as to how to appropriately categorize case studies. For our purposes, a relatively straightforward typology developed by Jack Levy (2008) will be used to describe four main categories of cases.[2]

First, **idiographic case studies** are designed to understand the complexity of a case for its own sake. These case studies are not used to generate theory or test hypotheses. Rather, an idiographic case study is used to provide a thorough description, interpretation, or understanding of a case that a researcher identifies as important or interesting for analysis. For example, a researcher could conduct an idiographic case study of a particular local government by watching committee sessions and plenary assemblies, interviewing representatives,

---

2   Jack Levy, 2008, "Case Studies: Types, Designs, and Logics of Inference," *Conflict Management and Peace Science* 25 (1), 1–8.

studying the letters that citizens write local officials, and analyzing both the proposed bills and the passed laws that the government produces. The purpose of the analysis is not to test any particular hypothesis or support a theory; rather, the ambition of the case study is to understand as much as possible about how a particular local government functions.

Next, **hypothesis-generating case studies** are used to generate hypotheses that could be tested in other contexts. Levy (2008) notes that hypothesis-generating case studies do not necessarily contribute to theory. Rather, they contribute to the process of creating theory by providing inductive observations about a case. (Remember from Chapter 4 that theory in political science is usually based on inductive observation, deductive reasoning, and insights from the literature. Hypothesis-generating case studies provide the inductive observations necessary to develop a theory, but the theory would also require deductive reasoning and insight from the literature to be complete.) In the case study of the local government, a researcher would perform a hypothesis-generating case study if he or she used the information obtained through the case study to develop a general hypothesis that could be tested with information from other local governments. For example, imagine that research on a particular local government concluded that committees are important arenas through which local politicians can work across party lines to accomplish mutual goals. The hypothesis that emerges from the work suggests that local governments that use committees extensively to draft and debate policies are more likely to pass policy outcomes that reflect the preferences of many different parties, as opposed to local governments that do not utilize committees extensively. This hypothesis, supported in the one case that was studied, could now be tested in other contexts.

The third type of case study is the **hypothesis-testing case study**, which is used to test a hypothesis that has been derived from a theory. More than one hypothesis-testing case can be involved in a single study. Hypothesis-testing case studies are often used for the comparative case study method that assesses how one value of a certain independent variable is associated with a specific value in a dependent variable for one or more cases at the same time. The ambition of including multiple hypothesis-testing case studies in a single design is to reproduce expectations about the predicted relationship between an independent variable and a dependent variable. This means that the cases are not necessarily chosen because of how they represent a research population, although they are still part of the research population. Rather, they are chosen because they either (1) demonstrate different relationships between the independent and dependent variables for theoretical reasons (i.e., one value of the independent variable is expected to produce a specific value of the dependent variable for one case, whereas another value of the independent variable is expected to produce a different value of the dependent variable for the second case); or (2) demonstrate similar relationships between variables (i.e., the cases exhibit the same relationship between the independent variable and the dependent variable). This distinction is analogous to most similar and most different comparative designs that were discussed in Chapter 5.

Let's return to the example of the research on local governments as an example of how case studies can be used to test hypotheses. Imagine that a researcher, through an extensive literature review, has established that legislative committees are important arenas through which politicians from opposing political parties can interact in a less adversarial way in local governments. The researcher borrows this insight and develops a theory to further suggest that size of a committee is an important variable explaining why some politicians behave more collegially than others in a committee setting in local governments. The size of the committees matters because collective action problems are more easily resolved when a smaller group of people is involved in making a decision. Thus, the smaller the committee, the more likely the politicians are to interact in a consensual way that integrates as many preferences as possible, and the larger the committee, the more likely the politicians are to interact in an adversarial way that privileges the interests of only the majority. To confirm these hypotheses, the researcher deliberately chooses two local governments to study further: one local government characterized by small committees and one local government characterized by large committees. The ambition of the research, then, is to assess how the size of the committees directly contributes to how politicians interact with each other, which influences the policy outcomes from each type of committee.

Finally, **plausibility probes**, of which **illustrative cases** is a common type, are used to demonstrate how a theory may be applied to different cases. These case studies are often short and are not necessarily designed to test specific hypotheses. Rather, illustrative cases "give the reader a 'feel' for a theoretical argument by providing a concrete example of its application, or to demonstrate the empirical relevance of a theoretical proposition by identifying at least one relevant case" (Levy 2008, 6–7). Illustrative case studies are sometimes used to complement large-n statistical analyses to show how some cases do conform to what was suggested in a theory. For example, imagine that a researcher had compiled a great deal of information about committees in many local governments and had determined through quantitative research that the policy outcomes from local governments with larger committees are indeed more partisan (reflecting the party with the majority representation) than policy outcomes from local governments with smaller committees. An illustrative case study of a particular local government could show how the variables (the size of committees in a local government and the degree to which policy outcomes reflect partisan preferences) "play out" in a particular local government to which a researcher happens to have access.

The case study you will perform for your project on political attitudes and values will be based on a single illustrative case. Your case will be the specific location where people who represent your research population can be found. For example, if you chose to study people in the millennial generation, your case will be your academic institution because the people you will interview for your case study will likely be your classmates.[3] However, if you chose a particular demographic characteristic in Chapter 3 to create a specific research population, the case you identify for your case study will be the place you visit to interview participants who represent your research population. If you chose to study older people, for example, you could visit a retirement community and interview participants there. The case for your case study would become the retirement community. Your illustrative case is the specific location where you find people who are representative of the characteristic you identified for your research population who agree to be interviewed for your project. (By now you should also have IRB approval to conduct the interviews for your project.)

The first step in conducting a case study is to identify the case and what type it is. This is important because how the case is chosen and how information from the case is gathered (step 2) will have implications for how any research conclusions are externally valid.

HOW TO CONDUCT CASE STUDIES: STEP 2, GATHERING INFORMATION

The specific information that a researcher chooses to evaluate when conducting a case study is usually selected carefully. There is no one specific method of gathering information that is always appropriate when conducting a case study. The best piece of advice is to determine which types of information best answer your research question. The most common methods for gathering information for case studies in political science are field research, a study of documents, or a combination of both.

---

3   Your instructor likely will set aside some class time so that students can interview each other.

Field Research

Field research involves a researcher leaving the workplace to gather data. As the name suggests, field research involves the researcher going "into the field"; the researcher must travel to where the respondents, participants, or events are to collect information. The field is defined by the parameters of the research. If you leave your classroom to interview people who represent your research population, you will be doing field research. The most common tools of field research are interviews, focus groups, and direct observation.

Interviews are one of the most popular methods of gathering qualitative data in political science. Interviews allow researchers to obtain firsthand information from selected subjects that will hopefully help a researcher answer a research question. Before conducting an interview, researchers usually write an **interview schedule**, which is a list of all the questions a researcher plans to ask a respondent. For qualitative analysis, interviews are usually either semistructured or unstructured. The interview schedule will likely contain questions that can serve as indicators for the independent and dependent variables in an analysis.

Semistructured interviews are common in political science. In semistructured interviews, a researcher begins with a formal interview schedule and asks specific questions in a particular order during the course of the interview, but then allows the conversation to deviate from the original questions when appropriate. This flexibility creates an atmosphere in which the respondent can guide the conversation in a way that the researcher may not have anticipated. After a respondent finishes with a particular discussion based on one of the interview questions, the researcher will then ask the next question on the interview schedule. In this way, semistructured interviews stay true to the original question list, but allow a respondent to deviate from the interview schedule where appropriate so that additional information about a topic can be obtained. You should use semistructured interviews when you interview the participants for your case study. Ask in-depth questions about the variables you included in your analysis. For example, if you would like to know about someone's placement on the left/right ideological spectrum, you could ask the respondent questions about when he or she decided to identify with a particular side, whether other people in his or her family or circle of friends share the opinions, or what experiences drove him or her to that point of view. Then, based on the responses, you could ask follow-up questions so that the respondent's answers can be as complete as possible.

Unstructured interviews are those in which the researcher asks open-ended questions that allow the respondent to guide most of the conversation.

Questions are not necessarily asked in a particular order, and questions that the researcher might have written in advance may not get asked at all depending on how the researcher interprets the conversation at the time of the interview. The main difference between semistructured interviews and unstructured interviews is the degree of spontaneity and control the researcher exercises during the interview. A researcher conducting a semistructured interview will likely return to the interview schedule, even when the conversation between the researcher and respondent occasionally goes off course. But a researcher conducting an unstructured interview will likely allow the conversation to veer dramatically from the original topic so that the information from the interview flows organically. This might allow the researcher to discover unanticipated patterns in the responses. As opposed to **structured interviews**, which are generally used for quantitative analysis (with closed-ended questions that are easily coded into quantitative-level data), the benefit of both semistructured and unstructured interviews is that a researcher can ask follow-up questions that flow from the interview process itself.

Interviews involve one researcher and one participant at a time. Another method of gathering information is the **focus group**, which is a discussion that a researcher conducts with several people at the same time. Rather than asking questions of specific individuals, in focus groups the researcher presents a topic and the participants begin a group discussion that hopefully provides the researcher with valuable information. One of the benefits of a focus group is that participants can respond directly to each other's comments. The idea of a focus group is not for the researcher to engage in a ping-pong style of conversation (one question/one answer) with respondents. Rather, focus groups provide opportunities for participants to agree or disagree with each other and to state why they have the opinions they do in a controlled, and hopefully civil, setting.

How you structure a focus group will depend on the research question. For example, if the purpose of the research is to understand why a group of people is expected to have a similar attitude about something, the researcher may deliberately put similar people together in a focus group so that the group can collectively provide information about why they hold that similar attitude. The participants in the group can build ideas from one another, although it is possible that the information from the group might reveal areas of difference that were originally unanticipated. But if the idea of the focus group is to understand why people differ on a particular issue, the researcher could deliberately place people who are expected to have different points of view in the same focus group so that areas of agreement or disagreement can be aired. The information gleaned from such a focus group is highly valuable because the presence of different perspectives coming from the diversity within a group allows individual subjects to provide reasons for agreement or disagreement on issues.

The number of people a researcher should include in a focus group will depend on the research question. Of course, as the number of participants increases, the ability to gather a lot of information from each participant in a given time frame decreases. But at the same time, if the number of participants is too low, there might not be enough variety of opinion among the participants of the focus group. As a general guideline, including between five and eight participants is a good target, especially for newer researchers. This keeps the number low enough that the researcher can meaningfully hear from each participant and at the same time allows for significant diversity of opinion among the group.

Any field work that requires you to interact directly with human subjects will require institutional review. Specifically, you must obtain informed consent from any person who agrees to participate in your research. This was covered in Chapter 3 and Appendix A; by now you (or your instructor) should have the appropriate documentation that demonstrates that your academic institution has approved your project.

The last method used in field research is **observation**, which can be a powerful tool in case study analysis. Observation allows researchers to collect data by watching a political process in real time to report on it. Generally, there are two types of observation, **participant observation**, in which the researcher actually participates in the process under study, and **direct observation**, in which the researcher simply witnesses the process from the side. Participant observation is often used in social science disciplines like anthropology or sociology, whereas most political science researchers use direct observation to gather data. Direct observation allows the researcher to understand how a process unfolds from beginning to end. For example, a researcher who wishes to understand how citizens participate in town meetings might attend a number of town meetings to see how citizens participate: noting how many citizens attend the meeting, what type of information is disseminated, how often citizens speak, and what types of questions are asked of the authorities. Direct observation allows the researcher to get a broad understanding of how a process works. Overall, the objective of the inquiry is to understand the process under study as deeply as possible so that the researcher can develop a detailed description of how the process operates in practice.

Analysis of Documents

Another way to gather information for case study research is through an analysis of documents. Although you will not use a study of documents for the case studies you will complete as part of your project on political values and attitudes, you will be encouraged in the last chapter of the book to analyze documents as a means to perform two hypothesis-confirming case studies as part of a second research project you could complete. Generally, researchers group documents into primary or secondary sources. **Primary sources** are original documents that were created during a particular event. Such documents may include different forms of communication, such as the transcripts of speeches or letters and, more recently, blogs or email messages. Primary documents also include official records, such as the constitution of a country, the standing orders of an institutional body, the text of bills and laws, or the verdict in a court case. Primary sources also include media stories found in the news, which may include newspapers, news magazines, Internet news sources, or the transcripts of television news. Some primary documents are housed in special libraries or archives where special access permission may be required in advance. Because they are located in a specific place, researchers will likely need to travel to where the documents are located to study them. However, many primary documents have now been digitized so that researchers can access them easily through the Internet. This is true, for example, for laws passed by democratic countries; many countries have online archives that are available for public use, such as Thomas at the Library of Congress in the United States or Hansard in the United Kingdom.

By contrast, **secondary sources** are documents created after an event took place that involve an analysis, commentary, or interpretation of something that has already happened. Secondary sources are most often found in the scholarly literature that can be accessed through a library. Research articles, books, working papers, and academic reports that study particular events are the most common secondary sources. Researchers access these sources when they want to understand how other scholars have interpreted something about their case. The use of such material in case studies is common in political science, where researchers often utilize the analysis, commentary, or interpretation made by other scholars in the reporting and understanding of a case.

A Word about Triangulation

Triangulation is the process through which multiple sources are used to answer a research question. One of the benefits of case study research is the ability to triangulate from multiple sources to gather information. Rarely is a case study based off of only one type of information. More often, a researcher will review multiple sources of information to provide as much evidence as possible for a particular claim the researcher wishes to make. For example, a researcher who wishes to do a case study on a particular political event could (1) conduct interviews with people who witnessed the event, (2) read news stories about the event as it unfolded through a media research, and then (3) study other scholar's interpretations of the event. In this way, the researcher will have created a case study research design that combines field work (interviews) with an analysis of both primary sources (news stories) and secondary sources (research articles and other scholarly materials that have been published about the event).

In general, researchers are limited in what they can do with regard to collecting information. Field work is often costly and time-consuming, and researchers may not have access to all the primary and secondary sources that would help them with their research projects. Constraints concerning time, money, and access are thus very real in case study research. The best advice is for the researcher to approach the research process as efficiently as possible to determine which types of information are the most accessible and will provide the best information to answer the research questions.

Sampling in Case Study Research

For both field work and the study of documents, a researcher must make important decisions about who to interview, what to observe, or how many sources to review for any given case study. We can return to the discussion of sampling from Chapter 5 to understand some of the different ways a researcher may make these choices. Rather than choosing information sources randomly, qualitative researchers overwhelmingly utilize nonprobability sampling methods. Specifically, he or she may select a quota, convenience, purposive, or snowball sample for the gathering of information for a case study. These nonrandom methods of gathering data for a case study have implications for external validity, mentioned earlier in the chapter. The way the information is collected will likely limit the generalizability of the results to the other cases within the research population.

Remember that a quota sample is chosen when a researcher is guided by a particular characteristic within a population and chooses a sample based on variation within that characteristic. Take, for example, a researcher who wants to conduct interviews at a particular university for a case study to understand why students vote in national elections. She knows that in general a bigger sample is preferable to a smaller one, but she has only a limited amount of time to conduct interviews. As a result, she decides to interview 10 college students at a local academic institution (let's call it College U). The case for the case study is College U and the research population for her case study is "students at College U." She knows from other studies that about half of College U's population leans toward a particular political party (we will call it Party A) and the other half leans toward a second political party (Party B). To create a quota sample based on party leaning, she deliberately chooses to interview 5 students who lean toward Party A and 5 students who lean toward Party B. (But remember that before she can conduct any interviews, she must obtain IRB permission, explain the project to potential participants, and obtain informed consent from those willing to participate; again, this is true for any research that involves direct contact with human subjects.)

Another sampling strategy is for the researcher to create a convenience sample for the case study, which involves the collection of information from the people, groups, events, or documents to which the researcher happens to have access. Continuing with the earlier example, rather than using a quota sample, the researcher could visit College U on a particular day when she knows a lot of students will be around and set up a table outside the main dining hall so she can recruit participants. The students who provide informed consent and agree to be interviewed constitute a convenience sample since the researcher interviewed 10 students she happened to meet at the table on the day she visited College U. Keep in mind that the people you will interview for your case study for your paper on political attitudes and values will form a convenience sample because you will interview people to whom you happen to have access on a particular day at the location that is your case.

Another type of sample is the purposive sample, which involves a researcher identifying people, groups, specific events, or particular documents that the researcher believes will provide the best and most helpful information for the case study. To create a purposive sample, the researcher studying the determinants of voting among students at College U could deliberately request 10 interviews only from members of College U's student government, with the reasoning that student government representatives will likely provide the best information about why students are motivated to participate in national elections.

Finally, the snowball sample involves the collection of information through a system of referrals from one person, group, event, or document to the next. In other words, the information gleaned from one of these sources gives the researcher an idea of what to study next. To create a snowball sample for the case study, the researcher interviewing students at College U could interview an influential member of the student government and then ask that participant to identify another person who might know about the research topic. The process continues until the researcher finishes 10 interviews.

These sampling methods presented above are also applicable to the other ways information can be collected for case studies, such as observation or the study of primary or secondary resources. For example, take another researcher who wants to do a case study on committee meetings in a specific state legislature to understand how they operate. He could choose to observe committees based on variation of a particular characteristic such as committee topic area (quota sample), the committees to which the researcher happens to have access on a given day (convenience sample), the committees he suspects might best help him answer his research question (purposive sample), or the committees that are referred to him by committee members on committees he has already studied (snowball sample).

How much Information is Necessary for Case Studies?

During the data collection phase for a case study, in which a researcher either conducts field work or collects documents, what defines "enough" information will change from researcher to researcher and from case study to case study. Generally, researchers can consider themselves finished with data collection once a **saturation point** has been reached. The saturation point is the point in a research program when the collection of additional information becomes redundant.

To give an example of when a saturation point is reached, let's return to an example mentioned above: the case study on how legislative committees function in a particular state legislature. Let's say that the researcher wants to understand how legislative committees contribute to the content of legislation that is eventually passed in the main legislative body. The researcher would like to understand how powerful such committees are in the revision of legislative bills and decides to conduct a number of interviews to collect information. After obtaining IRB permission to conduct the study, he contacts several state representatives who serve on committees and begins to conduct one-on-one interviews to ask specific questions about the research topic. In the beginning, each interview provides some new information and, as a result, the researcher is genuinely learning about how the committees contribute to the legislative process. However, during the 9th interview, the researcher realizes that every piece of information that was communicated through the interview was something the researcher had already learned from previous interviews. The same realization occurs during the 10th and 11th interviews. At that point, the researcher has evidence that the saturation point has been reached and that conducting further interviews will likely not provide additional information. This is the point when the researcher can feel confident about the information he or she has gathered for the case study and can probably stop gathering information. The saturation point may also be reached through observation and document gathering. It occurs when the researcher realizes that additional information will not add to his or her understanding of the case.

HOW TO CONDUCT CASE STUDIES: STEP 3, ANALYZING QUALITATIVE DATA

Regardless of how the qualitative data for a case study were accumulated, either through fieldwork or through the study of documents, researchers must have a systematic way of analyzing the information they collect. Just as there are different types of statistical tests you can perform using quantitative data, there are different ways of analyzing qualitative information. In this section we will briefly discuss two such methods, content analysis and process tracing. Content analysis is generally used on qualitative data that are collected from interviews, focus groups, observation, and primary documents, whereas process tracing is generally used when an analysis of secondary documents is involved.[4] The following discussion concentrates more on content analysis because you will use content analysis to analyze the interview data you will collect for your case study for your project on political values and attitudes. However, both content analysis and process tracing are common in qualitative research in political science.

Analyzing Qualitative Data through Content Analysis

For many researchers, **content analysis** is a popular way to analyze data gathered through fieldwork or a collection of primary sources. Content analysis is the analysis of nonnumeric text in a systematic way that allows a researcher to provide a description and analysis of what is contained in a qualitative dataset. Essentially, content analysis involves turning qualitative data into something that can be analyzed through some quantitative means.

The first step in content analysis is to create a qualitative dataset that can be analyzed. For field research, this usually includes the notes or transcripts from interviews, focus groups, or observation, depending on how the data were collected. Once the qualitative dataset is created, content analysis can be done in

---

4   Researchers can use content analysis for the study of secondary documents as well.

different ways. For researchers who are working with large amounts of text-based information, computer-based tools can help a researcher organize the material. Prominent examples in political science are NVivo and ATLAS.ti, which, among other functions, allow a researcher to code text-based data by quantifying how often a term appears in a word-based document or how often a particular word appears with other types of words in the same sentence. It is also possible to hand-code smaller amounts of qualitative data, as you will see in the paper progress section of this chapter.

The purpose of content analysis is to identify the codes, categories, and themes present in the qualitative dataset. **Codes** are particular words or phrases in the text, whereas **categories** are groupings of codes around a particular idea. To demonstrate how this works, take a researcher who wishes to understand whether participation in local political affairs (the independent variable) is related to political satisfaction (the dependent variable) among senior citizens in rural environments (the research population). To answer this research question, the researcher decides to conduct semistructured interviews with a number of senior citizens at a retirement community in a rural area. Since the researcher did not use an electronic device to record the interviews, after each interview he transcribes the detailed notes he took and creates a qualitative dataset. To understand words representing the dependent variable, the researcher must study the text from the interviews to look for specific words that capture the essence of being "satisfied" and specific words that capture the essence of being "unsatisfied." There are multiple ways to express being satisfied or unsatisfied. Words like "happy" and "pleased" and "content" would likely be assigned with a satisfied code, whereas words like "unhappy" and "displeased" and "discontented" would likely be assigned with an unsatisfied code. Although satisfied and happy are different words, they represent the same code because they represent the same term. In this way, the specific vocabulary used by the respondents can become an important and interesting point for analysis.

A category is created when different codes that represent a particular idea are combined. For example, for the independent variable of political participation the researcher could have developed categories based on codes that represent different forms of political participation that emerged from the qualitative dataset. These categories are not synonyms for codes. Rather, they are different codes that are related to a grouping category. For example, based on the codes that emerged from his content analysis, the researcher described above could create a category for "participation in elections" (codes = voting, campaigning, or donating money to parties during electoral cycles), another category for "participation in issues" (codes = writing letters or signing petitions), another category for "participation by protest" (codes = marching or engaging in boy-cotts), and yet another category for "personal participation" (codes = discussing politics with friends, writing political blogs, or participation in social media that pertains to politics). Note that the individual codes associated with each category are not synonyms like the adjectives for satisfied or unsatisfied were. Each distinct type of political participation merits its own category.

Once the codes and categories are properly identified, they can used to identify **themes**. Themes are relationships between codes and categories to produce a general idea. In some ways, the identification of themes in a qualitative dataset can be used as a means to test research hypotheses. Granted, you cannot test hypotheses in the same way you did when you performed quantitative analysis, but it is still possible to provide empirical evidence that a theme is present in a case study by making connections between the codes and categories in a qualitative dataset.

Themes emerge when particular codes or categories are systematically presented in the same space with other codes or categories to produce a general idea about something. Furthermore, if the presence of a code or category that represents the independent variable is consistently related to a code or category that represents the dependent variable, a theme that supports the research hypothesis may be identified. For example, do respondents who participate extensively in politics also report high satisfaction with the political process? Are the codes or categories linked in this particular way in the qualitative dataset? This type of analysis allows you to ask other detailed questions, too. For example, were certain types of participation—such as participation in elections or participation in issues—reported in conjunction with either higher or lower levels of satisfaction? Did respondents who do not participate in politics also report low levels of satisfaction with the political system? Identifying themes through content analysis in this way allows the researcher to evaluate whether research hypotheses have empirical support.

Analyzing Qualitative Data through Process Tracing

Process tracing is another qualitative method that allows a researcher to create an analysis of how an outcome occurred by developing a precise timeline and causal argument to carefully explain how one factor may have caused another. Process tracing involves describing important events or ideas that serve as key variables in an analysis as fully as possible to construct a plausible argument to determine how they developed over time. In-depth accurate description of each variable for the case is thus important. The main ambition of process tracing is to verify proposed causal mechanisms between variables. In doing so, it is not just a matter of showing how one value on an independent variable is associated with a particular value on a dependent variable. To the contrary, process tracing allows a researcher to show precisely why a particular relationship was observed. It is not enough to simply show that the relationship exists; the purpose of process tracing is to demonstrate *why* the evidence supports a particular hypothesis, which in turn supports a given theory. An important element to this process is ruling out alternative explanations that might have caused an outcome. The evidence that is presented to substantiate the claims made through process tracing can come from a variety of sources, including academic articles and books, reports, working papers, the news, and other forms of primary and secondary sources.[5] More information about process tracing is provided in Chapter 12.

Whether content analysis or process tracing is utilized, one of the benefits of in-depth qualitative analysis is the ability to further establish causality between variables. Here, we can return to the criteria for causality mentioned in Chapter 4 to determine whether the qualitative data support a researcher's theory about why one or more independent variables should be correlated in some way with a dependent variable. First, remember that the two variables should be empirically correlated. Second, the independent variable must occur before the dependent variable. And third, the correlation between the independent and dependent variables must not be caused by the presence of a third variable, which in reality is influencing variation in both the independent and the dependent variables. The relationship between the two variables should not be spurious.

Related to this point is yet another benefit of both content analysis and process tracing: the methods allow for the identification of additional explanations that may not have been anticipated in the beginning of the research process. Specifically, during the course of the study, a researcher may identify unexpected variables that provide clues as to why a specific outcome was observed. This is important because to this point we have been working with prespecified hypotheses about the relationships among variables; for most political science research, a researcher writes a theory, specifies a hypothesis, and then conducts empirical data analysis to determine whether the hypothesis is correct. Some scholars consider this a top-down approach: the theory comes first, and the empirical analysis comes second. However, one of the benefits of qualitative analysis—through content analysis and process tracing—is the

---

5   For more information on process tracing, see David Collier, "Understanding Process Tracing," *PS: Political Science and Politics* 41 (4): 823–30.

possibility of uncovering additional explanations for the outcomes we wish to explain. Since the nature of qualitative data is extremely complex and entails a much more complete picture of what people think, an event that happened, or how something works in practice, it is possible that a researcher will, in the process of qualitative data analysis, discover an important variable that was not included in the original theory. If the researcher becomes convinced that this new variable should be included in the theory, he or she may choose to add to or even rewrite the original theory to incorporate the new information. The result is called **inductive theory**. Inductive theory is useful when dealing with complicated data. In the creation of inductive theory, researchers remain open to the possibility that alternate explanations might emerge that better explain a particular outcome, as opposed to the ones that were originally proposed.

HOW TO CONDUCT CASE STUDIES: STEP 4, WRITING UP THE CASE STUDY

After a researcher has collected and analyzed qualitative data for a case study, he or she must write up the findings in a streamlined report. The best way to do this is to think about what in the data provides the most useful information for understanding the answer to the research question. Since data collection in case studies is often quite involved, it is necessary to determine which information is most relevant for the case study itself. Clearly, not every little point gleaned will be used; the case study would become too cumbersome and tedious and the reader would likely lose sight of the original focus. At this stage, it is useful to develop a hierarchy of information so that only the most relevant and powerful information is used in the case study itself. Information that is secondary can be referenced briefly or placed in a footnote.

The presentation of data for a case study is more of an art than an exact science. Case studies should be presented in a parsimonious and streamlined way that leaves the reader with an understanding of the general argument the case study is attempting to make. Some case studies will be extremely detailed; if this is the case, you must organize the material in a way that does not lose a reader. An introductory paragraph that outlines the overall case in the beginning of the text can also be helpful because it will give the reader an idea of what is coming next. Headers and footers in individual paragraphs may also help you organize the material. Always remember that other scholars will be reading your work and may even use it for their own studies; how you present the case study material will be crucial for how readers understand and digest it. More on how to present the results from a case study will be presented in the next chapter.

EXAMPLES FROM POLITICAL SCIENCE

Drutman, Lee, and Daniel Hopkins. 2013. "The Inside View: Using the Enron E-mail Archive to Understand Corporate Political Attention." *Legislative Studies Quarterly* **38 (1): 5–30.**

This case study of Enron attempts to understand the role of corporations in American politics and the importance that corporations put on their political activities, which the corporations hope will result in legislation that favors their interests. Studies that assess the relationship between corporations and politics are limited because most of the data concerning the relationship are often closed to the public. Thus, to further understand the importance corporations place on building relationships with political authorities, Drutman and Hopkins use a case study of Enron to create a qualitative dataset taken from 250,000 emails sent by high-level Enron employees to government authorities between 1999 and 2002. Enron was an enormous energy company that ultimately went bankrupt because of its accounting inconsistencies and rampant corruption. Emails sent between Enron employees and government officials were made public after Enron's collapse. The authors suggest that Enron provides a good case study for how corporations interact with political authorities because of Enron's interest in developing and profiting from deregulated energy contracts, specifically in electricity. Because of the potential benefits to Enron, Drutman and Hopkins suggest that the dataset containing the text from the emails should reveal information about how corporations interact with political authorities, what they prioritize, and how they go about achieving their goals.

Both automated and hand-coded content analyses were used to identify codes and categories in the emails' text. Of primary importance was the identification of emails that were "political" in nature. This was achieved by looking for specific codes among the emails that would flag a specific email as being political. Once the political emails were identified, coders were required to identify the following for each one: (1) the email's chief political concern, (2) the relevant government involved, (3) the government branch involved, (4) reference to any specific individual, and (5) reference to legislation. To make the case study more manageable, Drutman and Hopkins then concentrate specifically on the emails pertaining only to the "chief political concern" group. The ambition was to determine whether any codes or categories were consistently represented in these specific emails to describe

how Enron employees communicated with government authorities. The researchers developed five main categories based on the different political concerns found in the chief political concern emails. These categories were (1) campaign/elections, (2) monitoring, (3) legislative contacting, (4) opinion leadership, and (5) formal participation. For example, activities related to lobbying, fund-raisers, contributions, and serving as counsel for candidates were identified as codes and placed in the campaign/elections category. Specific codes for the remaining four categories were also identified and the chief political concern emails were then divided accordingly.

As part of the analysis, tables to demonstrate the total number of emails sent over time were presented. These tables show that the number of total emails sent by Enron employees increased steadily between 1999 and 2002. Of these emails, 41% were political in nature. Based on their elaborate system of identifying codes and categories for only the political emails, rich descriptive information about the emails in the chief political concern group was provided. A series of figures overwhelmingly demonstrates that the most common use of the political emails with a chief political concern was for activities related to the monitoring category. The monitoring category generally involved the exchange of information between Enron employees and government officials, such as the government's stance of electricity regulation or information collected by Enron employees or lobbyists. This category alone comprised 66% of all the political emails. Detailed information about the emails' content for the remaining categories (legislative contracting, formal participation, opinion leadership, and campaigns/elections) was also provided.

Contrary to expectation (that Enron employees were involved in trying to influence elections), a small portion (1%) of the political emails contained codes that were related to campaigns, elections, and fund-raising. Rather, most of the Enron employees' political attention was focused on information sharing (the monitoring category) and, to a lesser but still important extent, on formal participation in making rules. This suggests that Enron employees were using email to participate in everyday decision making rather than influencing elections. This is particularly relevant for massive companies like Enron that might have monopolies over certain types of information that policy makers find valuable. The final conclusion, then, is that the way corporations interact with political authorities is complex and involves more than what might have been expected. The case study would have external validity if it could be shown that other corporations exhibit similar patterns of interaction between employees and government officials.

Sawer, Marian. 2012. "What Makes the Substantive Representation of Women Possible in a Westminster Parliament? The Story of RU486 in Australia." *The International Political Science Review* 33 (3): 320–35.

In this case study of the passage of a particular law, Sawer investigates how legislation making RU486 available as form of chemical abortion for women in Australia was introduced and passed in the Australian parliament in 2006. To answer her research question about how the law was passed, Sawer conducted semi-structured interviews in 2007 with eight senators and several members of nongovernmental organizations that promote women's interests. The story of the passage of the legislation is a puzzle because the bill that was submitted to parliament was sponsored by four women representing four different political parties in Australia's senate. Two of the women came from parties in the government's coalition, and the remaining two came from parties in opposition. The passage of the RU486 legislation marked the first time that such cross-party sponsorship had occurred in Australia. Sawer's case study was designed to develop a theory to explain how this happened and what lessons can be gleaned for the prospects of cross-party collaboration in other legislative bodies, specifically in Westminster institutions in which such collaboration among parties in government and opposition is rarely seen or expected.

To develop her theory, Sawer borrowed from preestablished ideas of "critical actors" and "critical junctures." The four women involved in sponsoring the bill and the other women in the senate, representing 35% of the legislative body, were the critical actors. The critical juncture involves the fact that at the time of the bill's introduction, the legislature was nearing the end of its electoral term. The interviews Sawer conducted revealed that the four women who sponsored the legislation were nearing the end of their political careers as well, which meant that the female senators did not have much to lose politically in sponsoring the bill. The intersection of the critical actors at a critical juncture in large part explains the bill's successful passage in parliament. But in her analysis of the interview data, Sawer also noted the important role a specific "parliamentary friendship group" played in giving the women a space to collaborate in the first place. Parliamentary friendship groups are cross-body organizations that give legislators an opportunity to interact based on mutual interests that transcend party divisions. Thus, based on her analysis, Sawer understood that one particular parliamentary friendship group allowed the women involved to develop trust among them, which eventually led to their joint plan in bringing the legislation to parliament.

Most of the article involves a rich description in how the passage of the bill happened. But it is clear that Sawer's ultimate purpose is to demonstrate how parliamentary institutions, as independent variables, can help facilitate different types of exchange and explain variation in political outcomes. The group gave the women a space and opportunity to develop trust and identify areas of potential cross-party collaboration. This is the central message of the article. The case study of the passage of a bill making RU486 available in Australia can thus be used to promote a theory that might have broader application. Cross-party collaboration can occur in other contexts, Westminster parliaments especially, where institutions like the parliamentary friendship group exist. The study would have external validity if the theory about parliamentary institutions can be shown to explain how cross-party collaboration exists in other contexts.

CONCLUSION

There is no one correct way to do a case study, especially since there are different types of cases and different methods that can be used. Case studies can be performed in four steps. The first is to identify the case study. Generally, there are four types of case studies: idiographic case studies, hypothesis-generating case studies, hypothesis-confirming case studies, and illustrative case studies. The second step is to specify whether the information gathered for a case study will come through field research (through interviews or focus groups) or through an analysis of primary or secondary documents. This involves determining what type of sample of information will be used (the different types of samples are quota, convenience, purposive, or snowball). The third step is to analyze what was collected through some systematic means, such as content analysis or process tracing. The last step is to write up the case study in a streamlined report. Establishing external validity, the extent to which a case study's findings are generalizable, is an important part of case study research.

GLOSSARY

CATEGORIES   Groupings of codes around a particular idea.

CODES   Particular words or phrases in a qualitative text.

CONTENT ANALYSIS   The analysis of nonnumeric text in a systematic way that allows a researcher to provide a description and analysis of what is contained in a qualitative dataset.

DIRECT OBSERVATION   A form of observation in which a researcher witnesses a process from the side.

EXTERNAL VALIDITY   How generalizable a case study's findings are to other cases.

FIELD RESEARCH   When a researcher leaves the workplace to gather data.

FOCUS GROUP   A discussion a researcher conducts with several people at the same time to obtain information about a research topic.

HYPOTHESIS-GENERATING CASE STUDY   A case study used to generate hypotheses that could be tested in other contexts.

HYPOTHESIS-TESTING CASE STUDY   A case study used to test a hypothesis that has been derived from a theory.

IDIOGRAPHIC CASE STUDY   A case study used to provide a thorough description, interpretation, or understanding of a case that a researcher identifies as important or interesting for analysis.

ILLUSTRATIVE CASE   A type of probability probe that provides a concrete example of how a theory operates in practice.

INDUCTIVE THEORY   Theory that is created when researchers study empirical information and discover alternate explanations that better explain a particular outcome, as opposed to the explanations that were originally proposed.

INTERVIEWS   A meeting between a researcher and participant that allows the researcher to obtain firsthand information about a research topic.

INTERVIEW SCHEDULE   A list of all the questions a researcher plans to ask a respondent.

OBSERVATION   Allows researchers to collect data by watching a political process in real time to report on it.

PARTICIPANT OBSERVATION   A form of observation in which a researcher participates in the process under study.

PLAUSIBILITY PROBES   Used to demonstrate how a theory may be applied to different cases.

PRIMARY SOURCES   Original documents created during a particular event.

SATURATION POINT   The point in a research program when the collection of additional information becomes redundant.

SECONDARY SOURCES   Documents that involve an analysis, commentary, or interpretation of something that has already happened.

SEMISTRUCTURED INTERVIEWS   Interviews in which a researcher begins with a formal interview schedule and asks specific questions in a particular order during the course of the interview, but then allows the conversation to deviate from the original questions when appropriate.

STRUCTURED INTERVIEWS   Interviews that are generally used for quantitative analysis, with closed-ended questions that are easily coded into quantitative-level data.

THEMES   Relationships between codes and categories that produce a general idea.

TRIANGULATION   The process through which multiple sources are used to answer a research question.

UNSTRUCTURED INTERVIEWS   Interviews in which a researcher asks open-ended questions that allow a respondent to guide most of the conversation.

EXERCISES

1. Imagine that you want to conduct illustrative case studies to explore the following research topics. For each one, identify (a) where you could go to

conduct interviews on the topic and (b) what kind of sample (quota, accidental, purposive, or snowball) you could construct:

The relationship between political ideology and positions on same-sex marriage among people who identify as being religious.
The relationship between socioeconomic status and political party choice among college students.
The relationship between education level and views on welfare among national legislators.

2. Think of a research question involving some aspect of being a student. Identify one independent variable and one dependent variable for the question. For example, how do study habits influence academic performance? Write a brief theory for why you think study habits influence academic performance and derive a research hypothesis from the theory. Next, write an interview schedule with questions pertaining to the research question. Ask two or three classmates to answer your questions as completely as possible while you take notes. Then transcribe your interviews to create a qualitative dataset. Once you have created your dataset, identify codes and categories in the text. Next, identify whether there are any themes in the text, in other words, were particular codes or categories systematically presented with others that would allow to confirm your hypothesis and possibly your theory? If not, what other factors emerged as important from the data?

PAPER PROGRESS

By now, you should have completed your quantitative analysis using data from the WVS. The quantitative data analysis should have demonstrated which independent variables were the most significant for explaining variation in your dependent variable.

Step 1: Identify the case and where you will go to conduct interviews. For the qualitative part of your research, you will perform an illustrative case study that incorporates semistructured interviews with people who represent your research population. The definition of the "case" will be the specific location where people who represent your research population can be found. For example, if you chose to study people in the millennial generation, you should conduct a number of interviews with classmates in your classroom. In doing so, the case for your case study will be your academic institution and you will create a convenience sample of people who happen to be in your class. If you chose to study a different group of people, you must identify where you can go to do field work and interview willing participants who represent your research population. Where you go becomes the case (for example, a church if Christian people are your research population or a local party office if people who belong to a specific political party are your research population). The idea is to keep the case bounded so that the case study is clearly defined and has as much external validity as possible. Depending on the sample you create, your conclusions may be generalizable to other people who represent the research population within your case. The number of interviews you conduct should be determined by your instructor based on the feasibility of finding individuals who represent your research population who are willing to be interviewed for your project.

Step 2: Write an interview schedule.

Once you identify where you want to do your interviews, you must write an interview schedule. The interview schedule is the list of questions you want to ask every person you interview. Since the interviews you will conduct are semistructured, you may find that you stray from the schedule you have set. This is part of the process, but be sure that your interview schedule includes questions that pertain to all the variables you are investigating through your analysis.

A good way to start an interview is to ask about how the respondent would score specifically on your dependent variable (although be sure not to call it a dependent variable, since most people do not use research terminology in regular speech). Ask the question exactly how it appears in the WVS and ask the respondent to provide an answer for it from 1 to 10 (as in the WVS). Then ask questions about why the respondent responded in the way he or she did. Ask the respondents to tell you their "stories" about their point of view concerning your dependent variable. Possible questions could include "How long have you had this point of view?" or "How strongly do you feel about your particular response?" or "What influences can you identify in your life that have compelled you to have this particular opinion?" An interview question like the latter is important because it allows the respondents to think about why they answered the way they did about the dependent variable *before* you add questions about the independent variables. Let the interviewee guide the discussion about his or her point of view concerning your dependent variable as fully as possible before you begin asking questions about your independent variables.

Once you have some information concerning a respondent's point of view about the dependent variable, begin to add questions about your independent variables. Again, it is probably best to begin with the questions as asked in the WVS to have a point of reference when you begin your analysis of the data. Then, as you did with the dependent variable, take some time to ask questions about each independent variable to understand the respondent's point of view about them, just as you did for your dependent variable. Not all interviews are structured in this way (first asking questions about the dependent variable and then the independent variables), but for new researchers this method ensures that you ask questions about all the variables that you have included in your analysis.

Be careful, too, in how you phrase your questions in your interview schedule. Be as clear as possible when you write your questions so that every respondent can answer your questions as fully as possible. Do not create "compound questions," that is, questions that ask two things at the same time. Keep each question separate from the others. Additionally, do not create questions that steer a respondent into providing a particular answer, specifically one that supports your research hypothesis. For example, do not start a question with "Wouldn't you agree that . . .?" One way to ensure that you have asked good questions that do not "lead your witness" is to do one or two pilot interviews with classmates to determine whether your questions are clear and comprehensive, yet open enough to allow respondents to provide honest and unguided answers.[6]

Step 3: Conduct the interviews.

If you are doing field research for your interviews (in other words, leaving your classroom), you should introduce yourself to each person who has agreed to be interviewed and provide some information about your project. If you are interviewing someone who is not part of your class, you should have IRB approval for your project, which means that you must obtain informed consent from the participant before the interview can continue. Depending on the IRB protocol, this consent will be either

---

6   Most researchers do pilot interviews in the field before doing the formal research interviews to ensure that a given interview schedule is appropriate for conducting the research. Since you will likely not have this opportunity, conducting an interview or two with members of your class (regardless of the research population you are studying with your research) before you conduct your interviews is advised to ensure that your interview questions will solicit the information you need to address your research question.

verbal or written through a signature on a prepared document that you bring with you to the interview.

During the interview itself, you should do little talking. The best interviews are ones in which an interviewer asks questions and allows a respondent to provide complete answers. The nature of the semistructured interview gives you an opportunity to ask follow-up questions or to ask for clarification if you have misunderstood something or would like to make sure that the responses are as clear as possible. Make sure you ask questions related to each of the three variables in your study so that your analyses of the qualitative data will be as complete as possible.

If you take notes during an interview, take as many as possible, writing down the key words and ideas the respondent uses to express responses to your questions. These words will likely be the codes or categories you will find in the qualitative text after you have transcribed your notes. If you are able to record the interview with an electronic device, you must later transcribe the interviews (the IRB protocol should include whether recording is possible; if you do record the interview, the respondent should be made aware of it through informed consent).

You may discover after the first interview that you want to change how you ask a particular question concerning one or more of your variables. You might also need to add questions to ensure that your interview data are complete. This happens often when conducting interviews and is why doing a few pilot interviews with classmates before the formal interviewing begins is helpful.

Step 4: Transcribe your data and perform content analysis.

After you conduct your interviews, you must transcribe the notes you took to create a qualitative dataset. Once the qualitative dataset is complete, you can perform content analysis to determine whether your theory and hypotheses can be supported with the information you gathered from the participants in your study. Comb through the qualitative text you create to find codes and categories. Then determine whether you can identify themes based on how codes and categories were presented during the interview. This approach may reveal patterns among the variables that you anticipated in your research hypothesis. But the benefit of doing the interviews is that the respondents might be able to shed light on whether your theory and research hypotheses can be supported. In some interviews you may find empirical support for one of your hypotheses, but the reason the respondent provides for the association between the variables is completely different from what you had originally anticipated in your theory. This is an important reminder that correlation is not causation. It may also happen that the interview data do not entirely match your quantitative analysis; you may find, for example, that an independent variable that did not emerge as significant in your quantitative analysis is actually important for one of your participants in an interview. Likewise, the opposite may also be true: an independent variable that was significant in quantitative analysis may not be important for a particular respondent. Each scenario provides interesting results to interpret. Be aware, however, that the sample you create with the interviews is a convenience sample, which may compromise the external validity of your case study.

Your last step will be to write up the findings from your case study. This is covered more fully in the next chapter.

COMING UP

Now that you have completed both quantitative and qualitative analyses for your research, you are ready to write your final report. How to write complete academic papers is the subject of Chapter 11.

WRITING A FINAL RESEARCH REPORT

Let's take a look at what you have completed through the first 10 chapters of this book.

1. You identified a research topic concerning political values and attitudes and devised an analytical research question to examine the relationship between two independent variables and one dependent variable for a particular research population.

2. You wrote a concise literature review that provided a synthesis of the most important work that has been done on your topic.

3. You wrote a theory to explain why you expected a causal relationship between your independent and dependent variables and derived research hypotheses from the theory that could be tested with observable data.

4. You specified a mixed methods research design, one that included quantitative large-*n* data analysis and a single illustrative case study.

5. You measured the concepts you used in quantitative data analysis with indicators from the WVS and, when necessary, assessed those indicators for reliability and validity.

6. You performed quantitative analysis to determine whether your research hypotheses were empirically supported with data from the WVS.

7. You conducted a number of interviews with people who represent your research population and you performed content analysis on the qualitative data you collected to determine whether you can further support your hypotheses and theory.

Now is the time to analyze your findings and put everything together in a formal research report. For some students, writing papers can be an intimidating chore. However, many of the challenges students face stem from not knowing what to write. Hopefully by the time you finish this chapter you will discover that writing a final report can actually be enjoyable. This is the part of the process where you get to share with your readers what you have done and what can be learned from your efforts.

Each chapter in this book presented a separate component of research. As you piece together your paper, most of the components can be presented as separate sections of your eventual report. Research papers are often separated into standard sections. Each section's subheading gives the reader an idea of what will be presented in the section. Working with subheadings in a standardized **template**, a general outline organized by predetermined sections, makes a researcher's work much easier. The template gives you an idea of what to write in each individual section. See the following suggested template for your research paper. In the next chapter, you will see how you can modify this template for the writing of other types of research papers. For now, the template can be helpful as you prepare the final report for the research you have completed on political attitudes and values. You will likely not write the sections in the particular order in which they are presented here. Rather, most researchers write the "middle" of the paper first (the literature review, theory and hypotheses, methods and data, and results and discussion) and the "frame" of the paper last (the abstract, introduction, and conclusion). The numbers that appear in parentheses after the sections indicate the order in which it is suggested you write the paper.

GENERAL TEMPLATE FOR A RESEARCH PAPER IN POLITICAL SCIENCE

Abstract (7)
Introduction (6)
Literature review (1)
Theory and hypotheses (2)
Methods and data (3)
Results and discussion (4)
Conclusions (5)
References (8)

How to Write the Individual Sections of a Final Report

Researchers do not write their papers in order from the abstract to the conclusion. Rather, they write their papers in sections, beginning with the sections found in the paper's middle. You can present the individual sections in your paper as separate subheadings. Subheadings help you keep the material organized. Keep the sections separate as you write them and once the sections are all complete, weave them together in a single narrative. This strategy should help you with your writing. If you have followed the instructions in this book, you probably already have several sections completed. For example, you likely have completed a literature review, a theory and hypotheses section, and a methods and data section. You have also completed your data analysis. Next we revisit some of the sections we have already worked with before moving on to the newer sections that should now be written.

The Order of What to Write for a Research Paper

1. Literature Review

Many researchers create a separate section called "literature review" that they include in the text of their papers. Covered in Chapter 3, a literature review helps situate a study within the context of the literature itself. It also establishes the credibility of the researcher as an expert in a given field. Literature reviews vary in length based on how much work others have already done on a topic. If a topic is generally understudied, the formal literature review may be relatively short in length. On the other hand, if a topic has a well-known trajectory of scholarship, the researcher must synthesize the literature in a concise, useful way to demonstrate mastery of the subject at hand. During the peer-review process, reviewers will often comment that a researcher's literature review is not complete and will make suggestions of what to add.

However, remember that your literature review is not the main focus of your paper. It is required because readers need to know how the ideas surrounding your topic have developed over time. But the literature review should not detract from the research that you did to answer your research question.

Some researchers also choose to integrate elements of the literature in other sections of their papers. For example, a researcher may reference studies in the introduction of a research paper as a means of making a statement about the relevance of a topic. The theory section in a paper is also a place where important studies that advanced our understanding of a particular research topic are referenced, since such studies likely guided the researcher's thinking about the theory in some way. Others may choose to reference literature in the results and conclusion sections as well, especially if the findings of a particular research project either directly support or refute observations that have already been made by other scholars. How you choose to demonstrate your command of your research topic should thus be determined by what you deem appropriate. However, for new researchers, it is advisable to create a separate section in the final research paper called "Literature review" to ensure that the appropriate literature is cited and included in the final report.

2. Theory and Hypotheses

Social science researchers often craft a section devoted to the presentation of their theory and the hypotheses derived from the theory. Theories provide general explanations for why hypotheses are expected to be true. Like the literature reviews, how this section is presented may differ from researcher to researcher. For quantitative studies, hypotheses are usually listed explicitly after the presentation of a theory. For qualitative studies, the theory section may be more elaborate, since the detailed information from the analysis is provided as evidence for a general proposition. Studies that incorporate both quantitative and qualitative evidence to answer research questions will logically vary in how hypotheses and theories are presented.

If you look through mainstream journals or books in political science, you might find that some studies do not have a section designated for the theories and hypotheses that will be investigated by the research. But this does not mean that the study is not guided by a theory or hypothesis. Even if the terms "dependent variable," "theory," "hypothesis," or "evidence" are not explicitly mentioned, the overwhelming majority of studies will have some identifiable dependent variable, or what it is that the paper attempts to explain. Although the precise terminology may change from paper to paper, social science research studies generally involve (1) an analytical research question and (2) an answer to the research question, which, for most studies, can be restated as a research hypothesis that must be tested. The information presented in the results of the final report is an analysis of the evidence the researcher has identified as important for understanding the answer to the research question. Thus, although a researcher may not use the specific terminology you have learned in this book, it is usually possible to impose these terms on specific parts of a research report.

3. Methods and Data

The methods section in a research paper briefly outlines how a researcher answered his or her research question. Whether quantitative or qualitative methods were used is usually outlined in this section.

For quantitative analysis:

For studies that utilize quantitative methods, researchers will generally outline three key pieces of information. First, the progression of concepts to indicators to variables is often presented in the methods and data section. Use this section to argue why specific indicators were chosen and how the variables derived from them were measured. If needed, an assessment of the reliability and validity of the indicators used in the research should also be included here. This is important because the reader must judge whether the indicator you chose is an adequate representation for any concept studied through the research. Critics will often point to how concepts were measured as one of the weaker elements in a research project and argue that an alternate measurement of one of the key concepts (one that is more reliable or more valid) might have been a better choice. Hence, the methods and data section is a good place for you to justify the specific decisions that were made when the variables used in the empirical analyses were determined.

Second, for quantitative work researchers often use the methods and data section of their final papers to provide the source of the data they analyzed or whether they coded information themselves. In addition, it is important to justify how a sample was selected. For your papers you would state that you used the WVS, with reference to the specific country and year from which you took the data. You could mention that the WVS uses stratified random sampling at the country level. You should also provide a citation for the WVS as a reference or footnote.[1] This is also the appropriate section to explain how you limited the data based on your research population.

Finally, the methods and data section in quantitative studies is used to explain exactly which statistical tests you performed to determine whether and how your independent and dependent variables were related. This is important because most readers will want to know which statistical tests—such as regression—were performed on the data. Since there are many ways to utilize regression in research, researchers should provide an explanation for why a certain regression equation was used. Usually this will involve some discussion about the dependent variable and its measurement. For example, for your studies, a paragraph to describe the ordinary least squares regression equation you utilized would be helpful; you used ordinary least squares regression because your dependent variable was measured on an ordinal scale from 1 to 10. This transparency allows the reader to determine whether the methods you used were

---

1   Go to http://www.worldvaluessurvey.org/WVSDocumentationWV6.jsp for instructions on how to cite the WVS appropriately.

appropriate for the structure of your data.[2] Some researchers even opt to place the regression equation in the text. You could do this as well, using the equation provided in Chapter 8, substituting the specific variables you used for the Y and X's in the equation itself:

$$y_i = \alpha + (\beta 1 \times x1_i) + (\beta 2 \times x2_i)$$

where x1 = Independent Variable 1; x2 = Independent Variable 2; y = Dependent Variable

For qualitative analysis:

The methods and data section for qualitative research is similar but slightly different. First, you should discuss the single case you selected for your case study. You should mention that the case is an illustrative case because it potentially serves to provide an example to confirm the theory you developed. Remember that your case is the place where you interviewed the people who represent your research population. You would also state that because you interviewed people to whom you happened to have access on a particular date, you created a convenience sample of people who represent the research population for your study. Use this section, too, to provide information about the interviews themselves: for example, how many people were interviewed and what was the average length of the interviews? You could also include some information about the types of questions that were asked.

This section can also be used to explain how the information that you collected was transcribed. You should include the specific type of analysis you performed on your qualitative dataset for your research, which for your study on political values and attitudes was content analysis.

For studies with mixed methods:

For studies that utilize mixed methods, it is necessary to include methods and data information for both sets of analyses. Researchers in political science that utilize mixed methods will usually present the quantitative analysis before presenting the qualitative analysis, but not always. Since your study includes both quantitative and qualitative analysis, you must expand your methods and data section to include all the information you used to answer your research question.

The methods and data section is important because research findings should have some degree of **replicability**. If a second study uses similar data for

---

2   If you continue to work with political science research methods in upper-level courses or in graduate school, you will likely learn other applications of regression analysis, such as logistic regression (for dependent variables with binary measurement) or ordinal logistic regression (for dependent variables with ordinal measurement with a small number of categories).

the same research population and produces dramatically different conclusions about the relationship between an independent and dependent variable, something is wrong somewhere, with either the first study or the second study, or possibly both. Since the purpose of social science research is to develop general propositions that we expect to be true in multiple contexts, we should be able reproduce the research findings of a given study using methods similar to those the original study used. This is why transparency in the methods and data section is crucial. The methods and data section provides the important information that allows a second researcher to possibly replicate your analysis.

4. Results and Discussion
The results and discussion section of a paper represents the heart of the work. It is here that you provide evidence as to whether you can confirm your hypotheses and support your theory. The results section is usually the lengthiest part of a research paper since it is where you present the tangible findings from your analysis.

For quantitative analysis:

In most research studies that utilize quantitative analysis, the presentation of the descriptive statistics for each variable precedes the presentation of the data analysis. As explained in Chapter 7, descriptive statistics provide the reader a snapshot of what is contained in the quantitative dataset. Most researchers provide a descriptive statistics table and then offer a paragraph or two to discuss it. How the information is presented depends on the variables in the analysis. A table like the one presented in the paper progress section of Chapter 7 (Table 7.8) is helpful. Begin with the presentation of the dependent variable. Since it is variable with ordinal measurement, provide summary statistics for it: its minimum value, maximum value, mean, and standard deviation. The percentages for each relevant category should be included in the table for your binary independent variable. Likewise, you would present either the frequency distribution or the summary statistics for your independent variable with ordinal, interval, or ratio measurement, depending on the range of values associated with the values. (If a variable with ordinal measurement has only a few categories associated with it, a frequency distribution is preferred to summary statistics.) Having a table such as this provides a good snapshot of what is contained in the dataset. A researcher could also opt to provide bar or pie charts as well as visual representations for each variable.

After the descriptive statistics for each variable are provided, the researcher should begin the presentation of the data analysis. The results of bivariate correlations, the difference of means test and the correlation coefficient, are usually presented in the text. See the paper progress section of Chapter 8 for examples of draft sentences that you can use to report your results.

For single- and multiple-variable regression results, tables are helpful aids that provide large amounts of information in a streamlined way. The table with regression results from the paper progress section of Chapter 9 (Table 9.2) is a good example to use. The table lists the sign and size of each independent variable's coefficient and often uses a series of asterisks to denote significance for each model. In addition, each model's constant, adjusted R^2, and number of observations are included in the table.

Once all the quantitative data are presented to the reader in tables or in the text, the next task is for you to *discuss* the results of your quantitative analysis. This is one of the most important parts of the overall paper, where you explain what the results substantively mean. Discussing results is sometimes harder than it looks. The best advice is to begin by providing a discussion of each independent variable, beginning with whether the analysis provided evidence that a research hypothesis was supported with the data used for an analysis. The sign, size, and significance of each result all warrant extensive discussion. A good way to start is by discussing which variables included in your analysis had a significant effect on your dependent variable, which would allow you to reject the null hypothesis concerning that variable. Next, the sign of a result confirms whether the predicted direction of a research hypothesis was correct. Finally, the size of a particular result is also important. Some results may achieve statistical significance and allow you to reject a null hypothesis, but the actual effect (the mean difference between two groups, the size of a correlation coefficient, or the size of a coefficient from regression analysis, for example) is actually small. This is something you should include in your discussion. A significant result is important but it should be balanced with the magnitude of the result.

However, since correlation in quantitative analysis does not imply causation, it is now up to you to place your findings in context and to discuss why the results may imply causation between your variables. One way to begin a discussion of the findings is to revisit the original causal theory you provided as an explanation for why the variables were expected to be correlated in the first place. After all, if your research hypotheses are shown to be true with the WVS data, there is now some evidence that the theory that generated the hypotheses may also be supported, as long as the conditions for causality are met. In the discussion, you must utilize phrases such as "the results suggest" or "the findings imply" because the results do not prove that a hypothesis is true. Significant quantitative results simply suggest that what you predicted in a hypothesis is likely true for the research population from which your particular sample was derived. Thus, you should avoid using the word "prove" in your writing. Rather, the results suggest or imply that a causal theory may be supported because a hypothesis associated with it was shown to be likely true with observed data.

Also provide some discussion if your variables were not significant for explaining variation in the dependent variable. An insignificant coefficient is noteworthy because in the beginning you had a theory for why each variable should be included in the model. When a coefficient is insignificant, the results suggest that the null hypothesis cannot be rejected.

This is not to say, however, that the null hypothesis concerning the relationship between an independent and dependent variable is unequivocally true. Remember that the findings from quantitative data analysis are subject to many factors, such as the quality of the indicators used for measuring concepts and the quality of the sample used to represent the population. This is part of the reason that you must provide as much information as possible about the indicators and the dataset used for quantitative analysis in the methods and data section of a paper. The information allows readers to interpret the results for themselves. If a researcher has a suspicion that an unreliable or invalid indicator or the quality of a sample is what influenced a **negative finding**, a finding that runs counter to the researcher's original hypothesis, it is important that the researcher explain the shortcomings of the variables or the sample in the discussion or explain why the negative finding may actually be correct.

A negative finding may be disappointing, but it is important that you think carefully about why the data did not support a particular hypothesis, especially when you originally had a suspicion that it would be supported. Usually the reason that a hypothesis is not supported can be linked to one or more problems. Below are some possibilities. Each should be carefully evaluated in the discussion of the results.

1. The indicators that the researcher used to measure concepts were not reliable or valid.

   Generally, the results of quantitative analysis are only as strong as the dataset used to generate the results. If an unreliable or invalid indicator was used for a particular concept, the results may not be significant because the indicators used in the analysis did not adequately measure the concepts under study. Take, for example, a researcher who, in her study of the relationship between ethnic fractionalization and ethnic conflict in the Middle East, found insignificant results, although she had written a compelling theory for why the two variables should be correlated. What might the problem be? Could it be the indicators used in the analysis? Were they reliable and/or valid measures of the concepts under study? On further inspection, we learn that for the dependent variable the researcher used a self-coded measure for ethnic conflict based on a content analysis of news stories from a particular time period for a number of cities in the Middle East. Specifically, the researcher looked for news stories that contained the word "conflict" in the English-speaking news for a large number of cities and developed a coding scheme based on how often that word appeared in the news. The indicator for the dependent variable, then, was a measure based on the frequency of the word conflict appearing among a group of stories for a defined period of time. This coding scheme is faulty for several reasons. First, there are many different ways to express the term conflict. This means that the researcher neglected to review particular stories or reports because only one way to express conflict (specifically with the word conflict) was used. Chapter 10 suggested that performing content analysis requires us to think of all the synonyms that could be used to express a general idea; conflict, for example, may be expressed as "fight," "problem," or "struggle." In addition, by only using English-news sources, the researcher likely neglected to capture the full extent of conflict in a particular area that may have been reported by local media sources and not captured by English-speaking news. Hence, a negative finding about the relationship between ethnic fragmentation and ethnic conflict may be the result of a flawed indicator for ethnic conflict. Again, this is why measurement of concepts is important in empirical analysis. A flawed indicator will likely lead to insignificant results. If you have insignificant results with your analysis, you should ask whether the specific survey question you used through the WVS was a good indicator for the concept you had hoped to measure.

2. The sample was not an appropriate representation of the research population.

   If the sample you used to test a hypothesis was not fully representative of the overall population to which you hope to generalize the conclusions, the data may not support the hypothesis. Although the logic of probability sampling is geared toward the creation of a representative sample, there is always some likelihood, however small, that a sample is biased to some degree, which would tamper with your potential conclusions. If, for example, you believe that the sample the WVS generated was not adequately representative of the country's population, then any results you obtain through the survey might be suspect.

3. Other variables in the model explain more variation.

   One of the reasons researchers often present their quantitative results in different models in a single table is because an independent variable may achieve significance when included as a single independent variable, but fail to achieve significance when included alongside other independent variables. This does not mean that the insignificant independent variable is not important, but it does suggest that the other variables in the model have more power in explaining variation in the dependent variable. If this happens in your analyses, you could utilize part of the discussion section to explain why this is the case. In addition, you may wish to bring up any possible antecedent or intervening variables that you did not include in your analysis (see Chapter 3) that might help you further understand the relationship you observed between your independent and dependent variables. Since you included only two independent variables in your analysis, it is possible that important variables have been left out.

4. The theory is incorrect.

   Each of the reasons listed above may explain why a particular research hypothesis was not supported by quantitative data analysis. Yet it is also possible that there is another reason for why an independent variable failed to achieve significance in quantitative analysis. This may be harder to accept, but it is possible that the original theory you developed is simply incorrect. Remember from Chapter 4 that theories are usually crafted from three sources: inductive observation, deductive reasoning, and insight from literature reviews. It is possible that, even with careful thinking, you could have understood a social phenomenon incorrectly. When this happens, you should engage in what is called **ex post theorizing**, or the development of new explanations based on what you now understand. Many researchers engage in ex post theorizing when they discover findings that run contrary to their expectations. Ex post theorizing can be a powerful tool that gives future researchers important clues about what to study next.

For qualitative analysis:

How to present the results and discussion for qualitative analysis is harder to outline precisely because the nature of qualitative inquiry is more open. Nonetheless, there are a number of general guidelines you can follow when presenting and discussing the results from case studies, especially if you have used content analysis to analyze a qualitative dataset.

A good rule of thumb is to begin by presenting background information about the case you chose for your case study. Remember that for your papers, your case is the place where you went to collect interview data. If you stayed in your classroom, your case is your institution; if you did field work off campus, your case is the location you visited to interview people who represent your research population. The beginning of the results section should include background information about the case.

Since you used interviews to create your qualitative dataset, the next part of the results section should provide basic information about the people who were interviewed. Do not use anyone's name in your paper. Keep the interview subjects anonymous.

Next, what were the main codes and categories identified in the qualitative dataset that you produced based on your analysis of your qualitative dataset? What codes and categories emerged? How often were the most important codes and categories represented? To what extent was there variation among the respondents? Next, what were the themes that you were able to identify through your analysis of how codes and categories were associated with one another? Did any of these themes allow you to provide additional support for your research hypotheses?

As argued in Chapter 10, the identification of unanticipated codes and categories allows you to identify themes that you may not have considered when you began your research project. Imagine that respondents consistently brought up additional variables in their responses to your interview questions, for example, their political ideology or their religious beliefs. If you find that any new codes or categories such as these are continually associated with variation in your dependent variable, you could create new themes and discuss them in the report, perhaps as a means of creating inductive theory. You could also suggest that future research investigate these new codes as independent variables.

In the presentation and discussion of the material, qualitative researchers sometimes opt to include direct quotes from an interview, words, phrases, sentences, or even paragraphs, as part of the results and discussion section of a paper to help substantiate any results and to help readers understand how themes were created. This is useful because qualitative research often provides nuanced explanations and understandings that are not possible with quantitative analysis. Usually the quoted text is presented separately in a smaller font or indented from the main discussion to ensure that that the quotes are not mistaken for the researcher's regular text.

5. Conclusion

Now that the middle parts of the paper (the literature review, theory and hypotheses, methods and data, and results and discussion) are complete, it is time to create a frame around it. You must write a powerful frame for your papers. Think about this for a moment. When you are pressed for time and cannot read the entirety of a paper, what are the parts that you read first? Likely you will read the abstract, introduction, and conclusion of a study to understand the work's main points and, importantly, to determine whether the paper is one that you should read more carefully when you have more time.

A good conclusion should contain at least three main points for discussion. First, you should reiterate whether you were able to support your hypotheses with the data you collected and analyzed with either the quantitative or the qualitative analyses. If you were able to support your hypotheses, provide a summary of what the data could confirm. In addition, it is a good idea to revisit your theory in the conclusion, especially theory that may be supported by your data analysis (but again, do not use the word prove!). If you were not able to support your hypotheses based on the data analysis you completed, you can use the conclusion of the paper to identify the reasons for which your findings may have gone contrary to expectation and to engage in ex post theorizing if you believe your theory needs revision.

Second, a good conclusion will provide the reader an idea of how the research could have been improved and whether new questions based on the research findings have emerged. Remember that the presentation of your research is a conversation between you and the reader; a good conclusion will indicate where improvements could be made and what the next steps are to further our understanding about your research topic. Many conclusions have at least one sentence that begins: "Future research should . . ."

Last, a good conclusion will contain a discussion of how the findings from the research can be generalized to other cases. You should devote at least a full page or more to this particular task. If the main purpose of social science research is to understand patterns in social phenomena, it is important to know how the conclusions from one research project can inform other research projects. One way to do this is to think about the "bigger picture," that is, why other researchers should care about your project. In other words, place the findings from your research in a context that other researchers, who may not be working directly on your specific topic, will find interesting and relevant for their own work.

6. Introduction

Many beginning researchers think that the first part to write in a research paper is the introduction. But this is a big mistake! The introduction to the paper should among the last sections to be written for a paper, after the research is complete and the researcher knows exactly what the paper's conclusions are.

The introduction of a paper is just that: it should contain an introduction to the research topic. It should provide the reader with a clear idea of what the research question is and how it will be answered. It should also include the reason that a topic is relevant, important, or interesting. For many readers, the introduction to a research paper is a doorway to a metaphorical house. The reader looks in and determines whether he or she wants to continue exploring. If the door is not particularly inviting, the paper may get set aside. But if a reader discovers in the first paragraphs why the research topic is relevant or important, he or she will likely continue reading your paper.

In addition to stating the research topic and question and its overall relevance or importance, some researchers opt to mention the main conclusions in the introduction of the paper. A research paper is not a mystery novel; do not keep your audience guessing as to what the takeaway message will be. Instead, by providing some conclusions up front, someone who reads your paper will be able to understand what the goals of your research were and how you reached your conclusions much more effectively. A reader should never have to guess what the overall mission of the paper is and what the general findings are.

For many researchers, the introduction is often a difficult section of a paper to write. The difficulty may lie in not knowing how to begin. Although there is no one correct way to introduce a paper, below are some suggestions that you might use to get started:

- Start with a statement of the research question in the first sentence.
- Use an anecdotal story or example concerning the topic (something from the news, for example), and then end the story with the research question.
- Start with a summary of the most important literature as a means to establish the relevance of a topic and to show where the present study fits.

• Write a sentence or two to summarize the literature on a topic and then write a statement about what must be further explored (either to reinforce the literature or to refute it).

Once you have introduced the material you will cover in the paper, you can conclude the introduction with a paragraph that outlines the individual sections of the paper and the order in which they will be presented. This is so the reader will have an understanding of what will follow in the paper. This type of paragraph is common in political science research publications. See the following general example:

The rest of the paper is as follows. The first section provides a literature review. The second section presents the paper's main theory and hypotheses. The third section explains the methods that were used in this study and the fourth section present the results and a discussion of the findings. The last section concludes and provides suggestions for generalization and future analysis.

7. Abstract

An abstract is a condensed summary of your work that is placed at the beginning of a paper. Writing a clear and concise abstract is important because it is, beyond the paper's title, the first real information a reader will access about your paper. A good abstract will let a reader know whether the paper is worth reading, that is, whether the paper is relevant for the reader's interests. For example, if a reader wishes to know something about political participation in France and reads in the abstract that a paper is about ethnic conflict in Russia, he or she will likely not continue with it.

Abstracts are meant to be short, usually about 200 words. Generally, they contain four key pieces of information: (1) a statement of the research question; (2) the relevance or importance of the research question; (3) the methods used to answer the research question; and (4) the research paper's overall conclusions. Abstracts look a little like an annotated bibliography since both contain similar information. It is not necessary that you present the information in the abstract in this order, but a good abstract will contain all four points.

Examples of good abstracts from the political science literature start on the following page. The bibliographic references are provided, followed by the abstracts to the research articles. The abstracts are verbatim.

8. References

Every research paper that utilizes outside sources must include references. For most journals in political science, the reference list is provided either at the

EXAMPLES FROM POLITICAL SCIENCE

Gaskins, Ben, Matt Golder, and David A. Siegel. 2013. "Religious Participation and Economic Conservativism." *American Journal of Political Science* 57 (4): 823–40.

RESEARCH QUESTION: Note that the first two lines of the abstract contain the two main research questions.

METHODS: The next three sentences then explain to the reader what the present study will do.

RESULTS: The presentation of the results begins midsentence after "World Values Survey"

RELEVANCE: The last sentence tells the reader why this study is important and how the results might be generalized.

Why do some individuals engage in more religious activity than others? And how does this religious activity influence their economic attitudes? We present a formal model in which individuals derive utility from both secular and religious sources. Our model, which incorporates both demand-side and supply-side explanations of religion, is unusual in that it endogenizes both an individual's religious participation and her preferences over economic policy. Using data on over 70 countries from the pooled World Values Survey, we find that religious participation declines with societal development, an individual's ability to produce secular goods, and state regulations on religion, but that it increases with inequality. We also find that religious participation increases economic conservatism among the poor but decreases it among the rich. Our analysis has important insights for the debate about secularization theory and challenges conventional wisdom regarding the relationship between religious participation and economic conservatism.

Krieckhaus, Jonathan, Byunghwan Son, Nisha Mukherjee Bellinger, and Jason M. Wells. 2014. "Economic Inequality and Democratic Support." *The Journal of Politics* 71 (1): 139–51.

RESEARCH QUESTION: As in the previous example, note that the first sentence of the abstract contains the research question.

Does economic inequality influence citizens' support for democracy? Political economy theory suggests that in a country with high inequality, the majority of the population will support democracy as a potential mechanism for redistribution. Much of the survey and area-studies literature, by contrast, suggests that inequality

RELEVANCE: For this example, the relevance is that there are two competing theories for how inequality influences support for democracy.

METHODS: The authors state how they are going to test their hypotheses using information from 40 democracies.

RESULTS: The last two sentences provide the overall conclusions of the studies and what the findings mean in a general sense.

generates political disillusion and regime dissatisfaction. To clarify this disagreement, we distinguish between prospective versus retrospective evaluations as well as between egocentric versus sociotropic evaluations. We test the resulting hypotheses in a multilevel analysis conducted in 40 democracies. We find that citizens are retrospective and sociotropic, meaning that higher levels of economic inequality reduce support for democracy amongst all social classes. We also find a small prospective egocentric effect, in that the reduction in democratic support in highly unequal countries is slightly less severe amongst the poor, suggesting they believe that democracy might increase future redistribution.

end of the paper or through footnotes. Most journals (and instructors) have specific instructions for how the references should be listed. When in doubt, the reference style of the American Political Science Association (see Chapter 3) is a good default choice. For your papers on political values and attitudes, include a list of all the references you used in the paper at the end of your paper.

ISSUES IN WRITING

Although it is beyond the scope of this book to provide a comprehensive guide to academic writing, there are some general guidelines that new researchers should consider.

Structure

Research papers usually have a common structure that includes separate sections for the paper's introduction, literature review, theory, methods, results, and conclusions. The template provided earlier in the chapter should help you divide your paper into separate sections. You may decide to change the order in which they are presented, but most papers will divide the material into these recognizable sections, with clear subheadings.

Keep in mind, however, that not all research papers follow this specific format. Paper formats can vary, depending on what was done for an analysis and what the author deemed appropriate for inclusion in the final report.

Establishing a Proper Tone

There is a specific academic tone that researchers should utilize in academic papers. The writing should not be loose or informal. Do not write as you would talk; in other words, do not treat the paper as a casual conversation between two friends. Rather, your writing should be as tight and formal as possible. One way to evaluate whether your writing is appropriate is to picture yourself reading your paper aloud on a stage to a group of your institution's faculty and administrators in your best professional clothing. If you would feel comfortable using the language in your paper for a formal presentation, then the tone is likely appropriate.

Another important aspect to academic writing is clarity. Your prose should be clear and assessable. Make sure that every word you use reflects exactly what you intend it to mean. Also, use terms that are common in political science research, such as operationalization, content validity, research hypothesis, random stratified sample, generalization, or difference of means. You can use these terms without defining them, even if you are new to them yourself.

The "I" Debate

A common question among students new to academic writing concerns the use of the first person, specifically the words "I" or "we" and "my" or "our." Some researchers use the first person in different sections of a paper, whereas others avoid it completely. The use of the first person is tricky and it takes time to learn exactly when and how to use it appropriately in academic writing.

Most often a researcher will use the first person in specific sections of a research report, such as the introduction, theory and hypotheses, methods and data, or results and discussion. The first person denotes an action that the researcher has undertaken as part of the research process. We can revisit some of the papers we have used as examples of various themes for this book to provide examples of how to use the first person.

In the Introduction

Some researchers use the first person in the introduction to ask specific research questions and to lay out the research design. For example, after citing some literature to discuss how the use of cell phones has influenced political events in Africa, Pierskalla and Hollenbach (covered in Chapter 3) write the following sentences: "In this article, **we** ask whether modern communication technology has affected political collective action in Africa. Specifically **we** ask if the rapid spread of cell phone technology . . ." (Pierskalla and Hollenbach 2013, 207; bold added for emphasis).

In Methods and Data

The use of the first person is probably the most prevalent in the methods and data section for research papers that utilize the first person, since it is here that researchers justify the specific choices they made for what they did in their analyses. For example, Drutman and Hopkins's study on the content analysis of the emails of top Enron administrators (covered in Chapter 10) contains the following sentences in the methods and data section of the paper: "What targets of political attention are represented in these 2,559 Enron emails? To answer that question, **we** developed the coding scheme . . ." (Drutman and Hopkins 2013, 16; bold added for emphasis).

Although it is common to use the first person in certain sections of a paper, it is important that students new to academic writing in political science learn how to use it appropriately. Researchers should not use the first person in the literature review. This is because the literature review is a snapshot of what other researchers have written about the paper's topic and, as such, using the first person itself is not advised. Do not, for example, begin your literature review with "I reviewed six studies for my research and found that . . ." It is better to start a literature review with sentences that provide summary statements about the literature, such as "There is general agreement in the literature that . . ." See Chapter 2 for more examples of how to begin literature reviews.

Being Repetitive

The information contained in the abstract, introduction, theory and hypotheses, results and discussion, and conclusion reflect the same research process that was based around a central research question. As a result, some of the information in these sections may, at times, sound repetitive. For example, the research question can be stated in both the abstract and the introduction. The researcher's central hypothesis may be stated in the abstract, introduction, and theory and hypotheses sections. The main results may be stated in the abstract, introduction, results and discussion, and conclusion. Being repetitive may cause students new to academic writing some anxiety because they may believe that once information is provided, it cannot be repeated. To the contrary, the repetition of important information is how you signal to a reader that a specific piece of information is important. In other words, being repetitive about a specific conclusion in different sections of a paper gives the reader a chance to identify the paper's takeaway message.

Using Citations

Whenever you use present material from other studies in your work, you must cite the studies appropriately. Not citing material properly can lead to charges of plagiarism, a serious matter that should never been taken lightly. Plagiarism occurs when you present material that you have taken from other studies as your own in your work. Always use a citation if you are unsure when to cite to protect yourself. As mentioned in Chapter 2, parenthetical citations are common in political science. Furthermore, you must always include the page number on which a particular quotation appears when you use a direct quote in your paper.

CONCLUSION

Good writing is a skill and it takes time and practice for students to develop good writing habits. For academic research, working with a template with predetermined sections can be helpful when writing a final report. Most research papers contain sections for the abstract, introduction, literature review, theory and hypotheses, methods and data, results and discussion, and conclusion. It is best to write the middle sections of a paper before writing the paper's frame, which includes the abstract, introduction, and conclusion. New researchers can follow established general guidelines to ensure their final papers are as polished and professional as possible.

GLOSSARY

EX POST THEORIZING The development of new explanations about the relationship between variables that is produced after a research process is complete.

NEGATIVE FINDING A finding that runs counter to a researcher's original hypothesis.

REPLICABILITY Being able reproduce the research findings of a given study using methods similar to those used in the original study.

TEMPLATE A general outline organized by predetermined sections.

EXERCISES

Locate a research article of interest to you in the political science literature (perhaps from the *American Political Science Review*, *The Journal of Politics*, or *American Journal of Political Science*) and study it for the following information.

Concerning the paper's organization:

1. Study the organization of the material presented in the paper. See particularly how the authors titled and ordered their subheadings. Study the abstract, introduction, and conclusion carefully. For the abstract, see whether you can identify the research question, the relevance, the methods, and conclusions for the study. Next, study how the authors introduced their work to the reader. Finally, scrutinize the conclusions to determine whether and how research findings were reiterated to the reader, how suggestions were made for future research, and how findings were generalized.

2. Study the way the authors presented any quantitative or qualitative analysis. Look, for example, at the quantitative tables for descriptive statistics and data analysis (likely you will see different uses for regression analysis in these papers, too). Also, read through how different researchers present case studies if they are part of the research design.

Concerning the paper's writing style:

3. Take note of the academic tone used in the work. Also, note how different authors utilize the first person in the text of their papers. Use these studies as examples for how you might utilize the first person as well.

4. Note, too, how researchers write similar information in certain sections of their papers, specifically in the abstract, introduction, theory and hypotheses, results and discussion, and conclusions. Use these styles as a model for how you might present your work in the different sections of your paper.

5. Finally, note how citations were used throughout the papers when the authors presented work that was not their own.

PAPER PROGRESS

Step 1: Complete the middle sections of your paper.

By this point you should be ready to piece together your entire paper. The middle sections of the paper, the literature review, theory and hypotheses, methods and data, results and discussion, should be mostly complete.

You will likely need to add written material to the results and discussion section to supplement the quantitative and qualitative data analysis you performed as you worked through this book. Make your discussion as complete as possible for both your quantitative and your qualitative analyses.

Step 2: Create the frame for your paper.

Write your conclusion, introduction, and abstract in that order. Follow the instructions presented in this chapter to ensure that each section is as complete and informative as possible. Create a reference list.

Step 3: Use the template to present the sections of the paper in the proper order.

Although you used may have written the sections of your paper in a particular order, you now must rearrange the sections to create a full paper. Use the template to help you do this. Include subheadings to mark the beginning of each new section. Also, ensure that one section flows to the next.

Step 4: Proofread your paper several times before submitting it for evaluation.

Once the paper is complete, it is a good rule of thumb to read it several times before submitting it for evaluation to ensure that you have completed all sections and set the proper academic tone. One way to ensure that your paper is as polished as possible is to finish it well before you intend to submit it. Let it sit for several days or even a week. Then allow yourself some time to examine your work with fresh eyes. This maximizes the possibility that you will find any errors or inconsistencies in the text that you may have missed while you were writing the paper.

Also remember that good writing is a skill. The best way to learn to write is to write. Write and revise often and do not be afraid to discard entire paragraphs when you are unhappy with a particular part of your paper. Chances are that the second (or the third or the fourth . . .) time you write something will be better than your first attempt.

COMING UP

Once this work is complete, you should have a full-length paper in your hands. Now that you have completed this work, in the next chapter you will learn how to present your work to a larger audience and how you can modify the basic template you used to complete other types of research papers. Your future in research is just beginning!

CHAPTER 12

YOUR FUTURE IN RESEARCH

Congratulations! Your research boot camp is over. Take a moment to reflect on how far you have come. In a short amount of time, you have gone from being a consumer to a producer of research. You have learned how to conduct literature reviews on scholarly topics, ask analytical research questions that specify independent and dependent variables, write theory and derive hypotheses, devise a feasible research design, conduct basic data analysis, interpret findings, and write a final report. The writing of the final report was hopefully made easier with a template that demonstrated what types of information could be included in each section of your paper.

This last chapter has three purposes. The first is to suggest ways for you to share your work with a larger audience. Many students spend hours preparing excellent papers that never see the light of day once a course is complete. The first part of the chapter will discuss ways through which undergraduates in political science can present or publish their best work.

The second purpose of the chapter is to demonstrate how you can use what you have learned in this book for other purposes. Even if you never conduct formal research again, the information you worked with in this book is still helpful in developing your skills in critical analysis. In other words, it is hoped that you have also developed some transferable skills that you can apply both in and out of academia. The second section of the chapter includes a brief discussion for how what you have learned can serve you in other ways, such as critically examining information to which you are exposed on a regular basis.

The third purpose of the chapter discusses ways to modify the basic template to help you write other types of papers. There are many different ways to conduct research; what you learned in this book is just one way of structuring a research project. Although most research projects involve many of the steps we covered in this book (writing literature reviews, theory development, and different forms of empirical analysis, for example), in this chapter you will learn how you can modify these elements to create research projects in different ways. Your project on political values and attitudes used a basic structure of research that can be modified for other types of research projects you may pursue in your future.

DISSEMINATION TO A LARGER AUDIENCE

Students often write research papers for political science courses, especially upper-level courses. You have also written at least one research paper—the one you wrote with this book. What will you do with your work after you submit it for evaluation? Is your plan to let it sit in a computer or in a file on your desk? What if it is a really good paper? What else can you do with it?

Conferences

Dissemination is the process through which work is distributed to a larger audience. There are several ways students can disseminate their work. For example, research can be presented at a conference, either as a poster presentation or as a verbal presentation on a panel. A **poster presentation** is one in which the main points from a research paper are displayed on a large poster board. Generally, a poster presenter will provide a little information from each of the paper's sections, such as the introduction, literature review, theory and hypotheses, and methods and data. More space is usually reserved for the results and discussion section and for the conclusions, since these sections often contain the paper's takeaway message and how the research findings can be generalized. Visitors study the poster and ask questions of the researcher, who stands next to the poster. Poster sessions are an excellent and exciting way of getting a lot of feedback from many different people about a project in a relatively short period of time.

Papers can also be presented verbally on a **conference panel** at a conference. Conference panels are organized in advance, usually around a general theme. When a researcher presents on a panel, he or she will provide a brief oral summary of the work, usually between 10 and 15 minutes, to a group of people consisting of the panel's chair and discussant, other presenters, and visitors. The **chair** is usually the person who organizes the panel. He or she selects the panel's general theme and the individual papers that will be presented based on the abstracts that he or she received after issuing a **call for papers**, the general invitation to present research at a conference. The **discussant** is the person who reads the full papers after they have been submitted. His or her primary task is to summarize all the papers on a panel, to identify common themes among the individual papers, and to direct questions and helpful comments to each of the authors. The discussant's role is important because a good discussant can provide valuable feedback to a researcher who wishes to improve his or her paper. The other presenters and visitors on the panel may also offer useful insight during the question-and-answer period that often follows the formal paper presentation.

Presenting posters or oral presentations at conferences is an excellent way for students to gain experience in exposing their ideas to a larger audience. It is also an essential activity for scholars, so the more experience you can get with presenting your work, the better prepared you will be if you choose a career in academia. Check whether your institution has yearly conferences that give students opportunities to present their work. If your institution does host conferences during the year, consider responding to the call for papers. Your peers and the faculty and administration at your institution likely will come to visit your presentation and offer valuable feedback on your work. There are also numerous conference opportunities for undergraduates in political science in the United States; see Appendix B for some possibilities. Some of the conferences require a fee; others do not. Inquire within your department to determine whether any funding is available for travel and other expenses for undergraduate students who want to present their work at off-campus conferences.

Finally, if your institution does not host a conference or if you cannot travel to an off-campus conference location, it is also possible for you and your fellow students to organize a conference on your home campus. You could work with administrators and/or faculty to issue a call for papers for students within your own department, for example. If funding is not available, you could pursue funding opportunities through other organizations. Pi Sigma Alpha, the National Political Science Honors Society, is an example of an organization that offers small chapter activity grants that could be used to host a conference to allow students to present their work, either as posters or as oral presentations.

Publishing Your Work

If you believe that your work is well written and researched and if you have received positive feedback and encouragement from your professors on a specific paper, you can also seek out a publication outlet for your paper. Again, your institution may have a general review for undergraduate work. The review likely publishes work across several disciplines at the same time. In addition, you can submit your paper to publications that promote undergraduate work in political science. For example, through the American Political Science Association, Pi Sigma Alpha publishes the *Undergraduate Journal of Politics* twice a year. See http://www.psajournal.org/ for more details.

Using Your Papers for Other Purposes

Many students in political science pursue graduate studies once their undergraduate studies are complete. A well-written research paper can serve as a writing sample for a graduate school application. The paper will demonstrate that you have understood the basics of the social science research process and that you are able to complete a full-length project, from the identification of an important research topic to the generalization of your conclusions. If you choose to include a paper you have written as part of your application materials, you must ensure that your paper is written as clearly and professionally as possible. Also, if the paper's topic was something that you hope to pursue more fully in graduate school, use some space in your statement of purpose in the graduate school application to explain how the included paper laid the groundwork for your continuing interest in and knowledge about the topic.

A well-written paper can serve as a writing sample for other types of applications as well, such as job applications or grant applications. An excellent way to demonstrate command of a particular research area is to have conducted some form of research in that area. Hence, you should always keep the papers you write in case they may serve as a means for you to establish credibility, either in a particular research area or in using different research methods to answer questions.

USING THE TOOLS OF RESEARCH IN OTHER WAYS

Many students who graduate with a degree in political science may not conduct research the way you have here once their formal education is complete and they enter the professional world. A degree in political science can be used in several different ways; research is one of them, but it is not the only activity associated with the degree. Nonetheless, as argued at the beginning of this book, the tools of research you have learned can be used to help you become a better *consumer* of knowledge. This is where critical analysis plays an important role. Critical analysis involves the process through which we dissect information to assess how conclusions were reached. If the methods that were used in a particular study were reasonable, as critical thinkers we will be more comfortable accepting the study's overall conclusions. To this end, it is important to know the following:

- The study's main question, or *what was the study was trying to explain?*
- The study's theory, or *the reason that a causal relationship between two or more factors was expected. Is it possible that any of the relationships expected between variables could be spurious rather than causal? Are there additional variables that can explain variation in both the independent and the dependent variables? If so, the causal link a researcher identified between the independent and dependent variables may be suspect.*
- Why the study's indicators were chosen as measurements for concepts, or *are the indicators reliable and valid reflections of the overall concepts under study?*
- What the research design was for the study, or *what methods were used to answer the research question—was quantitative or qualitative analysis used, and was that choice appropriate for the research question? Were the results interpreted correctly?*
- What type of sample was used in the study, or *was the sample an adequate reflection of the research population to which the researcher hoped to generalize findings? Was it a probability sample or a nonprobability sample?*
- Finally, how can the conclusions of the study be generalized to observations that were not included in the study, or *what is the overall takeaway message that I should remember about this particular topic?*

Scrutinizing information that you come across in your regular life using these types of questions can greatly increase your skills in critical analysis. This is a crucial aspect to formal education. Critical analysis involves not only the ability of people to identify appropriate sources of information for analysis, but also the ability to evaluate the information they consume. In other words, it is not only about learning how to read scholarly material, but also about learning how to critically evaluate it.

When you identify an area of weakness in something you read or hear about at a presentation or the like, you may think about creating a new project to make refinements to improve on previous studies. If, for example, you read a study and do not accept its conclusions because you believe one or more of the steps in the research process was performed incorrectly or inadequately, you can endeavor to create a new research project that would fix the problems you identify. In truth, no research project is perfect. All scholars are limited by real-life constraints (such as time, financial resources, or access to data) that influence what we can do with our studies. Viewing research as an ongoing conversation allows us to do the best we can with what we currently have, with the understanding that future research may confirm what we already accept or even potentially change what scholars think about a particular topic.

MODIFYING THE TEMPLATE FOR OTHER WORK: REVIEWING THE STEPS OF THE RESEARCH PROCESS

The project you completed on political values and attitudes utilized a specific mixed methods research design that incorporated several standard steps in the social scientific research process. With this experience in hand, you should note that you can (1) use a similar design to pursue different research questions; or (2) modify the design to create different types of research projects.

Using a Similar Design for Different Research Questions and Instructions for a Second Project

It is possible to utilize a research format like the one you used for your paper on political values and attitudes to answer different sorts of questions for different research populations. One possibility that will be outlined in this chapter, for example, is a comparative most similar systems analysis with a mixed methods design, using the one dependent variable/multiple independent variables format that can provide an answer to a new analytical research question. To complete this new research, you would follow the same steps as you did for your paper on political attitudes and values, beginning with the identification of a research topic. Have you read something recently that piqued your curiosity? What issues are important to you? What would you like to know more about? The identification of a new topic that is interesting to you (and relevant to others) is the first step.

As with the first project, the next step in the research process is to become immersed in the literature that pertains to the research topic you wish to explore. Again, this is crucial; you must become engaged with the literature on your new topic. This is not only for the preparation of a formal literature review that you will likely present in the final report of this new work, but also to help you develop the theory you will write to explain why the independent and dependent variables you eventually choose are expected to be correlated with each other. You should spend considerable time reviewing the literature before you write your new analytical research question. The literature should provide guidance as to which variables you could include in your new analysis.

Once you understand which variables you would like to include in your new analysis, you can write your new analytical research question. Depending on your goals, you can include just two independent variables or you can vary the number. What you include will depend on what you found in the literature and what you believe is important for inclusion to explain variation in your new dependent variable.

You must also decide which research population you wish to study. For the most similar systems design, using geographic units as the unit of analysis is a straightforward way to proceed. Identify which area of the world you would like to study with your new research question. Remember that the general grouping of the observations is the unit of analysis (countries, states, or cities), whereas the research population is the group of observations within a unit of analysis that have particular attribute in common (democratic countries, German federal states, or cities in the United States with more than 100,000 residents, for example). Identifying the research population is important for the potential generalizability of your research conclusions.

Once you have identified your variables and specified a new research population, you can write your new analytical research question just as you did before, using the template in Figure 12.1 as a general guide:

As examples of different analytical research questions with this particular format, look at the following paper titles. Each title represents a research paper written by an undergraduate student after he or she completed the first paper on political values and attitudes.

> Exploring the Effects of Industrial GDP, Motor Vehicle Density, and Education Spending on the Production of Renewable Energy in Countries with Advanced Economies
>
> The Effects of the Minimum Wage, Educational Attainment, and Union Membership on Income Inequality among the Fifty U.S. States and the District of Columbia
>
> How Do Press Freedom, Annual GDP Growth, and Perceptions of Corruption Impact the Freedom of Sub-Saharan African States?
>
> A Decade in the Buckeye State: The Effect of Unemployment, Home Value, and Local Taxes on Population Change in the Counties of Ohio between 2000 and 2010
>
> Political Instability in the Middle East and North Africa: An Examination of Potential Determining Factors
>
> Telecommunication and Economic Development: How Does Access to the Information Economy Affect Asia?

The research questions indicated in these titles clearly differ from the questions you pursued with your project on political attitudes and values. Yet hopefully

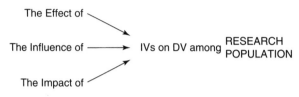

FIGURE 12.1:   Writing a New Research Question

you can see that they were asked in a way that is similar to the analytical research question you worked with for the project you just completed. Each title identifies a single dependent variable with ordinal, interval, or ratio measurement so that the same types of statistical analysis you learned in Chapters 7, 8, and 9 could be performed. Several of the titles also specify the independent variables used to explain variation in the dependent variable. Note that three independent variables are specified in some of these questions, which meant that each student had to write a theory and derive research hypotheses for three (and not two) independent variables. For these projects, students could choose independent variables with any form of measurement.

There is also wide diversity in the range of topics and the units of analysis covered among the students' paper titles. Since the studies used a most similar systems design, students were encouraged to choose a research population and group observations they included in their studies with the most similar systems logic (see Chapter 5). The observations had to have important characteristics in common that served as control factors that could not be used as independent variables. One of the student studies, for example, concentrated on "advanced economies" because advanced economies are expected to have certain commonalities. Likewise, the countries in the studies that cover different geographical areas of the world, specifically "sub-Saharan African states," countries in "the Middle East and North Africa," and countries in "Asia," also have a number of characteristics in common that made them suitable for inclusion in a most similar systems design. Grouping countries into general geographical areas is a common way to use the most similar systems design in comparative research. One research question covered the 50 states in the United States, whereas another concentrated on counties within 1 state (Ohio). Specifying the research population for the most similar systems framework for the students was crucial for two reasons: (1) the research population influences the generalizability of the eventual results; and (2) the identification of the research population within the most similar systems framework influences the number of observations that can be included in a dataset. The second point is not trivial because many of the tools of statistical analysis require a minimum number of observations. As argued in Chapter 9, a good rule of thumb is to have at least 10 observations for every independent variable you include. Thus, if you include two independent variables in your analysis as these students did, you should aim to include at least 20 observations in your new dataset; if you include three independent variables, you should include at least 30 observations.

Quantitative Analysis for the New Project

Like your paper on political values and attitudes, these student papers also utilized a mixed methods research design that incorporated both quantitative and qualitative analysis. For the quantitative section of the papers, each student identified publicly available websites that provided quantitative data that could be viewed or downloaded and inserted into a new SPSS data file. Students could identify different sources of data for their individual variables. Research projects generally draw their data from multiple sources. If you choose to use different data sources for your independent and dependent variables, keep the data temporally consistent. If you want to test the effect the independent variable has on a dependent variable, be sure that the data for the independent variable was measured just before or at the same time as the data for the dependent variable was measured. It would not be logically consistent to write a causal theory that explains why variation in an independent variable influences variation in a dependent variable and then to collect data for the independent variable for a time period that occurs after the time period for the dependent variable. Furthermore, keep in mind that since you are collecting data for only one period of time, your sample will be a cross-section of data from the population.

One of the most significant hurdles in a new research project is how to find good data that can be used to test hypotheses. Fortunately, there are many public online resources that researchers can use to access high-quality data that help answer different types of questions. To measure your concepts, you should identify the source of the data from which your indicators will be selected. Study the codebooks of the datasets you identify carefully so that the particular indicators you choose to measure the concepts you wish to study with your project are as reliable and valid as possible. See Appendix A for a list of possible data sources you could use. Include an appropriate reference to the website for the data you include in your study.

You may not be able to find data for a particular concept you wish to study through your research. If this happens, you must think creatively about how to operationalize the concept through an indicator. In the case that you cannot identify a measure for a particular concept, you may need to change the variable entirely. You must have a valid and reliable indicator for each concept you wish to include as part of your analysis. Otherwise, your results may be suspect.

Once you identify the Web-based data sources for the variables you would like to include in your study, you must create a new SPSS dataset. To create a new dataset in SPSS, click New Dataset after opening SPSS on your computer. Clicking New Dataset will create a blank spreadsheet (Figure 12.2).

Working with a new dataset is fairly straightforward. Since you are constructing the dataset with the information you have found through online data sources, you must first create variables in the Variable View and then populate the variables with data in the Data View.

To begin, create variables in the Variable View (Figure 12.3). Because the first column will contain nonnumeric data (you will need a list for the names of each observation in the dataset—such as country or state), the first variable must be transformed from a "numeric" variable that uses numbers to a "string"

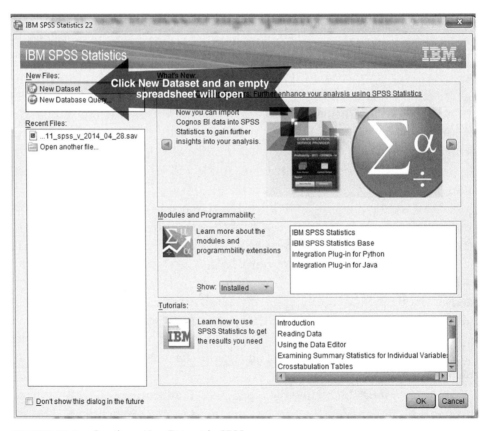

FIGURE 12.2: Creating a New Dataset in SPSS

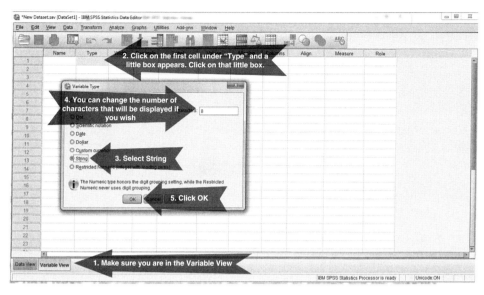

FIGURE 12.3: Creating Variables in SPSS

variable that can use letters rather than numbers for each entry. To do this, use the following steps:

1. Make sure you are in Variable View.
2. Click on the first cell under "Type." Click on the small box that appears in the cell.
3. Select "String," which will allow you to enter nonnumeric text for this column.
4. If desired, change the number of possible characters that will appear in the spreadsheet.
5. Click OK.

Once you have transformed the first column from a numeric variable into a string variable (leave the others as they are), you can create variable names for the variables you will populate with data. Before starting this process, save the spreadsheet as a new file. Under File, click Save As, and give the spreadsheet a new name.

The first column is the list of observations. In the first box in Variable View, under Name, type in the name of your unit of analysis: for example, the word "Country," "State," or "County." Since you transformed this first variable from a numeric to a string variable, you can now enter lettered text into the spreadsheet. (Note that SPSS does not allow you to include special characters or spaces in the variables' names.)

Next, add the variable names in the next few rows. You do not need to change the Type of these variables from numeric to string because these variables will use numbers, not letters. First, create a name for each variable. One way to organize your variables is to begin each variable's name with "DV" for the dependent variable or "IV1," "IV2," and so on for the independent variables. You can also change the number of decimal points that will be displayed for each number by clicking on the cell for "decimal" and changing the number (Figure 12.4).

1. Make sure you are in Variable View.
2. Enter your variables' names in each cell under Name.
3. Change the number of decimal places if you wish.

Once you have entered your variables' names, you can begin to enter data into the spreadsheet (Figure 12.5). To do this, you must be in the Data View screen. Click on Data View and you will see the variable names you have entered at the top. You can now insert the data you found online by clicking on the cells under the variable names and entering the value for each variable for each observation using your computer's keyboard. Do this carefully to ensure you do not make mistakes. Double check your work to ensure that each value has been entered correctly.

Once the data have been entered, you can perform quantitative analysis exactly as you did with the data from the WVS. First perform descriptive statistics on your variables, and then conduct bivariate and multivariate data analysis.

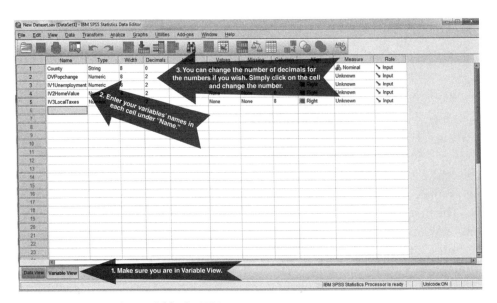

FIGURE 12.4:   Naming Variables in SPSS

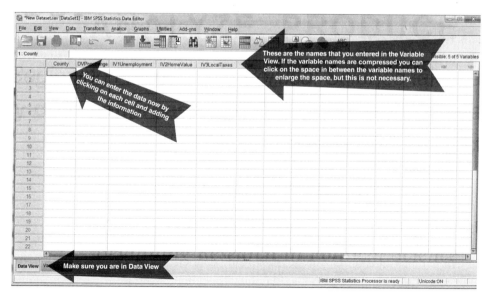

FIGURE 12.5: Entering Data in SPSS

When working with quantitative data from sources you collect from the Internet, you must include a citation to indicate where the data are officially stored so someone could potentially replicate your analysis. The possibility of replication, whereby a researcher reproduces a study with the same data from the same data sources, is an important part of the research process. If we replicate other people's studies and obtain different results using the same data, the results are suspect. This suggests that someone did not do something properly when performing statistical tests.

Qualitative Analysis for the New Project

Next, for the qualitative part of the papers, the students whose paper titles are listed above conducted two brief case studies that were included in the final paper after the results from linear regression analysis were presented. Specifically, these were hypothesis-testing cases (see Chapter 10) that were deliberately chosen for the most similar systems design framework. To determine the cases, the quantitative results were scrutinized to determine which of the independent variables were the most significant for explaining variation in the dependent variable. In this way, each student could determine which of the research hypotheses had the most explanatory power. The cases that were further explored were the ones that best confirmed the hypotheses that received the most empirical support in quantitative analysis. They were chosen from the original observations list used for the quantitative analysis. Importantly, the two cases each student chose represent two different values of the independent variable, which subsequently were associated with two different values of the dependent variable. For example, if one student's quantitative data analysis found that the average per capita income per state was positively and significantly related to voter turnout per state, the first case to examine further would be a state with low per capita income and low voter turnout, and the second case would be a state with high per capita income and high voter turnout. In this way, the two cases represent variation in both the independent and the dependent variables. As hypothesis-testing cases, they are expected to confirm the hypothesis.

Process tracing as described in Chapter 10 was then used to provide evidence for the causal relationship between the independent and dependent variables for the two hypothesis-testing cases. For example, the student who researched the determinants of political instability in the Middle East and North Africa found that political corruption was the only independent variable that emerged as significant in linear regression, controlling for the other independent variables that were included in the full model. Specifically, the student concluded that the level of corruption in a country was positively associated with its level of political instability. In other words, higher levels of corruption were associated with higher levels of political instability, and lower levels of corruption were associated with lower levels of political instability. The student returned to the list of observations from the SPSS dataset he created and identified two countries to study further: (1) Syria, which, compared with the other countries on the list, was characterized with high corruption and high political instability, and (2) the United Arab Emirates, which was characterized with low corruption and low political instability. To perform the case studies, the student searched the literature to find more detailed information that would help him create a precise timeline of events to connect a high degree of corruption with a high degree of political instability in Syria and a low degree of political corruption with a low degree of political instability in the United Arab Emirates. He looked through scholarly articles and books, current working papers and academic reports from think tanks, and news reports that would help him make a case for how the presence or absence of corruption explained the presence or absence of political instability for the time period under study. Specifically, the student accessed articles in mainstream journals such as *Comparative Institutional Development* and *The Journal for Developing Areas*, working papers and academic reports from the *Center for Systemic Peace* and *Freedom House*, and news stories from the BBC and Al-Jazeera. Through process tracing, the information the student amassed provided further evidence that showed not only that the degree of political corruption and the degree of political instability were empirically linked in Syria and in the United Arab Emirates, but also why. After gathering enough information from a plethora of sources, the student wrote a summary of his findings in two brief case studies that were presented after the results and discussion of the quantitative analysis.

The student who studied income inequality in the 50 U.S. states and the District of Columbia followed a similar strategy. In this study, the student found that of the three independent variables included in the analysis (minimum wage, educational attainment, and union membership), only educational attainment was shown to be associated with income inequality in linear regression.[1] The student returned to his SPSS dataset and decided to study Washington, DC (high educational attainment, high income inequality), and Wyoming (low educational attainment, low income inequality) more carefully to understand why this effect was observed. Like the student who wrote on political instability in the Middle East and North Africa, this student found studies from journals, official reports from reputable agencies, and stories from the mainstream news and used process tracing to create a timeline and argument for each location that would support his theory to explain why the two variables were causally linked.

Indeed, this is common way that hypothesis-testing case studies are used in the most similar systems design in political science. Many case studies in political science are constructed through process tracing that uses primary and secondary documents to help a researcher develop a concise, yet detailed and informative story that provides further evidence that a theory and specific research hypothesis are supported.

When doing research for your hypothesis-confirming case studies, you must be careful not to ignore information that might contradict assumptions you have made about your cases. Do not **cherry-pick** the information you find about your case. Cherry-picking is giving attention only to evidence that confirms a stated hypothesis while suppressing evidence that might contradict it. When researchers cherry-pick what they include in a case study, they introduce serious bias. If you find information from reputable sources that contradicts your expectations, chances are you have not fully understood everything about a case. The new information should help you develop a more nuanced

---

1   More than one independent variable may be significant in your quantitative analysis, which means that your eventual case studies could highlight the impact of more than one independent variable on the dependent variable.

understanding of your case that will complement the quantitative findings. Although the cases are expected to confirm the hypotheses, the benefit of doing in-depth qualitative analysis is the ability to provide more complete explanations for an outcome, which could potentially improve a theory.

Once you collect the information and perform both quantitative and qualitative analysis for your research question, you can write a final report for this second project. A template you could use follows.

TEMPLATE FOR A MOST SIMILAR SYSTEMS DESIGN PROJECT

Title

Abstract

Include the research question, the question's relevance, the methods used to answer the question, and the results of the research study.

Introduction to research topic and research question

Use this section to introduce the paper, to explain why the topic is important, and to show how the paper will proceed. Include a discussion of the most similar systems design and justify which observations were included in the analysis. Specify the two hypothesis-testing cases that were also explored as part of the research.

Literature review

Use the literature review to synthesize the work that has been done on the research topic and to place your study in context. Integrate the studies you review into a streamlined report. Include the appropriate parenthetical citations.

Theory and hypotheses

Use the literature to guide how you think about why there is variation in your dependent variable. Why do you expect a causal relationship between your independent and dependent variables? Based on the theory you write, what are your research hypotheses? List the null hypotheses for each independent variable as well.

Methods and data

Present the quantitative methods separately from the qualitative methods. First, for quantitative analysis: (1) Which indicators were used to measure your concepts and were those indicators reliable and/or valid for the concepts under study? (2) Where did the data you use come from and for what time period was each variable collected? (3) What statistical tests were performed on the data you collected? Second, for the qualitative analysis: (1) What were the two hypothesis-testing cases studied in the analysis and why were they chosen? (2) What information was collected and what method was used to understand the relationship between the independent and dependent variables under study.

Results and discussion

Again, you should present the quantitative results separately from the qualitative results. For the quantitative analysis: (1) present descriptive statistics about your independent and dependent variables; 2) present your data analysis as clearly as possible; and (3) discuss all your findings. For the qualitative analysis: (1) present background information about each case; and (2) use process tracing to explain why one or more independent variables are causally related to the dependent variable for the two specific cases.

Conclusions

Your conclusion should cover the following points: (1) Were you able to support your hypotheses with either the quantitative or the qualitative analyses? Why not? Engage in ex post theorizing where necessary; (2) Where do you see room for improvement? What should future research concentrate on? and (3) What implications do your findings have in a general sense? What else does your study help us understand; in other words, how can your results be generalized?

Reference list

Modifying the Design to Create Different Types of Research Projects

The preceding section showed how the structure of the project you completed on political attitudes and values could be used for different topics. But it is also possible to modify the design to create different types of research projects. Indeed, most research papers you will read as you continue your education in political science do not follow one standard design.

Perhaps the most straightforward change to the design you learned is the addition of dependent variables to the analysis. For example, a researcher could highlight a single independent variable and study its effect on several dependent variables in different equations. Sometimes, a researcher posits a general theme for a dependent variable and then uses several different indicators for the dependent variable, using each one in a separate equation. For example, imagine that a researcher wants to understand the effect the poverty rate has on economic outcomes in the 50 United States. The poverty rate is the primary independent variable, and different indicators to measure "economic outcomes" become the dependent variables. These might include economic growth rates, rates of income equality, and per capita income. Each indicator becomes a dependent variable and, as such, the researcher would have to present separate tables to show whether the key independent variable in question—the poverty rate—influences variation in each of the individual dependent variables. It would also be possible for the researcher to include additional independent variables in these models.[2] What the researcher chooses to add to the equation depends on which variables were argued in the theory to be the most relevant.

It is possible to design a single research project using *only* quantitative methods (extensive data analysis, for example) or *only* qualitative methods (through detailed case studies, for example). This book required you to do both types of analysis because both are used extensively in political science research and it is good for new researchers to have exposure to as much as possible as early as possible to understand the choices that are available for use. Researchers in political science utilize a variety of methods to answer analytical questions. The best advice in designing a project is to choose a research design that will help you best answer your research question based on what types of information are available and what is feasible given your constraints in terms of time or other considerations, such as monetary resources. For some projects, this will involve only quantitative analysis, for others it will involve only detailed case studies, and for still others a mixed methods design that incorporates both quantitative and qualitative analyses may be appropriate.

Finally, it is possible to utilize only particular research elements we have studied in this book to create full research projects. For example, some scholars produce papers that provide extensive literature reviews on a particular subject. Sometimes these literature reviews are organized by a theme and will usually include the methods and conclusions of several recently published books. These literature reviews are immensely helpful for scholars who are new to a particular field because they provide integrated summaries of the most recent and comprehensive work in a research area.

A second example involves studies that concentrate solely on concept measurement. These studies investigate how a particular concept, such as democracy, equality, justice, leadership, ethnic conflict, or political mobilization,

---

2   Some researchers include **control variables**, which are added to the regression equation. Control variables are not key variables under study, but they do serve an important purpose by holding certain factors constant while the independent effect of other variables is being assessed.

should be operationalized in research. These studies are instrumental in helping researchers refine the operationalization of particular concepts so that the concepts can be used consistently in other studies. Since many concepts that we work with in political science often defy precise measurement, these studies are crucial in helping us understand the best ways to measure concepts.

The project you completed on political attitudes and values has set you up to think about different kinds of research in political science. You could work with the template you have learned to write new papers on different topics or you could modify it to some degree to create different types of research projects. As emphasized at the end of the previous chapter, your future in research is just beginning.

FINAL THOUGHTS

Social scientific research is a process. It usually starts with the identification of a general topic of interest and relevance, a thorough study of the literature to understand as much as possible about the topic, and the subsequent asking of a good question within the research topic. Hopefully the framework provided in this book will help you continue to ask good analytical research questions in political science. Asking good questions is the cornerstone of the research process. Without a question, it is hard to know what to do next.

Research questions can develop in different ways. The best advice for someone who wants to identify a good research question in political science is, on the one hand, to continually study the academic literature and, on the other, to read and consume political news. Becoming immersed in the conversation about topics that are of interest to you—through both the scholarly literature and the mainstream news—is the key to becoming a good researcher over time. This is the best way to identify topics of relevance and concern for the political science community. More often than not, good research questions will emerge when you become *engaged* with a particular subject. Good research questions are born when you discover something you did not know about a subject and realize that there is so much more to learn. Hopefully the skills you learned in this book will help you as you continue to explore the political world and understand it just a little bit more.

GLOSSARY

CALL FOR PAPERS   A general invitation to present research at a conference.

CHAIR   The person who organizes a panel at a research conference.

CHERRY-PICK   Giving attention only to evidence that confirms a stated hypothesis while suppressing evidence that might contradict it.

CONFERENCE PANEL   A panel for the presentation of research that is organized in advance, usually around a general theme.

CONTROL VARIABLES   Variables that serve an important purpose by holding certain factors constant while the independent effect of other variables is being assessed.

DISCUSSANT   The person who provides formal comments on research papers after they have been presented at a conference.

DISSEMINATION   The process through which work is distributed to a larger audience.

POSTER PRESENTATION   A presentation in which the main points from a paper are displayed on a large poster board.

OBTAINING PERMISSION TO CONDUCT FIELD RESEARCH BASED ON INTERACTIONS WITH HUMAN SUBJECTS

Whenever you interact with another person for a research purpose, you must obtain special permission from your academic institution to conduct the research. For most institutions of higher learning, this is called **institutional review** and most institutions have a formal committee that reviews research proposals called the **institutional review board**, or **IRB**. Before conducting the actual research of a project (going into the field for interviews or focus groups), you must submit a proposal to your institution's IRB. The IRB will review the proposal to ensure that three specific criteria are met. First, you must show how each participant in your study will provide what is called **informed consent** before engaging in the project. Informed consent means that you have explained to your participants what the research is about and that you will obtain permission to utilize any data gathered from

them in the final research project. The IRB will look for some statement in the proposal that spells out how informed consent will be acquired from each participant. For many projects in political science, this is a document you must ask every participant to sign before the research process begins. The second requirement is that of **beneficence**, which ensures that the research process will not harm the participants in any way. For most political science research, you can satisfy this requirement by providing a list of the types of questions that will be asked in an interview or focus group. The questions must be vetted to ensure that the research process will not hurt any participant in any way, including psychologically. Finally, you must state that there is **justice** in your research process, which means that your participants will not be exploited and that the selection process for inclusion in the research project does not discriminate against certain groups or individuals. The justice criterion ensures that all participants who fit the profile for inclusion should be treated equally and respectfully.

Before engaging in any research project that involves direct interaction with human beings, you must obtain IRB approval. Usually the IRB will provide written documentation in an official letter that you should carry whenever you approach a new participant for your research. You should show this approval document to all participants before the research process begins. You should also ask participants to sign a form that you write in advance providing informed consent. Please refer to your institution's IRB office for further information about obtaining IRB approval for any research that puts you in direct contact with a human being.

GLOSSARY

BENEFICENCE Documentation that the research process will not harm participants in any way.

INFORMED CONSENT Documentation that researchers have explained to participants what the research is about; this includes either verbal or written permission from participants to utilize any data gathered from them in the final research project.

INSTITUTIONAL REVIEW Special permission from an academic institution to conduct research involving human subjects.

INSTITUTIONAL REVIEW BOARD A formal committee that reviews research proposals.

JUSTICE Documentation that research participants will not be exploited and that the selection process for inclusion in the research project does not discriminate against certain groups or individuals.

CONFERENCES IN THE UNITED STATES FOR UNDERGRADUATES DOING POLITICAL SCIENCE RESEARCH

Pi Sigma Alpha National Student Conference
http://www.psajournal.org/upcoming-conferences-for-undergraduates/

National Conference on Undergraduate Research
http://www.cur.org/ncur_2015/

Posters on the Hill: Council of Undergraduate Research
http://www.cur.org/conferences_and_events/student_events/posters_on_the_hill/

National Collegiate Honors Council
http://nchchonors.org/annual-conference/

Midwest Political Science Undergraduate Research
http://public.wartburg.edu/mpsurc/AboutMPSURC.html/

Undergraduate Conference on the EU: Scripps College
http://eucenter.scrippscollege.edu/student-resources/claremont-uc-undergraduate-research-conference/

The Student Conference on U.S. Affairs: West Point
http://www.usma.edu/scusa/sitepages/home.aspx/

Illinois State University Conference for Students of Political Science
http://pol.illinoisstate.edu/current/conferences/

Undergraduate Research Symposium: University of Pittsburgh
http://www.ucis.pitt.edu/ursymposium/
Wheatley International Affairs Conference: Brigham Young University
http://ce.byu.edu/cw/wheatley/

All Politics Is Local Conference: Walsh University
http://www.walsh.edu/all-politics-is-local-conference-registration/

Western Political Science Association for Undergraduate Research Papers
http://wpsa.research.pdx.edu/meet/posters.php/

DATA SOURCES FOR PUBLIC USE

This list represents only a fraction of the public data sources that exist. Consult your institution's library to see whether you can access data sources that are not listed here. Institutions often pay handsomely for database site licenses, so find out what you are eligible to use as a member of your academic institution.[1]

Data sources that contain links to other databanks:
Interuniversity Consortium for Political and Social Research
http://www.icpsr.umich.edu/icpsrweb/ICPSR/

Data sources for topics in American government: these websites contain links to databases that contain economic, political, and social data for the 50 U.S. states
The American Presidency Project
http://www.presidency.ucsb.edu/data.php/

Centers for Disease Control and Prevention
http://wonder.cdc.gov/

David Leip's Atlas of U.S. Presidential Elections
http://uselectionatlas.org/

Library of Congress:
http://congress.gov/

Pew Research Center
http://www.pewforum.org/religious-landscape-study/

U.S. Department of Labor
http://www.bls.gov/data/

U.S. Government
http://www.data.gov/

U.S. Census Bureau
http://factfinder.census.gov/

Data sources for topics in comparative politics: these websites contain links to databases that contain economic, political, and social data by country
Central Intelligence Agency World Fact Book
https://cia.gov/library/publications/resources/the-world-factbook/index.html/

---

1 It is also a good idea to keep a running list of the data sources you read about when you review other scholars' work in preparation for your literature review. You may be able to access these data sources for your own work, too. Word of mouth and sharing information with faculty and fellow students are also good ways through which you can learn about the availability of data sources.

Organization for Economic Cooperation
and Development
https://data.oecd.org/

Pew Research Center
http://www.pewforum.org/global-religious-
landscape.aspx/

Unesco Institute of Statistics
http://www.uis.unesco.org/datacentre/
pages/default.aspx?SPSLanguage=EN/

United Nations, general
http://data.un.org/

United Nations Statistical Yearbook
http://unstats.un.org/unsd/syb/

United Nations Demographic Yearbook
http://unstats.un.org/unsd/demographic/
products/dyb/dyb2.htm/

World Bank, general
http://data.worldbank.org/

World Bank Worldwide Governance
Indicators
http://info.worldbank.org/governance/wgi/
index.aspx#home/

**Data sources for topics in international
relations: these websites contain links to
databases concerning regime type, violence,
conflict, and terrorism**

Correlates of War Project
https://www.correlatesofwar.org/

Center for Systemic Peace
http://www.systemicpeace.org/inscrdata.
html/

CIRI Human Rights Data
http://www.humanrightsdata.com/

Freedom House
https::/freedomhouse.org/

National Consortium for the Study of Terrorism and Responses to Terrorism Peace
Research Institute Oslo (PRIO) Polity
Project
https://www.prio.org/Data/

INDEX

A

abstracts
    in literature review, 24–25
    in research report, 279
academic books
    citations for, 35*t*
    literature review of, 19–20
    publication of, 19–20
    as secondary sources for case studies, 247
academic reports
    literature review of, 20–21
    as secondary sources for case studies, 247
Academic Search Premier, 18, 18n2, 29
adjusted R^2, 214, 232
    in multivariate linear regression, 224
    in research report, 272
American Journal of Political Science, 17
American Political Association, 33–34
American Political Science Review, 17
analytical research question, 71
    correlation and, 40
    dependent variable in, 53–58, 70
    developing, 52–70
    independent variable in, 59–66, 61*t*–63*t*, 70
    measurement and, 48–52
    phrasing of, 44–48
    quantification and, 48–52
    research design and, 66–69
    research population and, 66–69
    variables and, 39–74
    writing, 69–70, 70*f*
    WVS and, 59, 65–69, 68*t*, 70

annotated bibliographies, for literature review, 26–27, 35
antecedent variables, 43, 71
applied research, 7–8, 13
archives, 111, 247
articles. *See also* peer-reviewed research articles
    citations for, 35*t*
    process tracing from, 254
    as secondary sources for case studies, 247
asterisk (*)
    for coefficient, 230, 231, 236
    for correlation coefficient, 200
    for *p* value, 236
    for regression analysis, 236, 272
    in search engines, 23
    for test statistic, 198
    for unstandardized beta coefficient, 230, 231, 236
ATLAS.ti, 252

B

"back" command, in search engine, 64n10
bar chart
    for frequency distributions, 162–63, 162*f*, 169*f*
    for values in life, 169*f*
The BBC, 21
bell curve. *See* normal distribution
beneficence, 307, 308
best fitting line, in linear regression, 211–12
binary variables, 71
    difference of means test on, 183–90
    logistic regression for, 232
    in multivariate linear regression, 223

Standard Grad Pack for, 150, 150n2
Statistics Data Editor of, 164
tables from, 209, 209n3
variables in, 296–98, 297f, 298f
Variable View in, 152–54, 153f, 154n5, 156, 166
for WVS, 150–58
Statistics Data Editor, of SPSS, 164
stratified random sample, 105, 105n3, 123
structured interviews, for quantitative research design, 245, 259
summary statistics
maximum value in, 170, 173t, 177
for ordinal measurement, 170–76, 170n7, 171f, 173f, 174n8
standard deviation in, 170n7
survey research
correlation coefficient and, 197
reliability for, 129–30
validity in, 133–34
systematic sample, 105, 123

T
tables
for regression analysis, 235t
from SPSS, 209, 209n3
television news, as primary sources for case studies, 247
template, 284
for new research, 292–305
for research report, 266–81, 302–3
testability, of hypotheses, 87, 93
test-retest method, 130–31, 140
test statistic
asterisk (*) for, 198
p value and, 212–13
themes, for content analysis, 253, 259
theory, 75–85, 93
building, 81–84
causality and, 5, 41, 78
causal research and, 9
deductive reasoning for, 82–83
defined, 76
deterministic, 80–81
empirical research for, 9
explanatory power of, 84, 85
ex post theorizing, 276, 284
hypotheses from, 5, 85–92
hypothesis-generating case studies and, 241
hypothesis-testing case studies and, 241–42

idiographic case studies and, 240–41
illustrative case studies and, 242
inductive observations for, 81–82
literature review and, 16, 83–84
negative findings and, 275–77
plausibility probes and, 242
probabilistic, 80–81, 93
probability, 103
research question and, 41
research report and, 268, 275–77
tone, of research report, 282
triangulation, 259
for case studies, 247–48
t test. *See* difference of means test

U
Undergraduate Journal of Politics, 290
unit of analysis, 72
measurement and, 99
in research design, 99
research population and, 99
for variables, 66
WVS and, 66
unstandardized beta coefficient, 233
asterisk (*) for, 230, 231, 236
independent variables and, 207–13
in linear regression, 207–13
logistic regression and, 232
unstructured interviews, 244–45, 259

V
validity
content, 132, 132n1, 134, 140
external, 240, 258
face, 132, 134, 140
of indicators, 131–39, 140, 273–74
values, ordinal measurement of, 168–69, 168f, 169f
variables. *See also specific types*
analytical research question and, 39–74
bivariate analysis for, 183–204
causality between, 41, 78–80, 254
correlation of, 40, 41, 78–79
deductive reasoning for, 82–83
defined, 40
difference of means test for, 183–90
interval measurement for, 51–52, 147–50
negative findings and, 275
nominal measurement and, 48, 66, 146–47, 148t, 158–66